Idol and Grace

On Traditioning and Subversive Hope

Idol and Grace

On Traditioning and Subversive Hope

Orlando O. Espín

ORBIS BOOKS
Maryknoll, New York 10545

ORBIS BOOKS
Maryknoll, New York 10545

Fathers and Brothers
MARYKNOLL™

Founded in 1970, Orbis Books endeavors to publish works that enlighten the mind, nourish the spirit, and challenge the conscience. The publishing arm of the Maryknoll Fathers and Brothers, Orbis seeks to explore the global dimensions of the Christian faith and mission, to invite dialogue with diverse cultures and religious traditions, and to serve the cause of reconciliation and peace. The books published reflect the views of their authors and do not represent the official position of the Maryknoll Society. To learn more about Maryknoll and Orbis Books, please visit our website at www.maryknollsociety.org.

Library of Congress Cataloging-in-Publication Data

Espín, Orlando O.
    Idol and grace : on tradition and subversive hope / Orlando O. Espín.
      pages cm
    Includes bibliographical references and index.
    ISBN 978-1-62698-062-4 (pbk.)
    1. Tradition (Theology) 2. God (Christianity) 3. Christianity. I. Title.
BT90.E87 2014
230'.2--dc23
                                              2013029808

If you understand, it isn't God.
Augustine of Hippo (ca. 354–430)

They might cut all the flowers, but they can't prevent the Spring.
Pablo Neruda (1904–1973)

What is the future of truth without faithfulness, or of faithfulness without truth?
Paul Ricoeur (1913–2005)

*Our falsified and inauthentic ways of dealing with our fellow
human beings are allied to our falsification of the idea of God.*
Juan Luis Segundo (1925–1996)

*We have, deep inside all of us, old blueprints of expectation and response . . .
and these must be altered at the same time as we alter the living conditions
which are a result of those structures. For the master's tools will
never dismantle the master's house.*
Audre Lorde (1934–1992)

*How a group names its God has critical consequences, for the symbol
of the divine organizes every other aspect of a religious system.*
Elizabeth A. Johnson (1941–)

The only true representation is one that also represents its distance from the truth.
Giorgio Agamben (1942–)

*Memory and history compete for the past. Because history can't always
trust memory, and memory can't believe a history that hasn't placed,
at its core, the memory of the struggle for human rights.*
Beatriz Sarlo (1942–)

Contents

Acknowledgments

Theology is not a monologue or a parroting exercise. Theology is crafted and engaged *en conjunto*, whether we are aware of it and want to admit it or not. It is an ongoing conversation. And, like every important conversation, it is shaped by and dotted with interruptions and silences, with many questions and some answers, with disappointments and cheers, with disagreements and agreements (including agreements to disagree), always seeking to understand *in order to live and act in the real world*. Theology is a shared intellectual adventure, with demonstrably important and sometimes subversive consequences for *this world*.

This book has been "in conversation" for about a decade. So I must thank my conversation partners—those whose names appear on this volume's dedicatory page and a larger group of colleagues and former students at my own university and at other institutions. Because of all of them, these pages represent a *teología de conjunto*.

Over several years, and through many conversations, these colleagues have helped me clarify ideas and intuitions while planting new thoughts and critically important questions in my mind. They have challenged, supported, agreed, and disagreed, and never left the conversation. They were heard.

Therefore, my thanks also go to these esteemed conversation partners:

Professors José de Mesa (De La Salle University, Manila), Raúl Fornet-Betancourt (Universität Bremen), Gustavo Gutiérrez, Virgilio Elizondo, and Thomas O'Meara (University of

Notre Dame), Gary Macy (Santa Clara University), Otto Maduro and Elías Ortega-Aponte (Drew University), M. Shawn Copeland, Roberto S. Goizueta, and Barbara Quinn (Boston College), Mary E. Hunt (Women's Alliance for Theology, Ethics and Ritual), Siegfried Wiedenhofer and Thomas Schreijäck (F. W. Goethe Universität, Frankfurt), Carmen Nanko-Fernández, Robert Schreiter, Steven Bevans, Gilberto Cavazos-González, and Gary Riebe-Estrella (Catholic Theological Union, Chicago), Jean-Pierre Ruiz (St. John's University, New York), Miguel H. Díaz and Neomi DeAnda (University of Dayton), Peter Hünermann (Eberhard Karls Universität, Tübingen), Peter C. Phan (Georgetown University), Daisy L. Machado and Sarah Azaransky (Union Theological Seminary, New York), Justo L. González (Columbia Theological Seminary), Paloma Olivares Guerrero (Universidad de Guanajuato), Luis Rivera Pagán (Princeton Theological Seminary), Bryan Massingale (Marquette University), Norbert Hintersteiner (Trinity College, Dublin), Patrick S. Cheng (Episcopal Divinity School), Milagros Peña (University of Florida), Víctor Carmona (Oblate School of Theology), Jacqueline Hidalgo (Williams College), Jorge Aquino (University of San Francisco), Jonathan Tan (Australian Catholic University, Sydney), Dale T. Irvin (New York Theological Seminary), Marion Grau, Bernard Schlager, Michael S. Campos, and the late Alejandro García-Rivera (Graduate Theological Union, Berkeley), Sharon H. Ringe (Wesley Theological Seminary), Jane C. Redmont (Episcopal Diocese of North Carolina), Pedro Ribeiro de Oliveira (Universidade Católica de Minas Gerais, Belo Horizonte), Néstor Medina (Regent University School of Divinity), Luis Rivera Rodríguez (McCormick Theological Seminary), Francisco Oda Ángel (Universidad Rey Juan Carlos, Madrid), Vítor Westhelle and José David Rodríguez (Lutheran School of Theology, Chicago), Maria Clara Bingemer and Paulo Fernando Carneiro de Andrade (Pontifícia Universidade Católica do Rio de Janeiro).

I am especially grateful to my colleagues at the University of San Diego for our many conversations on the "unsayability" of the Mystery, on religion, on interreligious dialogue, on culture, on theology . . . and on good cuisine: Bahar Davary, Evelyn Díaz Cruz, Mary C. Doak, Russell Fuller, Aaron S. Gross, Louis Komjathy, Lance Nelson, Susie Paulik-Babka, Emily Reimer-Barry, Karen Teel, and K. Lekshe Tsomo.

Jeremy V. Cruz, Robert J. Rivera, Anthony Suárez, Robyn Henderson-Espinoza, and Rafael Gómez—finishing their doctoral dissertations as I was finishing this volume— and other young scholars now on university faculties have also been my conversation partners over the past several years. They have raised some important questions that I have tried to address in this book. I am grateful for their generosity, their learning, and their intense commitment to justice and scholarship. Many conversations begun at colloquia of the Academy of Catholic Hispanic Theologians of the U.S. and at meetings of the Hispanic Theological Initiative have been continued on these pages.

But theology—it is evident—is not only a conversation among academics. All theologians have spouses or partners, families, friends, and neighbors, and mine too are crucially important contributors to the crafting of my theology. They know what and how to question, when to challenge, and when a shoulder is welcome. This volume of theology is no exception.

John Nevins, bishop, has been for me a model of mercy over his long life of service. Edgard Beltrán, teacher, still dares me to listen to the subversive hope of the Reign of God. My friends Carmen Chávez, Rubén Moreno Salinas, and Hugo Córdova Quero have repeatedly pushed me to reflect on what is important for real people in real families and communities, and on what real human struggles have to do with God, revelation, and theology.

Miguel G. Ramos (*Ilari Obá, Obá Oriaté*) of Florida International University (Miami), dared me to think "outside the box" in matters cultural and religious; I am in his debt for many years of friendship and for his scholarship and integrity. The Reverends Arturo Bañuelas, Mari Castellanos, John D. Gillespie, Eli Valentín, Rosa Frías, Joseph E. Stearns, Carla Roland Guzmán, Joseph Palacios, and Juan M. Acosta have contributed to this book by raising important social, doctrinal, pastoral, and ethical issues over the years.

But as always, the *abuelas* of the *barrios* remain my best and most insightful conversation partners—and critics.

Just as important is the gratitude I owe Robert Ellsberg of Orbis Books. His patient and efficient prodding, over more than a decade, finally led to the completion of these pages—which are probably not what he expected. To him, and to the entire staff at Orbis Books, my sincere thanks.

I recognize that I have been taught by many. I acknowledge my debt and gratitude to all those mentioned above and on the dedicatory page, and to many others. I know that the limitations of the present volume are wholly my own.

Orlando O. Espín

Introduction

The core of what Christians call God's revelation is the claim that God has begun to transform this world according to God's will and that this God is compassionate towards all, without limits, conditions, or exceptions. This was the center and anchor of the message announced by an insignificant Galilean Jewish peasant, executed as a subversive by Roman imperial authority two thousand years ago, and now standing at the dawn of Christianity.

Was this peasant right? Is God transforming this world, and is God limitlessly compassionate, as the message claimed? Christians are the ones who insist on this being so, without more proof than their own hope.[1]

Such fiercely subversive hope is the necessary core of Christianity.[2] Yet how has Christianity presented and interpreted itself in the many cultural and historical contexts in which it has found and now finds itself? How have Christians traditioned their hope? (As the reader will see, I use "tradition" as a verb.) How can Christians tradition their hope without adulterating its subversive challenge? A hope that subverts all that humans regard as definitive has been one of the crucial forces driving the complex of traditioning processes that created and have sustained the religion we call Christianity. Subversive hope, I will contend in these pages, is *the* crucial content of what Christianity refers to as revelation.[3]

This book studies and reflects on the assumptions, contexts, and processes employed and required for traditioning this hope—social, cultural, historical, philosophical, and theological—in multiple situations of hegemonic power asymmetries and also, today, in the context of globalization. For that purpose, the book discusses and critiques Christianity's historical inclination to "doctrinify" the subversive hope and the consequences of that inclination. Finally, and in consequence, these pages propose an understanding of Christian traditioning that can (even as it liberates) witness interculturally to the subversive hope that lies at the heart of Christianity.

Thus this book brings to the fore and engages multiple contexts required for a more complex and true to life understanding of traditioning in today's world—as the world is. There is a definite emphasis here on the crucial importance of a non-idolatrous understanding of hope, faith, revelation, doctrine, and traditioning.

All contents conveyed by traditioning—including all claims regarding revelation itself and the hope it provokes, and all doctrines, practices, and ecclesial polities developed therefrom—are always and have always been inescapably cultural, historical, contextual, societal, economic, and perspectival, molded and established by and within the non-religious processes of traditioning. This has very important theological consequences.

What have all claims, doctrines, and practices really traditioned over the centuries and across cultural contexts? To what have doctrines, claims, and practices really witnessed? To conceive of traditioning as the unfailing transmission of a set of doctrinal contents (a pre-established *depositum*) is to cheapen traditioning's importance as well as to ignore the cultural, historical, and contextual facts.[4]

Traditioning, I argue here, is about a radical hope that flows as demand from a trust in the credibility of Jesus' message regarding the dawn of the Reign of God. Obviously, this also implies and requires trust in the credibility of Jesus of Nazareth as messenger and "revealer"[5]—but not any hope or any trust. Faith is not for membership in Christianity nor for the individual salvation of our souls or persons—it is the most radical wager in and of life.

Below are other introductory clarifications that I want the reader to understand before we proceed.

These pages are, to a significant degree, a conversation and the result of ongoing conversations. The crafting of theology ("to theologize") is not a monologue or a parroting exercise. It is an ongoing conversation with many partners—who interrupt, challenge, question, or agree, sometimes agreeing to disagree, always seeking to understand in order to live, act, and transform the world in which all live.

Consequently, this volume represents an ongoing project, inevitably unfinished. It is composed of interacting and interdependent reflections on various contexts and assumptions within and from which traditioning occurs, and which inescapably affect and mold the processes of traditioning and the contents that traditioning is said to convey. These pages also include theoretical considerations (social scientific, philosophical, theological) to contextualize the necessary components, laid down here as initial steps toward, and signposts in, a longer journey in the theology of traditioning.

By definition, a conversation cannot and does not have its outcome pre-ordained. Hence this volume is not a work of denominational apologetics.

I am very much convinced of the accuracy of the insight of Yves Congar, who once remarked that no one person could ever pretend to accomplish or think through, in a single lifetime, all that is needed in the study of traditioning. The present book and its author cannot and do not have such pretensions.

Furthermore, these pages reflect multiple conversations on traditioning, seeking a theological understanding—specifically, a western Catholic theological understanding.[6] However, no claim is made or implied as to its being explicitly, implicitly, intentionally, or denominationally "Roman Catholic."[7] The very nature and intent of the book, as well as what is meant here by the expression "western Catholic," would make such a claim inappropriate and inaccurate. Several churches might very well be described as "western Catholic," but none of them alone is coextensive with the designation as used in these pages. I will discuss my definition of "western Catholic" in Chapter One.

This is an ecumenical conversation, though I realize that limiting the perspective to the churches within western Catholic Christianity might be deemed too narrow by those who are not within this ecclesial tradition. Much in this book's approach and proposal overflows and crosses broader denominational boundaries. Because it seems an undeniable demographic fact that the majority of Christians have historically identified themselves, and still identify today, with one or another strand within western Catholicism,[8] it is not unreasonable to focus, at least at this stage in the ongoing conversation, on this largest of all Christian traditions.

This is, however, an experiment with a clear, focused, and, I hope, "doable" scope. To attempt a more broadly ecumenical theology of traditioning—one that would also encompass all or most of western non-Catholic and eastern Orthodox Christianities—is certainly a worthy and necessary but still terribly daunting task for which I am clearly not ready and for which, I suspect, most other individual theologians are not ready either. A sustained, joint effort, however (an ongoing conversation!) might prove possible as it becomes more broadly and evidently necessary. I can and will make a similar caveat regarding the limitations imposed by my own (and every other author's) cultural context later in the book, when I discuss the current need for intercultural approaches to traditioning.

The same must be said regarding the interreligious dimensions of this book and conversation. I explicitly acknowledged above that my reflections and proposals are theological and western Catholic; hence the reader should not expect an interreligious or comparative approach.[9] Nevertheless, I have intentionally kept doors open and laid down bridges that western Catholic theology could cross (and in some cases has crossed) as it becomes increasingly and intentionally engaged in interreligious dialogue and more comparative methodologies. I have attempted to lay down bridges because I believe that interreligious dialogue will lead not to the erasure of each religion's distinctiveness but to the collective acknowledgment that there is, crossing all religious boundaries and distinctiveness, the Ineffable Mystery beyond all human knowing, all human saying, and all human comprehension—and beyond all religions. Christians call the Ineffable Mystery "God."

Who are my conversation partners? I have talked with colleagues and doctoral students (in the social sciences, philosophy, and theology) over years of meetings and discussions. These real-life conversations, some ongoing, have paralleled many others with real-life individuals and families in real-life communities. My conversation partners, therefore, have been and are real people with real lives, some of them are explicitly mentioned in the dedicatory page of this book as well as in the Acknowledgments. The bibliographic references throughout these pages will inform the reader of other important thinkers and sources that have also influenced my thought.

It is my hope that the present volume will be engaged by theologians as well as by scholars in other fields of learning, and by a broader spectrum of thoughtful readers.

This is a book on tradition*ing* and not mainly on tradition, although the two presuppose each other in many ways.

All religions known to humankind, including Christianity, of course, are "traditional," in the sense that all religions exist only in time and are necessarily situated in history and in cultures; they are heirs of history and cultures, whether they perceive or explain themselves historically and culturally or not.[10] Religions survive and prolong their existence in time because they have managed to create the means of transmitting their beliefs, holy stories, and rituals, from one generation to the next and from one culture to another, selecting what to remember, prioritizing among that which is remembered, and interpretively adapting the meaning of these vital elements of religious life to new historical and cultural contexts. These are "processes of traditioning." They are always and inescapably historical and cultural, with all that histories and cultures contain and imply.

Human beings too are necessarily traditional in the sense meant here; they cannot be otherwise.[11] From preceding generations, and by varied means of transmission, human beings are entrusted with meaningful worldviews, languages, customs, values, and thought patterns. While in human trust, these elements are further selected, shaped, reinterpreted, and made to grow. It is no exaggeration to say that human beings receive much of their self-understanding, and the tools for expanding, adapting, and building on it, through processes of traditioning.

My focus in these pages is on the *processes* of traditioning of the Christian religion, as the religion is understood in and by its western Catholic strands, and on the *transformations* that occur and have occurred within western Catholicism precisely *because* of those processes of traditioning. I note that we cannot forget the consequent changes that affect the processes of traditioning themselves as they occur historically and socially within the dynamics of cultural and intercultural contexts.

More to the point, and more importantly, *this book attempts to construct experimentally (or to lay the foundations for) a theology of traditioning from real-life historical, cultural, and intercultural perspectives, in a dialogical context.*

All traditioning, and therefore all that may be understood as Christian traditioning, is inevitably and inescapably cultural. Nothing human is ever a-cultural.[12] Hence even revelation (to the degree that it is received and understood by humans[13]) is inevitably and inescapably a cultural event. Consequently, to construct responsibly any theology of traditioning we must admit the culturalness[14] of such theologizing. We must also acknowledge the unavoidable historical and cultural contextualizations, and asymmetrical social uses, of all doctrinal and theological statements on traditioning and of all doctrines and theological claims and statements on God, revelation, church, and other core articles of Christian faith.

More specifically, if traditioning has to do with the contextually cultural and historical handing over of what is affirmed as revelation, and if revelation is ultimately the call (and hope) for the subversion of all that humans regard as definitive, then traditioning and whatever is understood as "the content of tradition" are also ultimately about the handing over of a Christian subversive understanding of the unsayable Mystery.[15] This Mystery is grounded in what Christians claim has been revealed and present in the person by whom Christians claim it has been revealed, and it is expressible only analogically.[16]

Western Catholic Christianity, however, has never been culturally monolithic. It has always been *asymmetrically intercultural*, although the categories and terminology to name, reflect on, and analyze cultural and intercultural reality may not have been available[17] to theologians in earlier centuries. Christian history, unfortunately, has witnessed many attempts by the socially or ecclesiastically dominant to enforce monochromatic cultural uniformity as if it were a requirement of, or coextensive with, Christian unity.

The majority of communities and persons within western Catholicism are now in what is often referred to as the "Third World."[18] This geographic, social, political, economic, and cultural fact is not theologically irrelevant because the most basic western Catholic ecclesiological understanding is that *the Church is the People of God.*[19] Consequently, given today's increasingly globalized and globalizing world and its demographic and cultural diversity, it is ethically and methodologically necessary that all theology be done interculturally and committed to justice—or face the justifiable accusation of Eurocentric tribalism or colonialism or of instrumentalization by the dominant.

This book is not, and it is not intended to be, a comprehensive western Catholic "theology of Tradition," or a general theory of traditioning.

Centuries of reflection offer us an enormous amount of data not easily summarized in these few pages. Furthermore, this long historical reflection cannot be simply or conveniently assumed to be only or mainly European, Mediterranean, or North Atlantic. History does not allow us to continue making such tribal claims. In fact, even the encyclopedic and brilliant Yves Congar was very modest in the claims he made for his now classic *Tradition and Traditions: An Historical and a Theological Essay*.[20]

Equally daunting can be the effort of synthesizing and analyzing the contemporary cultural, economic, social, and political dimensions of our world. No one individual could conceivably do a sufficient, apt synthesis and analysis covering every corner of the planet—and it would have to include every corner, because western Catholicism today is no longer western in a North Atlantic or European sense. No single individual or group of individuals can any longer pretend that a truly "general," "worldwide," or even "intercultural" approach to traditioning (and/or to the contents traditioned) can be valid beyond the always limited cultural contexts and perspectives within which it was proposed. Thus I also make no claims in this regard.

I do hope, nevertheless, that this volume may be received as a contribution to the yet to happen intercultural dialogue on traditioning among those Christians who identify themselves as western Catholics.

Just because a theology seriously commits itself to theologizing from the lived reality of people, it does not follow that it will not contain unexplained "blind spots" in reference to significant portions of reality. Needless to say, I admit that there will be unexplained and unintentional blind spots in this book.

This work is, therefore, neither a general or comprehensive history, nor a general theory, nor a full systematic study, of western theologies of Tradition and traditioning. Nor is it a thorough presentation of the contemporary world's globalizing, diverse, and increasingly intercultural reality, even when frequent references to all of these are made.

This is a theological book in intent, assumptions, and method. It is also a book in dialogue with philosophy, history, and the social sciences which allows all dialogue partners to critique and nourish each other.

Western Catholic theology has a long and fruitful history of dialogue with philosophy and other sciences. In engaging other disciplines, therefore, I am doing nothing new. However, in this work, I have intentionally allowed the discomfort and serious questioning raised by the non-theological dialogue partners to appear without any attempt at alleviating or downplaying the difficulties they raise. As this book is one moment in an ongoing conversation, the reader can understand why this must be so.

One very obvious discomfort and serious difficulty, as will be noted elsewhere in this volume, is raised by the use of the word "culture." Culture is so fluid a concept, and so critiqued by many social scientists and philosophers from the marginalized peoples of the world, that one must be careful in the use of the term and pay close attention to the critics and their arguments. Given today's globalizing yet emphatically diverse world, and because of the prominence of culture and of interculturality in the ongoing conversations that led to this book, we will be examining the notion of culture with care.

After four decades of studying theologically the daily religion of western Catholics—what is so often called "popular Catholicism"—it is clear to me that the popular religious universe is the primary and ordinary transmitter of western Catholic Christianity among most self-identified western Catholics throughout the world. It is also the ordinary means used by most western Catholics to gauge the authenticity of any doctrine, practice, or lifestyle that might claim their assent and/or participation. The present volume is, in important ways, a further development of my earlier work on daily, real-life—"popular"—western Catholic Christianity.[21]

Popular Catholicism has been much maligned historically, misunderstood theologically, and abused pastorally. The people's daily religion has been ignored, manipulated, or dismissed by denominational institutions, structures, and personnel as well as by most in the theological and social scientific disciplines. In this volume, as in my earlier work,[22] I take it very seriously theologically.

However, forty years of studying people's daily religion have taught me the perils of romanticizing it as well as the perils of not considering popular Catholicism with all due seriousness. We must search for a critical *and* respectful way of theologizing on and because of popular Catholicism. If we do not, theology becomes an insiders' dialogue about a religion of the sociologically dominant, a theology of "books speaking with books," Eurocentrically.

What western Catholics (and all Christians) remember and believe as their religion is that which has been preached, catechized, prayed, ritualized, witnessed, and thus transmitted *to them*. The processes of this complex transmission have shaped Christianity as today's Christians know, live, and profess it.

Today's Christians (always cultural, always gendered, always classed, always racial, always contextualized) shape Christianity in ways unexpected and unknown to the apostolic generation. This is inevitable if Christianity is going to make sense to contemporary women and men. Christians of today and Christians of yesterday have shaped Christianity in *their* cultural images, and it could not be otherwise because every proclamation, every explanation, every witness, and every reception of Christianity assumes cultural and other interpretations, perspectives, and lenses without which Christianity would become an unintelligible museum piece. The Christian religion (and very emphatically its western Catholic strand) is not a contextually disembodied, cerebral, doctrinal creed, but a way of *living* grounded on faith and commitment, which in turn requires understanding—all, if Christian faith would be honest, sustained by God's grace.

Christians believe a Christianity that is what *they* believe Christianity is. This is no play on words because Christianity does not exist and has never existed as a living religion apart from Christians. *This is, precisely, the core issue with which any theology of traditioning must deal.*

It is not enough to refer to written texts from the past (e.g., the Bible, ecumenical councils' decrees and creeds, patristic works, episcopal or papal statements) as if these were *the* Tradition and as if their transmission and repetition were *the* traditioning. Tradition and traditioning are not, have never been, and cannot be mainly about transmitting written texts, even if these texts are the biblical ones!

Christianity is not and has never been a text or a collection of texts or even an interpretation of texts. Consequently, Christian traditioning cannot be doctrinally or theologically reduced to the written word, no matter how wise, true, or inspired it might be. Christianity is not (and has never been) the texts of the Bible or the written texts of conciliar statements and other ecclesial authorities. Theology, specifically, cannot be reduced to the interpretive analysis of written texts.

Furthermore, it can be historically and easily demonstrated that most Christians have been illiterate during most of Christian history. Consequently, to identify the content of tradition and its traditioning with written texts alone (or primarily) is the same as reducing Christianity, and its witness to revelation, to a cultural product of the literate (and conveniently dominant) elites.

Christianity is a meaningful way of *living*, of being human, grounded on specific memories, hopes, and experiences that *sometimes* have found *some expression* in written texts, but what came to be written is not, and has never been, coextensive with Christianity as a meaningful way of living. Just as importantly, because Christianity is a way of living, it must not pretend that it can be lived apart from the social, historical, and cultural realities, hopes, and struggles that are the inescapable contextualization of all humans and of all things human, because Christian living is very much *a way of being human.* And because Christianity is first and foremost a way of living, it cannot be understood apart from the lives of the vast majority of Christians who, throughout the last twenty centuries, have been mostly poor, illiterate, and marginalized. A telling of Christian history that mostly reflects the faith, theologies, and lives of the literate, dominant elites in Church and society over the past twenty centuries is a suspect telling.

I do not doubt the need for God's grace, but God's grace, as western Catholic perspective has typically understood it, "builds on nature." Furthermore, whatever can or has been claimed and understood as "human nature" has been and remains inescapably a historical, social, and cultural construct. The theological or doctrinal appeal to the grace of God, therefore, cannot be a cover for an escape from *real* human reality, with all this implies in a world of asymmetric power relations, of poverty and violence and abuse, of racism and cultural colonizations, of androcentrism and heterosexism. The appeal to the grace of God cannot be an invitation to disregard or downplay the real lives of most Christians, who are often the victims in this human reality constructed for the benefit of the socially or ecclesiastically dominant.

The processes of Christian transmission have never been only or mainly ecclesiastical[23] or the exclusive province of the ordained. Families, communities, neighborhoods, villages, and other collective formations have played (and continue to play) the preeminent role in the traditioning of western Catholic Christianity.

Furthermore, the processes of transmission have never been exclusively intra-ecclesiastical, because extra-ecclesiastical (as well as extra-ecclesial) transmitters have played and continue to play a crucial role in traditioning beliefs and practices to Christians. Today, for example, one cannot deny that the so-called "secular" media (or, occasionally, the "fundamentalist" media of the far right) and websites and webpages of all sorts also "educate" Christians about their religion and act as "missionaries" to non-Christians—whether correctly or not and whether they want to or not. Many cultural products and cultural producers purport to know and convey "real" Christianity to the public today, and these products and producers are often believed to be accurate enough by Christians and non-Christians alike—again, even if incorrectly or without reason or foundation. I have no doubt that today's social media (Facebook, Twitter, YouTube, and others) have as much impact on the transmission of Christianity to Christians and non-Christians alike as all the sermons delivered from all the pulpits on all the Sundays in any given year. (It is possible that they have even more impact than those sermons.)

In other words, the processes of traditioning western Catholicism have not been and are not limited to what we might label "intra-ecclesial" or "ecclesiastical" processes. In real life, factually, clergy are immensely less important for traditioning Christianity than grandparents, extended families, neighborhoods, social media, pop artists, and many others people and communities.

News reports, blogs, Twitter, YouTube, social scientific explanations, Facebook, and conversations around kitchen tables, in markets and laundromats, and on street corners, all present to us popular (and sometimes academic) stereotypes about Christianity in general and about western Catholicism in particular. The stereotypes and explanations abound, often presenting themselves as factual and correct, and they are not, for the most part, produced by believers, by well-informed interpreters, or by "clergy approved" communicators. In other words, other cultural products and producers importantly contribute to what Christians will hold, do hold, and have held to be authentically Christian.

I think that we need to take extra-ecclesial, non-ecclesiastical, and even outright non-Christian transmissions of Christianity seriously, searching for a theological explanation of traditioning and of the contents traditioned that can honestly acknowledge the impact of these other means of transmission, while also critiquing their limitations, biases, inaccuracies, and naïveté, since the extra-ecclesial cannot honestly, by their own criteria, claim more access to truth and fact than believers.

Some western Catholics might not like this intromission by outsiders in the business of transmitting Christianity, but whether they like it or not is irrelevant. In today's globalized and globalizing world, no one religion can or should control the flow of information about itself or even within itself. Unfortunately, most western Catholic theologians (including many in the clergy) still have not acknowledged the traditioning role of "outsiders." This omission bears serious, potentially negative consequences for western Catholic Christianity today.

Whether one holds that continuity in western Catholicism is guaranteed by this or that condition or requirement, no one may forget that any content transmitted goes through, and is understood, selected, and shaped by the cultures, conflicts, genders, social classes, sexual orientations, races, biographies, and interpretations *of the transmitters*, whether these are intra- or extra-ecclesial transmitters, and whether the transmitters are aware of these influences and contexts or not.

Cultures, conflicts, genders, social classes, sexual orientations, races, biographies, and interpretations inevitably select what to remember and what to modify as they transmit Christianity,[24] and this selection occurs according to criteria that are not always conscious and not always admirable.

We do not have today, as the content or the story of Christianity, the same Christianity preached, practiced, and prayed by the generation of Jesus' first followers. No Christian denomination can seriously claim this. What we have today (and I hold this to be legitimate) is what has been transmitted over twenty centuries of traditioning: what has been handled, selected, and shaped by countless generations, with and through their own cultures, conflicts, and social formations, who nevertheless *believed* that *what they held to be the Christian Gospel*, and therefore what was preached, catechized, lived, and prayed by them, was *in authentic continuity* with the Christian Gospel preached, catechized, lived, and prayed by the apostolic Church in its earliest generations. To me, among many other things, this also means that it is nearly impossible today (if it ever was possible in the past) to do a theology of traditioning as if there were a content to be exactly and wholly recalled generation after generation, or as if there ever was a content so exactly or wholly recalled at any point in Church history. Memories and practices have been gained and lost, reinterpreted and reintroduced, in content, understanding, expression, and contexts.

What can and must be done is a theology of the *processes of traditioning*, Within these processes we can then understand the contents traditioned by Christianity, not as if these were identical copies of original versions, but as contents *intended* to be so in *intended loyal continuity* with the supposed originals.[25] We need to understand *the processes* of traditioning as they occur and have occurred as well as *the contexts* of all transmission and all theologizing of Christianity, including our own, since *contexts are also "traditioners,"* shaping, selecting, and determining the contents and stories as well as all their interpretations. Any theology of Tradition, if it wants to reflect human, ecclesial reality and revelation's cultural reality, must really be a theology of tradition*ing*.

Western Catholic faith must be reasonable. But faith is not grounded exclusively in reason. Grace and the Spirit of God have indispensable roles. Yet faith cannot be devoid of reason if it is to be received, understood, and committed to by reasonable and not fanatical humans.[26] The Church as People of God—its living practices and polities, its memories and its doctrines, its ways of praying and witnessing—must be open to and engage reason's queries, even if reason must admit that it alone cannot justify or understand all of the depth that is Christianity as revelation, as community of faith and compassion, and as transmitter of the hope, message, and meaning of Jesus.

Consequently, the theological study of traditioning, and of the contents traditioned, selected, and shaped by the processes of traditioning, cannot be equal to or defined by historical, sociological, or cultural research exclusively, although the processes of traditioning (as well as the contents thereby traditioned) cannot avoid undergoing historical and social scientific research and philosophical confrontations. More crucially, traditioning and what is traditioned cannot avoid the real-life questions and confrontations raised by real-life people. In brief, any theology of traditioning will surely acknowledge the roles of grace and of the Spirit of God, but it must also critically dialogue with and be confronted by (and not run away from) history, the social sciences, human reason, and human reality, as well as acknowledge that what humans say of grace and of the Spirit of God are neither grace nor the Spirit.[27] Otherwise it would not be theology—or responsibly Christian.

This book organizes our ongoing conversation into four chapters. The chapters are parts of a process whereby each contributes a set of elements, further expanding on and elucidating the other chapters and elements. The last chapter acts as the gathering and summarizing moment.

I. Clarifications. Here readers will find my understanding of basic terms, perspectives, and starting points which they will need throughout the remaining chapters; these are the basic building blocks for this volume. However, it should be clear to readers that each one of these understandings or building blocks will be significantly expanded later in the book, and that their presence in this chapter is only by way of clarification and not as a sufficient reflection on any or all of the topics involved.

II. Contexts. Several contexts are introduced here in order to set the perimeters within which, and the ground on which, I have crafted the following two chapters. This second chapter requires the same caveat as the first: each of the contexts discussed deserves a much broader and more complete reflection. My present discussions of these contexts, therefore, are not intended as sufficient reflection on any or all of the topics involved.

III. Theological Elements. No theological reflection on traditioning can avoid discussing revelation, hope, and faith. These "theological elements" receive more extensive consideration in this chapter, as does anti-idolatry as crucial theological perspective. The chapter also discusses the roles of doctrine in traditioning. All of the theological elements are studied from the perspective of Jesus' subversive claim that God has begun to transform this world drastically according to the divine will, and that this will is compassion toward all, without limits, conditions, or exceptions.

IV. Traditioning: A Theological Proposal. Finally, I gather all of the preceding chapters, and their discussions, as I propose an understanding of traditioning, with special emphasis on the crucified as "effective analogy" of the Ultimate Mystery's compassion, and on hope and faith as inseparable and inescapable for those who would recognize the analogy. But I do not mean any compassion, any hope, or any faith, as the chapter will make clear. A few synthetic statements will serve to gather the book into a whole.

After this book is finished, the conversation will need to continue.

As in a culinary creation, the various elements and parts in this book were chosen, measured, and prepared because of their potential contributions to the conversation and because of Chapter Four's contribution to the ongoing conversation—and only for that purpose and to the degree they serve that purpose. As in good cooking, the resulting meal will always seem much simpler and more "evident" than what was required and involved in its preparation.

This author could not and cannot say it all, explain it all, or think it all. That is why the notion of conversation keeps reappearing, because to reflect effectively on traditioning is like traditioning itself: it takes place only and always *en conjunto*.

The approach taken in this volume, furthermore, cannot and does not claim to be the only possible approach to a western Catholic theological reflection on traditioning, or to any of the elements brought into our conversation. Only God is definitive, not our understandings of God or of God's self-revelation.

Following the dedicatory page of this book are several sentences from the works of a few eminent thinkers. These epigraphs represent insights that guided the reflections in this book. They also represent their authors' (and this author's) passion. Without passion there would be no justice, no love, and no hope. Thus, Christians could add, without passion we would not know God.

The goal of Christian theology is to understand in order to transform: to understand the world, and within it God's revelation and Christian faith, in order to transform *this* world.[28] Theology is a moment of critical awareness and understanding. That is why I believe theology can be a powerful tool for a critical, perhaps subversive reflection on real religion—specifically, in this volume, the Christian religion—in today's real world.

I also believe that it is mainly among and from among the "disposable," the unimportant and insignificant, the forgotten and the marginalized, as well as among those accused of being morally sinful or socially dangerous, that we may discover the most scandalous and definitive Christian understanding of the Ultimate Mystery—the effective analogy of the unsayable Mystery. It is deeply relevant to the argument proposed by this book that we recognize that the vast majority of today's western Catholic Christians are still counted (as most western Catholics have always been counted) among the disposable of the world.

Every work of theology is contextual and biographical before it becomes theological, whether we care to acknowledge it or not. The contents and reflections in this book, therefore, assume and implicate their author.

This book was conceived and written within a cultural context and from a contextualized methodological perspective, as is all theology. I am a western Catholic Latino,[29] and this is a work in Latino/a theology. I earned doctoral degrees in western Catholic theology and theological methodologies.[30] To affirm my *latinidad*, among other things, emphatically means that my theological work is done with, from within, and among real-life validating communities of real people.[31] But it also means, and very emphatically, that this book is not just for Latinos/as and not just about Latinos/as.[32]

This volume, therefore, is as contextual as all works in the long history of theology. There is no such thing as (and there has never been) a general or universal methodology or theology, because all are and have always been contextual, historical, cultural, gendered, ethnic, racial, and limited *by* the theologians' various social locations and contexts and by their personal biographies, social dominance (or lack thereof), and social interests. The present book is no exception.

The renowned historian of doctrines Justo L. González once wrote:

The new theology being done by those who are aware of their traditional voicelessness is acutely aware of the manner in which the dominant is confused with the universal. North Atlantic male theology is taken to be basic, normative, universal theology, to which then women, other minorities, and people from the younger churches may add their footnotes. What is said in Manila is very relevant for the Philippines. What is said in Tübingen, Oxford or Yale is relevant for the entire church. . . . Such a notion of "universality" based on the present unjust distribution of power is unacceptable to the new theology.[33]

I cannot agree more.

I

Clarifications

We begin by gathering a number of different terms, assumptions, perspectives, and starting points that require explanation
beyond the brevity of an Introduction. We also need to clarify
what is meant here by the expression "western Catholic." Before
we proceed to laying the groundwork and develop our argument
in the subsequent chapters, the reader will want the clarifications
below. The several parts of this chapter do not yet pretend to "fit"
together; that will be a goal for the final chapter.[1]

First, the obvious that often isn't.

Jesus of Nazareth stands at the start of the religion we call
Christianity. He stands at the start of all Christian theology. So
here too we must begin with him.

Jesus: His Context and His Message

The message of Jesus' earliest followers included his person as
inextricably linked to whatever he had said and done. But Jesus
did not preach Jesus. His followers did. Given the arguments in
this book, it is methodologically important that we start with
the historical Jesus, as best reconstructed and inferred from the
historical and cultural data we have.[2] Christianity stands or falls
on the content, understanding, and credibility of the message of
the messenger: they are what and whom Christianity claims to
tradition.

What do we know of Jesus of Nazareth, of his message, and
of his context?[3]

Jesus was a day laborer in a small village in the southern region of Galilee.[4] He and his family probably were among the poorest and most vulnerable in his village, needing to earn each day what was needed for that day's survival.

Jesus was a Galilean Jewish villager in Roman-occupied Palestine. This means that he was subject to the violence and abuse, as well as the heavy taxation and toll systems, of the imperial occupiers and their local allies (Herodians in Galilee and the high-priestly families in Jerusalem and Judea).

All indications suggest that Jesus was completely committed to the ancestral religion of his people and to the observance of Torah.[5] But, as can only be expected, his commitment to and understanding of Israel's religion were typical of the Galilean Jewish peasants of his day—because he was one of them.[6] He was not one of the educated, or one of the city folk, or one of those who placed ritual purity above all else. He was not a "recognized" religious leader;[7] in fact, he seems to have gone out of his way to challenge (sometimes through ridicule) the learning of the pious, the understanding of ritual purity of many religiously-motivated leaders, and the abuses of the dominant.[8]

Jesus was an interpreter of Torah—not the only one, certainly, but one of the more radical. His understanding of revelation and covenant reflected the reality, needs, and concerns of his fellow Galilean Jewish peasants. The "will of God" seems to have been paramount in Galilean Jewish village contexts in Jesus' day, a will expressed in Torah, yet misunderstood by those (mostly from the cities) who attempted to doctrinify and codify Torah, reducing it to compliance with ritual and purity requirements and with proper tithing. Jesus proposed a different, radical interpretation of Torah, wherein a compassionate way of life outweighed all other demands and practices.[9]

Jesus' interpretation of Torah—this would perhaps surprise many Christians today—did not concern itself with an individual's eternal salvation. In his cultural, political, and economic context, such concern would have really been the effective denial of compassion: to be compassionate in Roman-occupied Galilee (given the Jewish peasant belief that God was compassionate toward them also in Roman-occupied Galilee) meant to stand with the victims, with the abused, and with the poor, even when the local beneficiaries of Rome's occupation would invoke God and Torah in order to appease the imperial authorities and control the people's minds by reinterpreting the memory of God's subversive behavior in Israel's history.[10]

Jesus' radical stance was subversively anti-idolatrous and totally committed to a life of compassion because he understood the will of God to be radically compassionate, as expressed in Torah, because he understood God's compassion to be the ultimate cause for subverting all systems of dominance over the poor and vulnerable. These are also the two sides of another coin: to understand compassion as the will of God, above all that could claim religious value or importance, is to stand against the idols that religious persons sometimes make of their explanations and of their practices, thereby turning their explanations and practices into the criteria by which to measure commitment to God and God's will. Compassion, not the explanation or practice, is the criterion.

According to Jesus, compassion and justice are absolutely more crucial than ritual, obedience, purity, or tithing, hence his deep disagreements with other Jewish groups of his day.

Not all members of the Jewish religious leadership supported Rome's interests or involved themselves in sacerdotal politics. Yet Jesus seems to have distanced himself from, and at times fiercely disagreed with, most of them as well. Their interpretations of Torah and of "God's will" still passed through ritual and religious observances and practices (especially rituals and practices of purification) that declared "impure" those who could not keep up with the high standards of a "pure" life. As a consequence, the poor and the "disposable" of rural Galilee (and elsewhere) were effectively dismissed because their daily struggle for the basics of life did not allow them time and resources for the observance of purity rituals and practices.[11]

Jesus simply placed compassion—for victims and for the poor, as well as for the impure and the sinner—at the core of his radical interpretation of Torah and of his understanding of the will of God. Nothing was more important than compassion, and nothing was to curtail, diminish, or domesticate it or explain it away. Compassion was scandalous, it could provoke violent backlash, and it might prove very difficult, but it was the only absolute because God had been compassionate towards the people of Israel when they were insignificant and enslaved in Egypt, as well as throughout their history.

God's compassion toward an insignificant, enslaved people was the sole reason for and foundation of Torah. God had remembered God's promise of compassion and had acted accordingly. Consequently, any correct interpretation of Torah (and of the implied revelation of God) and any legitimate interpretation and organization of the life of Israel had to place compassion at their very core, as compassion was God's founding behavior and remembered promise. However, compassion was no mere feeling: it was to be a lived behavior (again, like God's) that actually and effectively liberated, and that effectively[12] promoted justice, social responsibility, and participation.

What would the world of Jesus and of his Jewish Galilean contemporaries be like if it were according to this will of God? It would be a world where God reigned! This was the core message of Jesus of Nazareth. He announced it as a Jewish Galilean peasant among other Jewish Galilean peasants. For them, undoubtedly, this was good news, especially in the cruel and violent world of Roman-occupied Palestine. God was beginning to interfere with and intervene in this world, and had finally begun the process of transforming it according to God's own compassionate will. The "Reign(ing) of God" was at hand!

Jesus of Nazareth was a Jewish "popular prophet,"[13] living in rural Galilee during the period of imperial Roman occupation of Palestine. His concern seems to have been the radical, hopeful reform of his people's ancestral religion and not the establishment of a new one, much less of a new religion that would come to be regarded as superseding his own.

Jesus was condemned by the Romans to die by crucifixion[14] following a political "show trial" that resulted in a death sentence to be carried out in a manner Rome reserved for subversive outsiders. Jesus had become a potential leader of subversion against established rule—Roman, Herodian, and priestly.

Jesus announced the hope-filled dawn of the "Reign of God." In order to make clear what he meant by that expression, he also spent considerable effort describing and acting out his radical understanding of the God of Israel, since the God whose Reign was dawning was none other than the God of Israel. Jesus was adamant that the God of Israel, because of God's promises made and kept, was especially compassionate toward all whom the dominant and the pious considered to be sinful and impure. Jesus announced, in his words and in his deeds, that God took the side of the "disposables" of his world—excellent news among peasants like himself![15]

Jesus spoke of the impending dawn of the Reign of God. In his rural Galilean Jewish context, the expression "Reign of God" was known among some radical circles, and the hope it represented had been, and was again to be, the source of several subversive movements during Second Temple Jewish history. Jesus' message about the Reign of God was also deemed subversive of the Roman occupation and of the locally dominant groups that had negotiated the status quo with Rome.[16]

Consequently, Jesus' appeal to the Reign of God, and his announcement that the Reign was dawning, were neither innocent nor naïve. He must have known full well what his contemporaries were hearing and understanding as he publicly spoke and acted. Jesus' message and actions did not occur in a cultural or historical vacuum: his context allows us, as it did his contemporaries, to understand what he said and did, and to understand why these words and deeds led to his trial and execution by the dominant of his day. Without his specific context, Jesus' message and actions could easily be misinterpreted—as, unfortunately, they have been in more than a few periods in Christian history.

Historical studies and reconstructions of Jesus' message agree on the following points as being the crucial elements of Jesus' core message.[17] God is transforming this world, in its structures of power, in its structures of ownership, and in its very understandings of what "religion" is, to make this world a different world that reflects the compassionate will of God. This new world according to the divine will is to be constructed by radically living a life of compassion toward all, but especially toward the sinners, the impure, and the poor (i.e., the disposables of the world built by and for the dominant and the pious); no doctrine, no religious practice, no power relation, no obligation (no matter how "holy" it might be) can stand in the way of this radical new world and this radical new way of being human, because this is God's will and because this is how God acts in order to be faithful to God's own promises.

For proclaiming the above, and for credibly acting on it in his own life,[18] Jesus of Nazareth was executed by the Romans (with the connivance of the high-priestly families, of the Herodians, and of other supporters of the *status quo*). As Marcus Borg notes, "Jesus died a martyr, not a victim."[19] Soon after Jesus' crucifixion, a handful of his followers began to make claims about him: he was not dead because God had "raised" him. *This meant that Jesus was right* about God, about God's transforming intervention in the world, and about compassion, because God would not raise a liar or a misguided fool and because "resurrection of the dead" was code language, among many Jewish groups of Jesus' time, to indicate or refer to the dawn of the Reign of God.[20]

Therefore, Christianity stands or falls on the *hope*—a reasonable and realistic hope, and not wishful credulity—that Jesus of Nazareth was right.[21]

Christianity stands or falls on the reasonable hope[22] that God, as Jesus said, is really intervening in this world, transforming it according to God's compassionate will. Christianity exists because of the effectively subversive hope that God really does care for the most vulnerable and disposable members of humankind, that God is really compassionate, and that the ultimate moment of history will be compassionate and not the now all too frequent abuse of the poor and vulnerable.[23]

Christianity stands or falls on the reasonable hope that God's will for the world is only compassionate, because, as the earliest Christians came to say, God *is* compassion. Because Jesus, as a sign of God's will, reached out to the disposables of the world built by the dominant and the pious. Because Jesus announced that only compassion, and especially compassion towards the disposables, will be the criterion for participation in the new world God is fashioning.

But is any of the above true? Is *this* world being transformed by God? Is God nothing but compassionate toward humankind, especially toward those whom the powerful and the pious would dismiss or judge as sinful or disposable?[24] Is compassion *the* behavior really demanded of all who would act according to God's will, regardless of any and all other conditions?

Christianity stands or falls on the reasonable hope that, in all of the above, Jesus of Nazareth was right. And because Christianity has always held that in all of the above, Jesus was right, it holds Jesus himself as model and revealer of a new way of being—a new creation—in accordance with the new world that is dawning. Jesus, who never preached himself, has come to be understood in Christianity as the effective analogy of what Christianity claims of God, of compassion, and of God's Reign.[25]

To hold that Jesus was right reasonably demands a leap of (hopeful) faith.[26] But there will still be no credible claim to Christianity until the leap becomes the wager or bet—the wager of one's life for the reasonable and subversive hope that God is as Jesus said, and that the world is in fact being transformed according to the compassionate will of God. To bet one's life on that hope is to place compassion at the center of one's life, and to trust ("faith") that this is a reasonable option and not an illusion or a credulous fantasy.

A Christian is one who bets that effective compassion toward and with the most disposable of the world is worth all the risks—even the risk of being wrong! This is Christianity's subversive hope.

Yet how do we[27] transmit, how do we tradition—used here, again and repeatedly, as a verb—Christianity thus understood? How do we avoid making doctrinal statements or stipulating religious practices, turning them into criteria of Christian identity and orthodoxy? How do we assure the continuity of Christianity in a world of relentless change and diversity of cultures? How can Christianity tradition itself without becoming what it was never supposed to be—another religion? More crucially, how can Christianity remain a subversive message and compassionate way of living among and for the disposables of this world?[28]

Christianity has never forgotten Jesus and his subversive message, although historically it seems often to have forgotten both. This loss of subversive memory is one of Christianity's enduring temptations. This context grounds much of this book.

Traditioning

As we continue clarifying terms, assumptions, and starting points, we need to discuss the meaning of and reasons for the term "traditioning."[29]

"Traditioning" focuses on and refers to what occurs when we understand "tradition" as a verb or process much more than a content.

In fact, the "contents of tradition" are not and cannot be reduced to propositional doctrinal statements, not even when we claim that these doctrinal statements are part of revelation.[30] The contents that are traditioned by Christians have been and still are molded and affected by human histories and human cultures, by power asymmetries and conflict, by ethnic bigotries and social prejudices, by racism and gender biases, as much as by courageous attempts at compassion and truthfulness, by dogged hope and self-giving, and by a faithfulness to revelation that is far greater than mere obedience or repetitious orthodoxies. All contents traditioned by Christians, in other words, are shaped by the same dynamics and processes that mold and impact all things human. It cannot be otherwise.

The contents of traditioning, in the final analysis, are time-bound and culture-molded attempts by one generation or community to witness to another generation or community what the first regards as "our faith": what this faith has meant and why, what "we" claim and believe has been proclaimed and received since the days of the apostolic generation. Some of the witnessing transmission might occur through texts, some through speech, some through daily life and actions, some through prayer styles; the transmission occurs in many other ways. But no understanding of "our faith" can ever claim permanence or immutability, because all claims and all acts of faith are human, transitory, and changeable. Nevertheless, and squarely in the midst of inescapable human contexts and time's transience, Christians still claim to witness to—and therefore, to tradition—the subversive hope that is the core and ground of revelation.[31]

What is transmitted is what one Christian community, though not necessarily another, decided was more important or more indispensable. All Christian communities, aware of it or not, choose what they think is most necessary from a wider pool of contents witnessed and traditioned to them by others.[32] These choices have not been the same throughout history. Some have led to splits and rejections, while others have brought about deeper understanding and consensus. "Reception" must be historically understood in this context.[33] Unfortunately (or maybe not) not all that Christians have traditioned throughout twenty centuries has survived time, contexts, and the traditioners' own various interests or understandings, although the elements that did survive have typically been claimed to be "all." Remarkably, the memory of Jesus' radical core message has not been forgotten, although it has undergone myriad explanations, some of which have dismissed the radicality of the message, reinterpreted its meaning, or doctrinified its defiance. Even for Christians, Jesus and his message have been mostly dangerous and in need of pious or learned domestication.

All choices made by Christians (and the reactions that followed them) have occurred in daily life, in history, and in culture, and none of these has ever been innocent or sinless. Consequently, all that is traditioned is traditioned because it is regarded as important by the traditioners, yet this in no way determines that the recipients will regard in the same way what was transmitted to them or that they will accord it the same importance. For the recipients, and their processes of reception, are also enmeshed in history and culture, and are also affected and molded by biases and prejudices and by courage and hope. Just as there is no innocent traditioning, so too there is no innocent reception.

The contents of tradition exist only as contents of traditioning in the processes of traditioning and reception.[34] It is reception that allows what was held by one generation or community to be "our faith" to become, for another generation or community, also "our faith." The authority of the traditioner does not determine the reception and understanding of the recipient; otherwise, instead of evangelization, we would have colonization.

In other words, the "what" that is traditioned does not exist and has never existed except within contexts (cultural, historical, political, economic, et al.) and in and through processes (also cultural, historical, political, economic, et al.).[35] Therefore, the *contents*, the "what" of traditioning, will not explain themselves if we do not first understand their *contexts*, because the contexts not only make them intelligible but also, and more importantly, choose, determine, shape and, convey the contents. The "how" and "when" and "why" and "who" shape the "what" immensely more than vice versa. Even more importantly, the "how," "when," "why," and "who" decide that this and not that "what" is, or is not, part of the content of Christian tradition, in this and not that way.[36]

The Latin noun *traditio* (and the verb *tradere*) and the Greek noun *paradosis* (and the verb *paradosein*) bore similar meanings in western pre-Christian antiquity. Both implied the handing over of something into someone else's care. The terms came to signify "tradition" (in antiquity, in Christian usage, and in today's meaning) because of the implied and required tradition*ing* in the most basic understanding of *traditio* and *paradosis*. In other words, *traditioning was the context that birthed and defined tradition.*[37] It still is.

In some western Catholic churches (and more emphatically among the churches in communion with Rome), some doctrinal claims have proposed, and also assumed as correct and necessary doctrine, that what is and has been traditioned is a "deposit of faith" (*depositum fidei*), which itself is coextensive with the definitive and complete revelation of God in Jesus, as expressed by and contained in the Bible and the apostolic tradition.[38]

Although the terminology of a "deposit of faith" seems unusual or strange to theologians outside of the Roman Catholic communion, these theologians would not find it unusual to claim that in Jesus of Nazareth God's revelation to humankind is final and complete. This has been part and parcel of Christian faith since the apostolic generations. Nor is it controversial to hold, in contemporary theology and biblical studies, that the Bible may be understood as a part (albeit an indispensable part) of the broader Christian traditioning.[39]

Some New Testament texts clearly indicate or suggest that certain practices and beliefs received from Jesus himself, or from his immediate followers, must be transmitted to and by the Christian communities, whether or not these practices and beliefs were reflected in the New Testament canon.[40] This is not the theological issue.

The theological issues—I use the plural intentionally—are raised by history and cultural contexts. By this I mean the history and contexts of the apostolic generations as well as ours, and those of every generation between the two.

If there is a *depositum fidei* coextensive with the definitive revelation of God in Jesus, and if this revelation is expressed and contained in the Bible and in tradition, then this deposit of faith cannot be reduced to (or be understood mainly as) a set of doctrines, a set of practices, and/or a set of interpretations of those doctrines and practices. This is the case because doctrines and interpretations are contingent human expressions, in human languages within human cultural contexts, that attempt to say or explain what cannot be definitively or ultimately said and explained if revelation is God's *self*-revelation in Jesus.

It would be acceptable and perhaps useful to hold on to the claim of a deposit of faith if the latter were to imply that there can be no new revelation beyond the self-donation of God that occurred in Jesus. The expression "deposit of faith" might theoretically be useful if by it we also meant that nothing could be deleted that was held and proclaimed since the apostolic generations. Unfortunately, in real history, these understandings of a deposit of faith have not always been clear, or even held by all Christians, and historical data might not support them.

Although the expression *depositum fidei* came into western Catholic use, and specifically into Roman Catholic terminology, during the mid-sixteenth century, as part of the Council of Trent's arguments against Lutheran and Calvinist theologians, it was with the First Vatican Council (1869–70) that the expression "deposit of faith" entered Roman Catholic theological discourse. Unfortunately, the meaning of the expression was narrowed in the nineteenth century to mean an objective understanding of revelation, itself reduced to doctrinal affirmations. It further made bishops and popes the only legitimate custodians and proclaimers of the doctrinal contents of the *depositum fidei*.[41] The Second Vatican Council (1962–65) rejected this propositional, doctrinal understanding of revelation, and hence of the centrality of the deposit of faith,[42] but since the 1980s, many bishops in communion with Rome appear to be returning to the nineteenth century propositional claims regarding the deposit of faith as content of tradition.

Consequently, although it might be acceptable to refer to the contents of traditioning as a *depositum fidei* coextensive with God's definitive self-revelation in Jesus, this reference and these contents can become problematic when historically and culturally de-contextualized, and especially when doctrinified.

Traditioning, as process, is the best antidote for the idolatrizing tendencies in the doctrine of a propositional deposit of faith. Without denying the legitimate roles of doctrine, we must admit that the reality of traditioning does not historically allow doctrines to have any legitimate role outside of their specific cultural and historical contextualizations, and then only as contingent means for human attempts at understanding and articulating God's self-revelation in Jesus of Nazareth.

Western Catholicism as Perspective

As I mentioned in the Introduction to this book, I write from within a western Catholic perspective. "Western Catholicism" will be the last clarification in this chapter. What do I understand by this expression?[43]

Western Catholicism is a *perspective* within which (historically and numerically speaking) most Christians have understood and traditioned, and still understand and tradition, their faith. Western Catholicism is a way of "doing" and living Christianity, and only secondarily a way of doctrinifying or explaining it.[44] Those are among the reasons why western Catholicism cannot be reduced to a denomination or even an ecclesial communion. How then do I describe this perspective?

When travelers enter a modern city on any given day, they may do so by car or bus on a highway, by train, by airplane, or perhaps by seafaring vessel or on foot.[45]

Will all of these travelers enter the same city? Yes. But they will not be seeing the same buildings, the same pedestrians, the same streets as they enter it. What each sees of the city is factual and yet different—and always limited. The complete city is not even the sum of all the travelers' views, because the travelers will not see the insides of homes and of workplaces, or hear the myriad conversations, or capture every movement in the lives of the city's inhabitants.

A city is a finite human-inhabited construct, not fully seen or fully understood by any traveler entering it, regardless of means of transport. Some means might provide ample views (e.g., travel by air) while others might more easily lead to engaging the city's inhabitants (e.g., travel on foot), but none will be all-encompassing or all-understanding. Travelers into a modern city will all experience the same city from necessarily limited perspectives, and yet all the perspectives will be "true."

The same conclusion must be affirmed of those who believe in and practice the same religion, because each believer "enters" the religion from very distinct contexts—of generation, of culture, of gender, of social class, of race, of ethnicity, of sexual orientation, of social position, of level of education, of family experiences, of social power asymmetries. Believers believe according to (and are shaped by the possibilities and limitations inherent in) their contexts, their perspectives, their abilities to understand, and so on. All faith, consequently, is perspectival if it is real, and thus every religion is internally diverse.[46]

For some who do not regard themselves as "western Catholics," as well as for many who do find themselves included under that umbrella term, the expression might seem problematic, and possibly too laden with historical (including recent) "unfortunate baggage" to make it desirable. That is one reason for my repeated insistence on there being here no explicit or implicit connection between "western Catholic" and any one denomination or group within this perspective.[47]

Nevertheless, this umbrella term is useful when pointing to a historically real and widespread manner of living and traditioning Christianity. This manner of living, understanding, and traditioning developed, beginning in apostolic times and continuing to the present, in what is geographically the western Mediterranean basin. The expression is especially important as an umbrella term, considering that it is mainly from this geographic area that Christianity spread throughout most of Europe and north Africa, and later to the Americas, central and southern Africa, Asia, and the Pacific. For historical and cultural reasons, therefore, western Catholicism has represented (as an umbrella term) the historically and demographically largest and most widespread perspective within Christianity. I find it a viable term today, despite my misgivings.

Western Catholicism, employed as an umbrella term, can be said to indicate the broad (though diversely contextualized and always perspectival) manner in and through which most of the world's Christians are Christian. This is a demographic, "statistical" statement and, like all statistical statements, religious affiliation statistics are nothing more than maps.[48]

Prior to the sixteenth century, Christians were mostly "western" or "eastern," although these two geographical labels did not, throughout the first millennium of Christian history, signify rupture. At most, these geographic terms represented cultural styles and various apostolic heritages. The world's western Christians began to self-identify as belonging to this or that ecclesial community or denomination only after the sixteenth century. I am deriving the meaning and use of the expression "western Christian" from the first millennium's usage.

It is not irrelevant to acknowledge that within western Christianity, after the sixteenth century, there is still a demographically significant majority that self-identifies with what I describe in these pages as "western Catholicism" although the denominational and other boundaries established by five centuries of acrimonious disagreement could suggest otherwise.[49]

As I mentioned above, the expression "western Catholicism" as I use it echoes the first millennium of Christianity by focusing on the ways in and through which the religion has been lived, understood, and traditioned, from apostolic times to the present, in and from the western Mediterranean basin. I also acknowledge,

under the "western Catholic" umbrella, the colonizing and colonized peoples who spread the religion beyond the western Mediterranean basin, especially since the late fifteenth century, and
the power asymmetries among them; obviously, without these
asymmetries, western Catholicism would not have spread beyond
its Mediterranean lands of origin. In its long history, therefore,
western Catholicism became a religion of both the oppressed
and the oppressor.

This, among other important issues, raises the question of the
meaning of "western," given the hegemonic, conquering, and now
globalizing tendencies of the western world. How could the subversive religion of the peasant Jesus of Nazareth and of his earliest
followers become a "western" religion? What do I mean by "western" in the expression "western Catholicism," given the history
and the cultural, economic, and political realities of this world?

"Western," of course, has geographic roots. The term, however, is not a noun but an adjective. It refers to what and who is
from the "west," but even "west," geographically, is a term relative
to east, north, and south . . . and raises the question "Whose east,
north, and south . . . and whose west?" Therefore, it is important
that we realize that "western" as used here is an adjectival term
that is far from naïve or ethically innocent, precisely because it
refers to the "West." This also requires that we keep in mind that
by "West" are implied not just those with imperial pretensions
and hegemonic dominance, but also the dominated, the enslaved,
and the conquered *in* the West. Western Catholicism, because it is
western, cannot free itself from its contextual history or from its
responsibilities within it; but because it has also fed and continues
to feed subversive hopes and movements against the hegemony
of the powerful, western Catholicism cannot ignore or downplay
its roots and roles in the struggles for justice, for the rights of all
humans, and for freedom.

Eurocentrism and the "western" in western Catholicism
are not coextensive. They do not necessitate each other. Again,
though, it would be useless and ethically questionable to pretend

that Eurocentrism and western Catholicism have not had a significant impact on each other.

"Eurocentrism" refers to the cultural attitude and assumption that what is western European (or European in general) is superior to the rest of the world because it is the world's evolutionary cultural crown, or its destiny, or its logic, or the standard by which all that is non-European should be judged and measured. The Eurocentric cultural attitude or assumption is present, whether we like it or not, in much of today's exact and natural sciences, philosophies, theologies, historiographies, social sciences, and other fields of learning. The Eurocentric is in their methodologies and in their starting points and in the criteria for judging "truth" and "falsehood," for making theoretical claims, and even for determining what is a "fact." Eurocentrism is not *necessary*, however, for western cultures or within them—or within or for western Catholicism. In fact, Eurocentrism has been an oppressive hegemonic tool (*within* western cultures and western Catholicism) in the hands of the hegemonies' dominating minorities.

The western cultural tradition, as well as the Catholicism within it, is the ambivalent mixture of the dominant and the dominated, and neither side can claim to be sole representative of this tradition. Both are representative of the western cultural tradition, though clearly asymmetrically. That is why Eurocentrism does not represent the western cultural tradition any more than other allied and hegemonic tools of the dominant. In other words, Eurocentrism is tied to the dominant side within the west, a side certainly not representative of the west's cultural and religious majority, though a side whose impact we cannot ignore.

In these pages I will argue against a Eurocentric western Catholicism. I will not, however, pretend that Eurocentrism has not played, or that it does not continue to play, an important role—an ethically and methodologically compromising one—in theology and religion. It is certainly possible, and history gives us many examples of this, to critique and subvert Eurocentric dominance from within, utilizing the scholarly tools of the western cultural tradition. In the west we seem to have little alternative, since even new tools would be fashioned from previously held knowledge and previously existing tools, but these tools need not be used for the same purposes or in the same manner as the dominant have taught and utilized them. A drastic change in purpose, agency, and perspective can transform a tool of hegemony into a tool of subversion. Therefore there is a serious need, when confronting Eurocentrism, not to fall into analytic or terminological Manicheism.

Most of today's western Catholics (according to the meaning used for expression here) live in countries of the so-called Third World. Many are also members of minoritized communities in the countries of the so-called First World.[50] Ecclesiologically this is of enormous importance, because if western Catholicism claims that the Church is the People of God, and the People of God are factually of and in the Third World, then there can be no legitimate western Catholic ecclesiology that ignores or dismisses the conclusion that *the real faith of the Church is the faith of the real People of God.*

Western Catholicism is a manner of being Christian and of traditioning Christianity. It emphasizes, assumes, and cherishes the several distinct elements in historical Christianity that we will be describing immediately below.[51] However, not all of those elements have been held by western Catholics as having equal value, equal importance and authority, or equal provenance, even though western Catholicism has historically identified with them.

The following nine elements have, in my view, molded western Catholicism's identity.

Revelation

In western Catholic Christianity, the grounding initiative belongs to God alone, and thus to God's revelation. Although we will be discussing revelation later in the book, it is important to understand first that by revelation, here and elsewhere, I always mean

God's self-revelation (i.e., God's self-donation) to humans.

It is obvious that, if there has been a self-revelation of God to humans, these persons cannot have been addressed or engaged by God except as humans.[52] Consequently, they could not and cannot be addressed or engaged by God except as cultural beings. God alone is not bound by culture, but humans are. This means that revelation *qua* God's self-revelation (and self-donation) is not bound by culture, but that any human acknowledgment, experience, statement, or claim regarding revelation is cultural, and inescapably so.

Revelation, therefore, because it needs to be acknowledged, received, experienced, and understood by humans in order to be claimed as revelation, must also be a human cultural event. And because revelation, Christians claim, is not for a handful of people but for all of humanity, it must also require an intercultural (i.e., "catholic") perspective in order to reflect more authentically the revelatory event as God's self-donation to humankind and for the benefit of humankind.[53]

God's self-revelation, i.e., God's self-donation, constitutes the People of God: humans across history and across cultures have experienced and heard that God is radically transforming the world according to God's compassionate will. The People of God[54] are thus constituted by the faith *response* of those who bet that effective compassion toward and with the most disposable of the world is worth all the risks, even the risk of being wrong![55] Faith is the wager that this subversive hope is ultimately right and worth risking it all. Without God's grace-full initiative,[56] which makes possible the human faith response, there would be no western Catholicism.

It is in this diverse and inescapable context of cultures, of history, of experience (of God's self-revelation and self-donation), of hope, and of faith, that the texts of the New Testament were written, collected, and trusted as hermeneutical response of the People to God's revelation.[57] The New Testament is part of the faith-full response to God and an irreplaceable witness to the Christian wager (i.e. faith) for and in the hope that what Jesus said and lived (and for which he was executed) was right and that it remains the ground for the most profound, radical, and subversive human future.

It is historically evident that the majority of Christians, throughout most of Christian history, have been illiterate. This must be seriously taken into account when one makes claims about written texts, which obviously require readers. One must not ignore the unspoken power asymmetries embedded and hidden in claims made regarding the writing and the reading of texts in a universe of illiteracy.[58] Therefore, the texts of the New Testament cannot be (and are not here) prioritized above the faith of the People of God, and certainly not made coextensive with God's revelation: to prioritize a text above faith or revelation amounts to the dominant literate elites' control of the texts' interpretation, and ultimately to these dominant literate elites' claims over revelation itself.[59] Christians claim that the New Testament texts were inspired by God,[60] but in no circumstance does an inspired text (or a doctrine developed from a text) ever stop being a culturally, socially, and historically contextualized product.

It seems that, historically, the literate dominant elites have assumed, and attempted to convince themselves and all other segments of the People of God (and of civil society), that the only way to assess and guarantee the validity and purity of the People's faith is to measure it against the standards of written texts (biblical, creedal, ecclesial)—texts, of course, declared to be the standards by the literate dominant elites that produced and "authoritatively" interpret them.

God's definitive self-revelation and self-donation in Jesus of Nazareth preceded the New Testament canonical texts. So did (and still does) the faith of the People of God. Therefore, the New Testament can be legitimately claimed to be an indispensable witness to God's definitive revelation *because* its texts reflect the faith of the mostly illiterate (because poor!) People of God. Therefore, any valid interpretation of the New Testament (and of doctrines or claims developed therefrom) must also factually reflect and be congruent with the faith of the poor among the People of God, who are still the majority of Christians today.[61]

An interpretation of the New Testament may be correct as long as it is congruent with the faith of the real (not ideal or theoretical) People of God. And the faith of the People of God is correct if it is in accord with God's self-revelation. Therefore, there is here a dynamic akin to an interpretive dance among the real faith of the real People of God, the texts of the New Testament and their interpretation, and the event of God's definitive self-revelation in and as a Galilean Jewish peasant. These dance partners cannot be understood or interpreted apart from each other. Consequently, I am in no way denying the irreplaceable and even normative role of the New Testament within historical Christianity. I am, however, inviting the reader to remember that the New Testament did not canonize itself, and has never interpreted itself; humans have done so and still do. This fact assumes and poses many challenges to historical Christianity.

To complicate the picture even more, we recall that western Catholicism has always claimed that it is possible (and, indeed, that it is historically a fact) to know and encounter God outside of the parameters of Christian claims regarding revelation. It is possible to encounter, and thereby know, God through nature, reason, experience, and other religions. Yes, Christianity will say that those encounters, and all knowledge of God derived from them, are and will be insufficient as compared with God's definitive self-revelation in Jesus of Nazareth; but what Christianity cannot do, and does not pretend to do, when making this claim of definitiveness, is to sink into self-idolatry. "Definitive" is not an "idol."[62]

Part of Christianity's admission that the God who definitively self-revealed in and through Jesus of Nazareth can be truly encountered outside of this definitive revelatory event is the Christian claim that the Hebrew Scriptures are part of the Christian Bible.[63] Perhaps it is here useful to remind ourselves that the very claim that another religion's scriptures have been received

as their own by Christians is, in itself, a powerful anti-(self)idola-
trous statement within and about Christianity. Yes, it is clear that
the acknowledgment of the Hebrew Scriptures had everything
to do with the historical fact that Jesus was Jewish, as were all of
his earliest followers. But it is very relevant to this book's argument that the followers of Jesus who acknowledged the Hebrew
Scriptures as their own were not regarded (by other Jews) as
having any religious authority. Indeed, most were regarded as
ignorant, or impure, or in one way or another religiously and
socially disposable.[64] This act of acknowledgment and "reception"
(of the Hebrew Scriptures as Christian Scripture) is important,
as it can also open the doors to an interreligious conversation on
the possibility and conditions of similar receptions.

Sensus Fidelium

Revelation is God's self-revelation and self-donation, and, Christians claim, definitively so in and as the Galilean Jewish peasant
Jesus of Nazareth. He was executed, Christians remember, because he proclaimed (and lived accordingly) that God was intervening in this world, transforming it according to the divine will.
Jesus further proclaimed that this God is compassionate, and only
compassionate, towards all whom the world regards as disposable or impure. Christians bet their lives on the subversive hope
that effective compassion towards the disposable of the world is
worth all the risks, even the risk of being wrong. They bet their
lives subversively, hoping that the definitive way to act and live
according to God's will is compassion, which supersedes all other
religious expressions or expectations, including Christian ones.
This Christian wager is Christian faith, implicating and risking
all one is and has on the subversive hope.

    Faith, itself originating in God's self-donation, is an indispens-
able hermeneut among the People of God; it is a "truth recognizer."[65] This leads me to incorporate briefly here a clarification
on the meaning of the *sensus fidelium*.[66]

Cultural differences, diversity of languages, and all sorts of other contexts make the theological study and interpretation of the faith of real Christian people a very difficult task indeed. To complicate things even further, the "object" of study (expressed through cultural categories and idioms that run the full gamut of human diversity) is to be found at the level of *a lived life wager*. It is this faith-full bet that makes western Catholic Christians *sense* that something is true or not vis-à-vis the Gospel, or that someone is acting in accordance with the Christian Gospel or not, or that something important for Christianity is not being heard.

This sense in turn allows for and encourages a belief and a style of life and prayer that express and witness the fundamental Christian message: the subversive message and hope proclaimed by and in Jesus of Nazareth. The faith-full intuition that causes believers to stake their lives on the compassion of God and for the God of compassion is called the *sensus fidelium* (or the *sensus fidei*).

The whole People of God has received the revelation of God and accepted it. The People of God have bet their lives on the subversive hope announced by Jesus.[67] As a consequence, the whole People of God is charged with proclaiming, living, and transmitting the fullness of revelation. Therefore, the necessary task of traditioning the hope is not and cannot be limited to the ordained ministers of the Church. The whole People of God has this mission, and the Spirit was promised to the whole People for this task. All Christians, consequently, are indispensable witnesses and bearers of the Gospel. Furthermore, because the foundational origin of the *sensus fidelium* is the Holy Spirit, it can be said that this "sense of the faithful" is infallible, preserved by the Spirit from error in matters necessary to revelation. In other words, the faith-full sense and real-life wager of real Christian persons infallibly tradition Christianity, and thus infallibly sense the proper interpretation and application of the Scriptures and of doctrine.[68]

The main problem with the study of the *sensus fidelium* as a necessary component in any adequate reflection on traditioning is precisely its being a "sense" that relies on a "bet" and a "hope." This sense is never discovered in some kind of pure state. The *sensus fidelium* is always expressed through the symbols, languages, and cultures of the People of God and, therefore, is always in need of intense, constant interpretive processes and methods similar, but not identical, to those called for in relation to the written texts of Christianity (biblical, doctrinal, and theological). Without this careful examination and interpretation of the means of expression and transmission of the true faith-full sense of the Christian people, this sense could be inadequately understood or even falsified. This is where theology and the consensus of and among the People must play their indispensable hermeneutical roles, though, as we shall see, this process is not without its own limitations and problems.

The means through which the *sensus fidelium* expresses and traditions itself are extremely varied, showing the cultural wealth of the Christian people. Given the global demographics of today's Church, the means of traditioning tend to be more as they have been throughout most of Christian history: oral, experiential, and symbolic . . . and from among the disposable poor. These expressions also show, because of their origin in human cultures,[69] the wound of sinfulness capable of obscuring (but never destroying) the faith-full and infallible sense of the Christian people. The interpretation and discernment needed in the study of the *sensus fidelium* must, therefore, try to ascertain the authenticity of the intuitions (i.e., their coherence and fundamental agreement with the other witnesses of revelation) and the appropriateness of the expressions (i.e., their validity as vehicles for the traditioning of revelation). Those interpreting and discerning must also realize that no human expression is sufficiently transparent to the God of compassion or to the compassion of God.

The sense of the faith must be capable of promoting the results expected of the Christian subversive hope. The means through which the sense of faith expresses and traditions itself (given the fact that all of these means are cultural, historical, and social) must somehow be congruent with Christianity's necessary proclamation and practice of compassion, justice, peace, liberation, and reconciliation as indispensable dimensions of a world according to God's will. Consequently, the expressions of the *sensus fidelium* must facilitate and not hinder the People's participation in the construction of a world according to God's compassionate will. This obviously demands an awareness of culture and of economic and political reality, as well as awareness of hidden (but certainly present) class and ethno-cultural biases and interests which may blind the People of God, and their ministers and theologians, to dimensions of revelation present in the faith-full sense of the People.

If the infallible, faith-full sense of the People of God can only be expressed through culturally given means, then it is possible that the same intuition could be communicated by different Christian communities through different cultural means. It is in this context, and as a consequence of what we have been discussing, that I believe popular Catholicism is the most frequent culturally possible expression of the Christian faith. Popular Catholicism is indeed a means for the communication of Christians' *sensus fidei.*[70]

Spirituality, Prayer, Liturgy

Without the human encounter with the Ultimate Mystery we call "God," there would be no western Catholicism. There is, of course, the originating revelatory encounter, God's self-donation in and as the peasant Jesus of Nazareth, his message, and his life. But the self-donating God who is compassion has not ceased to self-donate, and consequently, human encounters with the Mystery remain not only possible but, for Christians, necessary. Without the possibility and experience of encountering God, Christianity would be a theory or a memory—in other words, a museum piece without a present that can defy human lives.

Encounter with the Mystery grounds and defines what we often call "spirituality."[71] Theology does not ground or lead to a spirituality; it is the other way around. I do not exaggerate if I say that Jesus' spirituality made it possible for him to be the subversive popular prophet he became. Likewise, spirituality grounds the best in western Catholicism.

Spirituality is made of the real life, the compassionate commitments, the wager and the hope, of anyone who honestly and honorably (hence truthfully and reasonably) claims to have encountered the Mystery. For Christians, at least two conditions must be evident in the life and commitments of the one making such claim: (1) daily life must be transparently compassionate and (2) the Mystery encountered must remain the Mystery.[72] In other words, in any Christian spirituality God must remain Ultimate Mystery beyond all understanding or "sayability," while human life is staked on the subversive hope that God is transforming the world according to the divine compassionate will, because the unsayable Mystery self-revealed and self-donated in the peasant Jesus, who is, in Christian claim, the "effective analogy" of the Mystery.[73] Without these two conditions, and without this cause, any so-called Christian spirituality is no more than a falsehood— perhaps well-meaning and naïve, but no less false.

The term "spirituality," furthermore, implies (and is frequently used for) naming a Christian life's founding insight or perspective—always retaining the two conditions mentioned above: that daily life must be transparently compassionate and that the Mystery encountered must remain the Mystery.

If the Mystery is beyond fully "saying" and beyond full understanding, can a human encounter with the Mystery (always at the initiative of the Mystery) "say something" about the Mystery to that human? And in so "saying," has the Mystery not made that "something" somehow "understandable" to the human? The contrary would make the encounter with God impossible for real humans (who are always contextualized in cultures, history, and perspectives). Nevertheless, whatever is "sayable" or understood of the Mystery cannot claim to be

absolute or total truth,[74] and it cannot be credibly asserted except as part of a real life of effective compassion, because only
compassion reflects for and among humans (albeit opaquely)
the Mystery as encountered, understood, and sayable in, by, and
because of Jesus of Nazareth.

Spirituality is necessarily expressible because it grounds life
and perspective. It points to the compassion that is the Christian
claim regarding God's "donating self," a claim made possible by
God's initiative in God's definitive self-revelation in and through
Jesus. Among the expressions of spirituality is prayer, both private
and communal.[75]

Prosper of Aquitaine has often been called upon to justify the
importance of liturgy in western Catholicism. He has been quot-
ed as having said *lex orandi lex credendi*, "the rule of praying [is]
the rule of believing," or paraphrasing, "what we pray is what we
believe." Such ideal equality of importance between prayer and
belief, however, does not appear in the phrase he actually wrote,
lex orandi legem credendi statuat, "the rule of praying establishes
the rule of believing," or paraphrasing, "what we pray establishes
what we believe." Here there is no equality, since praying is the
guiding force.[76]

Western Catholic Christianity is clearly a "liturgy emphatic"
manner of being Christian and of traditioning Christianity. This
is so because it is also "community emphatic." If anyone wants to
know what western Christianity really believes, the liturgy is the
place to go: not all will be there, but much will be—and arguably
what is most important. Liturgy is a culturally authentic gathering and public moment for Christian shared prayer.

Nevertheless, the idea of "liturgy" requires some reflection,
as does "prayer," because liturgy is not the collection of rituals
established by ecclesiastical authority; it is *Christian common prayer
expressed culturally*. Liturgical traditions have served, and continue to serve, as models and molds for communities to establish
their own culturally authentic styles of shared, public praying.
These liturgical traditions developed regionally, initially around
the Mediterranean basin, out of cultural needs and shaped by

cultural means, at times influencing each other. Liturgies, ecclesially and customarily, canonized the ways in which the Eucharist
and baptism, among others, were celebrated and were to be celebrated.[77] There is no one liturgy or liturgical tradition mandated
or "preferred" by revelation or by the apostolic generations of
the western Church. In fact, Prosper of Aquitaine's insightful *lex
orandi legem credendi statuat* can help us understand why there
must be diverse liturgical traditions, and also, more importantly,
why the liturgy is an indispensable element of western Catholicism, because common praying establishes what comes to be
(doctrinally) believed. I do not, however, see Prosper's thought
as justifying liturgy's doctrinal role unless we first admit, as I did
above, that liturgy is not ritual but the cultural (and culturally
authentic) expression of the Christian community's shared praying. *The praying*, when Christian and shared, is the crucial shaper
of belief. Therefore, liturgy establishes belief to the degree that it
is shared Christian praying. Its inclusion of ritual (and its performance of ritual), though evident, is theologically of immensely
lesser significance.

One point I need to underline here is that, because they are
cultural expressions, liturgies are also subject to the wounded-
ness of human sin, including the power asymmetries between
and among Christians and in the societies where Christians live.
Dominance and imposed uniformity, more than faith or hope,
seem at times more important in western Catholic liturgies. One
example of this is the preponderance of discussions on "liturgy"
that invariably consider under that label only the ecclesiastically
mandated and clergy-sponsored liturgies of the Church, disdain-
ing or marginalizing the public shared praying of the People of
God, expressed through the People's cultures and expressive of
their faith, priorities, and lives.

Under no circumstance, therefore, should we think that
"liturgy" is always and only coextensive with what is ecclesiastically mandated or approved. All liturgies are always and
only to be culturally authentic, shared (and consequently, public) Christian praying. The vast majority of western Catholics

have always prayed together, since apostolic times, in authentic liturgies that have been marginalized[78] by the ecclesiastically powerful. These liturgies arguably remain today the more frequent, shared, public praying of the People of God—and are still marginalized.[79]

The key to understanding the role of liturgies in western Catholicism, and also to understanding claims regarding encounters with God or claims about God, is prayer.[80] Without pretending to offer here a complete or even sufficient reflection on prayer, I do need to reflect on its import for understanding western Catholicism. From apostolic times to the present, western Catholic Christians have emphatically claimed the centrality of prayer in their lives.

Praying is what fuels the continued hope of Christians and their faith, but not praying as some today might understand it: as repetition (even very sincere repetition) of established "prayers." The repetition of canonized prayers is not the problem; after all, even two of the three synoptic gospels say that Jesus asked his followers to say what we now call the Lord's Prayer,[81] as Christians have ever since, customarily using Matthew's version over Luke's. The problem is the assumption that the repetition (or the lack thereof!) *is* praying.

Praying is an attitude, a risk, and an openness to the Mystery we call "God." This attitude, risk, and openness are radically anti-idolatrous, and radically subversive of all our certainties, because openness to the Mystery cannot be programmed or induced. It is literally a "radical" risk (from the Latin *radix*, root). Openness to the Mystery must also defy our certainties regarding the Mystery and our own openness to it. Openness to the Mystery is neither key nor guarantee of the encounter with the Mystery. At most, openness is just that: a dangerous openness, which is an attitude and a risk before it is a condition.

The Mystery that remains Mystery, especially in our encounter with it, is the one we may call "God." Furthermore, before God[82] we cannot program our response, because a programmable encounter or response would be a sign of the idol[83] and of human desire for security and certainty, and not of the Mystery we call God or of risky, faith-full and dangerous trust in the Mystery. Praying is a risky and defiantly anti-idolatrous attitude; it is radical openness to the Mystery we call God.

Praying, however, is human. The Mystery does not pray; we do. And we (with everything we do) are inescapably contextualized in culture, in history, and in society. Therefore, praying, if it is human, can only be contextual—in culture, in history, in society. This also means that praying must not be, if it is truly praying, a tool or occasion for cultural colonization of the human other.

Western Catholicism has constantly pointed to the centrality of praying in the lives of Christians. It has always admitted the cultural contextualization of praying as well as the impossibility of containing or exhausting prayer (or more exactly, pray*ing*) in canonized forms. And yet there seems to be on the part of many Christians a serious ambivalence in regard to these canonized forms, i.e. what is often simply referred to as "prayers." What value do these canonical forms have in relation to praying as described above? We may ask, given the real and *constatable*[84] poverty and the subaltern social and ecclesiastical position of the vast majority of western Catholics throughout history, whether what the educated elites (including theologians) might perceive as shortcomings or flaws in the praying of the vast majority of the real People of God might not be a result of the elites' often-demonstrated inability to see and understand from the perspective of those marginalized by the elites (and, intentionally or not, by most theologians).

Communal Dimension of All
Human (Hence Christian) Life

Western Catholicism is clearly communal. Its basic insights into human life, social issues, modes of praying, and much more, are grounded in a vision of humanness that is communal. Individualism, as an ideological perspective, is foreign to western Catholicism.[85]

"Community" or "communion," however, is not coextensive with a sociologically measurable institution. It incorporates the institutional, without question,[86] but it is not exhausted by it. Consequently, it is not acceptable to reduce western Catholicism to ecclesiastical institutions led by (or even perceived as coextensive with) the ordained who have abrogated exclusively to themselves the power to determine who or what may be regarded as orthodox or as "pure."[87] The most basic of ecclesiological insights would defy such reduction.[88]

The community-emphatic character of western Catholicism, with deep and evident roots in the New Testament notion of *koinonia*,[89] is also the basis for much in western Christian liturgies, ethics, ways of biblical interpretation, theologies of grace, soteriologies, and more. Hence, without community, western Catholicism is not possible as a way of being Christian. Furthermore, "community" is not and cannot be a theory if it exists *as community* in human reality.[90] The subversive hope announced by Jesus, which is the core of Christianity and the ground on which it ultimately stands or falls, *constatablemente* assumes and affirms the inescapable communal dimension and responsibilities of humanness.

"Apostolic Succession" of the Episcopate

There are bishops in all of western Christianity, and the necessity and importance of their ministry in the Church has never been challenged, at least within western Catholicism.[91] Nevertheless, there has been and still is a significant variance among western Catholics regarding the doctrinal definition and ecclesial authority of episcopal ministry, as well as regarding the meaning of the expression "apostolic succession." In these issues (and variance) lies the main cause of the denominational diversity within western Catholicism. This clarification item, as its title specifies, refers exclusively to apostolic succession and not, more broadly, to the ministry of bishops, except as the latter is derived from the apostolic ministry.

Western Catholicism has understood the episcopate (the bishops, jointly) as "successors to the apostles." The apostles, then, are the key to a proper understanding of the episcopate's "succession." More specifically, *apostolic ministry* is this key.[92]

The New Testament and some other early Christian texts (e.g., the *Didachê*) mention the varied roles played by the apostles in early Christianity.[93] The term "apostles" is employed in reference to leaders of communities, missionaries, teachers or itinerant preachers, healers, founders of new local communities, and others. The apostles were acknowledged as Christians "sent" (from the verb *apostello*, to send) to serve through any or several of the roles just mentioned.

The apostles were, first and foremost, witnesses to the subversive (yet reasonable and realistic) hope that Jesus of Nazareth was right when he announced that God is really intervening in this world, transforming it according to God's only-compassionate will. They witnessed to the meaning of resurrection as God's corroboration of Jesus' message and life. For their witnessing, and for their traditioning of the hope and the faith (as the betting of one's life on the credibility of the hope), the various roles played by the apostles came to be regarded as facets of one apostolic ministry, a ministry of witnessing to the transformation of the world as announced by Jesus and to the executed and risen Jesus as model and argument for the faithfull, who bet their lives for God's compassionate transformation of reality.

Therefore, the various elements that have historically been named as parts of the ministerial role of bishops are only truly apostolic when the witness to, and the wager for, the subversive hope announced by Jesus remains at the core of the episcopal ministry, and when it is *the* criterion by which the apostolicity of that ministry is judged.

"Apostolic succession" is then a provocative way of stating that the apostolic ministry as described above crucially survives in the Church. It survives and it continues to empower and justify the episcopal ministry.[94] It remains a necessary element of western Catholicism. Apostolic succession is succession in, and incorporation into, the apostolic ministry.[95]

The (Expressed) Faith of the Early Centuries

If faith is betting one's life on the subversive hope that is the core of Christianity, then unavoidably, that faith will always be expressed first of all in life's deeds, values, and commitments, because faith without lived compassion is false.[96] But faith will also express itself through symbol, through text, through narrative, through performance, through affirmation, and through art and song, because the wager for hope will always occur in culture(s) and through culture's means. This is a way of affirming that to be an authentic expression of faith, an expression also has to be culturally authentic.

But it would be naïve to forget that symbol, text, narrative, performance, and affirmation, and arguably many other forms of expression, are *human* expressions of faith, and thus subject to culture and history and to the power asymmetries that always have an impact on the cultural and the historical. Revelation is God's *self*-donation, God's *self*-revelation, but the many culturally authentic means that witness to revelation, as well as the Christian doctrinal statements about and because of revelation, always remain *human* expressions subject to culture and history.

Among these expressions of faith are intra-Christian statements of belief composed during the first several centuries of Christian history.[97] These affirmations were expressions of consensus and clarifications of meaning—of internal conversations— that signaled the interpretive perimeter for developing Christian identity. The statements claimed that their justification was "apostolic preaching," i.e., that this was what the apostles and the Christian mainstream of the apostles' generations were said to have proclaimed, or would have proclaimed had they faced the newer questions. "Apostolic preaching" thereby became a consensually accepted criterion by which to judge Christian expressions of faith and belief. Of course, the issue soon became: "By what criterion or criteria are Christian communities to determine and assess 'apostolic preaching'?" The New Testament canon became that privileged criterion, although at no point did the communities of the first several centuries assume that all of apostolic preaching was contained within, or reducible to, the texts of what became the New Testament.[98]

The western Catholic churches have always accepted the ecumenical councils of Christian antiquity, and the churches in communion with Rome also accept later councils unique to their ecclesial communion. The authority of the councils, however, is not the same across western Catholicism. Suffice it here to say that there is within western Catholicism a shared respect for the doctrinal decisions of those ecclesial gatherings and a shared willingness to understand the conciliar affirmations and be open to their reception.

In western Catholicism, few would advocate the dismissal of the ecumenical councils of early Christianity, because the teaching of these councils received the consent of the immense majority of their Christian contemporaries, and because conciliar teaching still reflects the faith of the People of God. These are powerful rationales within western Catholicism. Nevertheless, we cannot forget that all conciliar statements are inescapably bound to culture and history and to the political and social power asymmetries so often displayed in each council's particular history. It is thus irresponsible for us in later generations to appeal to a conciliar decision of antiquity without regard for its proper historical contextualization and subsequent cultural hermeneutic.

The creeds and other doctrinal statements of ecumenical councils are important, and many will argue, indispensable, but they must always be understood as culturally and historically bound *expressions* of the faith of the People of God. Acknowledged as always contextualized, the creeds and other doctrinal affirmations can (and do) offer a rich testimony to Christian faith.[99]

Human Reason and Human Experience

I recognize that there have been periods in western Catholic history (and in Christian communities in every historical period) that seem to us to represent the opposite of the reasonable. One may ask, though in no way as a justification, what our contemporary reason might be judged to represent to those living centuries into the future, especially to the descendants of today's victims, often the victims of those who today understand themselves to be so "reasonable."[100] In any case, I will not make excuses for the abuses and irrationalities of the western Catholic past. I only point to an unquestioned fact: human reason also has a history and it is also and only experienced and expressed within culture. In other words, reason is not devoid of its own biases (historical, cultural, and other). And because it is human, reason is also wounded by human sin.

Wounded and contextualized as reason always is, there is a very solid and well-documented respect, within western Catholic Christianity, for the indispensable role of reason in Christianity, as well as an equally well-documented trust in the ability of experience to teach and guide Christian life and understanding.[101] From the earliest period of Christian history to the present, western Catholicism has engaged (whether to incorporate or to argue against) the most important contemporaneous currents of thought. This is historically so obvious that it hardly requires further elaboration. Reason and experience[102] help understand western Catholic theologies' engagement with philosophies, with historical and social scientific studies and theories, and with other currents of thought.

More importantly, reason and experience lead to our privileging daily life as it is lived (and this is not unnecessary redundancy) as the primary *locus theologicus*. Daily life as it is lived is often referred to as *lo cotidiano*.[103] It is there that the People of God, individually and communally, have experienced revelation and encountered God. It is in *lo cotidiano* that sin is experienced as well as compassion and grace.

Lo cotidiano is the context of all other contexts, and hence the one existential space and ever-present moment in which God reveals Godself and humans respond in faith (or not). It is the experience of *lo cotidiano* that has allowed western Catholicism to see the presence and workings of grace in daily life as it is lived.[104] We experience grace as humans, inescapably in our respective *cotidianos*, which also evoke and bring forth the myriad other contextualizations that make us human, not as theories but as living beings.

Western Catholicism may be described (correctly but perhaps not completely) as a manner of being Christian, a manner that is inseparably both individual and communal and that is culturally and doctrinally shaped and expressed by the faith of the People of God. Because there is (and has to be) obvious and welcome diversity among the People of God, the shapes and expressions of western Catholicism, culturally and doctrinally, exhibit the catholicity of western Catholics.

No one culture or group of cultures, however, can claim dominance or any sort of *magis*[105] in western Catholicism. Such claims would contradict the logic of the message regarding the Reign of God as well as other New Testament witness.[106] Consequently, it is impossible to claim that within western Catholicism a single cultural logic is necessary for the comprehension of the Christian message, and this applies to the logic of the dominant as well as to the logic of the "western."

Colonization in the name of the Gospel is ethically and doctrinally not acceptable to the Gospel. Therefore, western Catholicism cannot be captive to western "centers" that often equate their specific cultural ways of expressing their western Catholic faith with the whole of western Catholicism. Being a historically traditioned manner of being Christian, western Catholicism is not and cannot be hostage to, or reduced to, any one present-day "authority" or any one present-day interpretation of the Tradition, regardless of the historical and cultural present in which western Catholicism might find itself. The historical, cultural traditioning of western Catholicism demonstrates that it is the multifaceted transmission of and witnessing to a variety of elements by a variety of traditioners that constitute traditioned western Catholicism, and not any one of its traditioned elements, traditioning processes, or traditioners.

One might then ask: "Whose western Catholicism and whose traditioning of it?"[107] These are far from idle or secondary questions.

When it comes to revelation and traditioning, the Church is of paramount protagonic importance. But if the most basic of ecclesiological definitions is taken seriously, then it is evident that it is the People of God who *are* the Church and, therefore, who are of paramount protagonic importance. It is *their* faith and real faith-life, therefore, and *their* traditioning, to which we are referring here. Western Catholicism is the *cotidiano* religion of western Catholic persons and communities, *their* religion lived and expressed in *their* many *cotidianos*, with all that the *cotidianos* imply.

Traditioning and its contents, therefore, are not "culture neutral," and consequently, not social class neutral, gender neutral, poverty neutral, sexual orientation neutral, ethnicity neutral, or race neutral. There is no antiseptic neutrality or objectivity in traditioning and in the contents traditioned if traditioning and belief are human activities. There is no neutrality possible if traditioning and belief are attempts at witnessing to the scandalous message that an executed Jewish peasant *is* the definitive revelation of God. It is the real, lived faith of the real People of God that is the faith of the real Church, and nothing else. The history of this real faith of real people is sufficient proof.[108] Therefore, it is far from irrelevant to remind ourselves that throughout Christian history as well as today, the vast majority of Christians have been poor, illiterate, disposable sheep in the eyes of the dominant. And today, certainly, most of the real People of God are in the Third World or among the minoritized in the First World.[109]

This book will not forget.

II

Contexts

Theology is constructed by theologians.[1] No one can question that obvious fact. But, perhaps because it is so obvious, theologians (and other scholars, as well as ecclesial leaders) have all too frequently not paid all the attention required by the obvious.

Theologians are human beings, members of families and communities, they have to earn salaries, eat meals, should take care of their health, and need housing. Theologians, like all other human beings, communicate via languages, think only culturally, and identify themselves (and are identified by others) according to social class, educational status, gender and sexual orientation, race and ethnicity, and other factors. Therefore, theologians are as contextualized as all other human beings. Consequently, their theological constructs (because they are the constructs of humans) will always be inescapably contextual, perspectival, historically and culturally bound, and expressive of asymmetric power relations. Whether theologians acknowledge it or not, their theologies are produced and shaped in a complex web of contexts. That is why their work is not necessarily relevant in sociocultural and historical contexts outside their own.[2]

This chapter will discuss the main contexts of theologies today. We will consider history, culture, and globalization as key contexts of all theologizing in these first decades of the twenty-first century.[3] We will then reflect on what "saying" the "unsayable" might require, specifically focusing on analogy, metaphor, and *experiencia*. These contexts will allow us then to proceed, in the last two chapters, to the book's explicitly theological proposal.

I cannot overemphasize the importance I attach to the discussions in this chapter. They will ground and allow us to reflect on Christianity's claims about revelation, Jesus of Nazareth, and the importance (or not) of doctrines. Perhaps more importantly, this chapter will help us understand the notion of "effective analogy," which is crucial to my theological argument.

As the reader will deduce, I cannot address everything that could or should be said about each of the various contexts and topics discussed in this chapter, or about the thought of the scholars I engage. This chapter focuses only on some specific issues about a few (albeit crucial) specific contexts raised here because of the succeeding chapters.

This chapter is divided into two parts. The first will discuss the contexts that are inescapable for any human person, group, or endeavor, because they are human. The second part will reflect on our methodological approaches, given the inescapable contexts.

Inescapable Contexts

History

We always and only live in time. All humans are time-bound beings; this is obvious. To speak of time, therefore, is to speak of one of the most grounding of all contexts. To speak of time is necessarily to speak of transience as well: nothing human is permanent or final.

But neither time nor transience is "history."

Reality is also historical,[4] but only for human beings, because history is a human cultural construct. History is not just time or transience or the sum of all events in the past, although time, transience, and past events are intimately tied to any understanding of history. Only history constructs an interpretation of the past, and only history mines the past for "important facts," "important events," "important people," and "important relations," preferably those claimed to be "causal" in relation to history's interpretive constructs. History, therefore, inescapably includes a judgment on what is or was real and on what is worth remembering as fact, as event, and as important. History is always and only a human construct because it is humans who interpret and select past events and determine from among these which are "real," "important," and "factual." This means that *history is never innocent.*

History never "tells it as it was."[5] It is always a present endeavor pursuing and building an interested interpretation, selectively ascribing meanings to the past for the sake of present interests. This, of course, raises important questions regarding the identities and purposes of the hegemonic power interests that benefit from history's selective constructs of any one point in human time.

We create history as much as history creates us, because by creating it we give it a reality and importance it would simply not have had solely in transient time. We also give ourselves a memory that names and shapes our identity by selecting and interpreting what we regard as "important" and "ours." This "realness," this identity and importance, are culturally created tools employed to give meaning to our present. They always benefit or justify an asymmetric configuration of hegemony and social relations in our present.[6]

Inescapably, therefore, one must consider that what Christians claim are the "contents of tradition," because they refer to past events and to past teachings and practices, have also been selected, remembered, and interpreted throughout history to benefit every generation's present-day claims and the present-day hegemonic interests that propose these claims in every generation.[7] But for this reason, and in the same way as with history, the contents of the same tradition can *also* be remembered, selected, and interpreted subversively by those in any generation whose interests challenge the pretensions of the dominant to permanence and definitiveness.[8]

History is traditioned. It is not "there" unless tradition points it out to us as meaningful, important, and real. Tradition culturally creates history—with a difference: Tradition acknowledges that there is intentionality in itself and that it has a place in either

hegemony or subversion. Tradition acknowledges that there is interest in an outcome, in a use, and in an interpretation of the past,
although it rarely names the hegemonic or subversive interest.
Tradition knows that it is not innocent, and that it is "interested"
in hegemony or in subversion—and maybe in both.

Tradition hands on to us, collectively and individually, a "history"—and with the tools, meaning and "facts" of that history,
we construct ourselves. Tradition admits that not all that was is
remembered. Unfortunately, it does not tell us either why what is
remembered is remembered, or why what is forgotten was (and
is) deemed unimportant. We construct ourselves,[9] therefore, on a
selective memory with pretensions of permanence and facticity;
but do we question the selection of memory or its beneficiaries?

Tradition turns "time" into "history" because tradition trans-
mits the meaning of "human" to (and in) every community and
person.[10] The traditioning of the meaning of "human," and of
all human meanings, creates identities and constructs meaningful presents, but it will be up to human societies and persons to
make the ethical choices that would lead to humans experiencing those identities, meanings, and presents as humanizing or
dehumanizing. History is the product of these ethical choices.
The experience of time, therefore, is not the same as the experience of history, because what we experience as history requires
and assumes ethical choices. As I stated above, history is never
innocent.[11]

Present-day historians, and those who at any time would
pursue history, find themselves always as outsiders to the past
events they judge important or worth remembering. They never become participants or actors in those events. Historians
can never judge past events as if they had been there. Because
their task is to make sense of the past for the present's interests, historians are always outsiders, at times only vague tourists,
hoping (when not pretending) to understand motivations, nu-
ances, connections, and relationships, in cultural and linguistic
contexts not their own. They also assume that their present in-

terpretive tools and criteria are adequate and sufficient to judge, assign, and interpret past events accurately and "objectively." However, there have been too many instances of tendentious misinterpretations in every period of "history."[12] The past does not need or care for our "history."

It is clear that historians cannot dismiss texts, artifacts, and other "evidence," but historians cannot deny that all too frequently their evidence speaks only of and for the interests and perspectives of the dominant. Ethically speaking, the voices and the lives of the immense majority of humans who could not write or whose artifacts were not preserved by nature or humankind cannot be left out of history.[13] Their absence cannot constitute objective "history" or justify the naive identification of "history" with the archives, memories, and artifacts of the dominant. Not ethically, not reasonably, and certainly not when discussing Christian tradition and traditioning.[14]

Christian tradition, as seen and defended by the dominant, has often been turned into an immutable, transmitted content, a content determined and doctrinified by the dominant themselves. On the other hand, the memory of most Christian people's faith and faith-full living, of their struggles for life, of their witnessing, and of their peaceful or dangerous transmission of the subversive hope first announced by Jesus is frequently a dismissed memory.[15] And yet, a duty of Christian traditioning is to keep alive the memory of those—including Jesus himself—whom the dominant regard as disposable, and whose lives and faith are deemed as unimportant and forgettable. Faithfulness to history and tradition is also faithfulness to the meanings and hope constructed by their victims.[16]

To be human is to be in time and transience. To be human is to be in (traditioned) history. Nothing human is a-historical, including human cultures. For the same reason, therefore, all human experiences, including experiences of the Mystery, and all religions of humankind, are historical; they exist in time and they are transient.

Culture

Culture is inescapably historical because it is human. All human reality is historical *and* cultural. All that is human and all who are human occur and live always within culture, and cannot ever be a-cultural. Culture, therefore, is a context we cannot avoid or even imagine to escape. We are only and always in culture.[17] Culture itself is always within time and transience—which necessarily means that all cultures change and pass.

To define "culture" is in itself a cultural act, because it is a human act. The act of defining "culture," furthermore, is not ethically innocent or interest-neutral. This is especially so when we attempt to define or understand the culture of another: we must then be very aware that such act occurs from, within and because of *our* culture. This means that the ethical non-innocence of our culture assumes and reinscribes its biases in the cultural definition or description of the other. These biases may be neither present nor necessitated by the culture of the other, but our biased cultural glance needs to see them in the other for its own non-innocent, interested reasons.[18] To define another culture is an exercise of hegemonic or subversive power.[19]

In our western cultural milieu,[20] how do I define "culture"? All human cultures are primarily *the historically and ecologically possible means and ways through which a people construct and unveil themselves* (to themselves, and secondarily to others) *as meaningfully human,* constructing the meaning of "human" in the same process. The values, meanings, and goals of cultures, which define the human communities that construct them, have effective impact on the social organization of the contextual-material universes that these communities affirm as their own because *they are in them.* Even the most marginalized cultures are still meaningful vehicles of meaningful interpretations of life and reality for the communities that construct and claim them. And it is within, and from within, this meaningfulness, that human communities create and speak their logic, their perspectives, and their sense of life and that they engage in the quest for truth. It is within and from within this meaningfulness too that human communities universalize their interpretive universes.[21]

Culture, therefore, has primarily to do with the construction of shared meaningfulness and humanness, the latter two terms being mutually imbricating. We are human because we have constructed the meaningfulness of our being human. Meaninglessness is the opposite of culture.[22]

Furthermore, no culture is peacefully monochrome. Culture is meaningful humanness shared (or claimed to be shared) by many groups within any culture's society. These groups are incessantly involved in internal and society-wide struggles over which interests, and which representatives of which interests, are to play the dominant role of constructing the hegemonic definitions of the culture's society. Who *has* the "right" or the "power" to define what it means to say "we are" as a culture and a society? Who *should have* that right and that power? Who has convinced the rest of society that they, and only they, are best qualified to decide who is included or worth including in the "we are"? And who has the power to decide what the relationship should be among those allowed in the "we are"? The struggle for hegemony is the struggle for the power to define who is human (like "us") and what it means (for "us") to be human. No society has ever permanently settled those questions, except as a deluding act of hegemonic power which can never and will never escape its own transience.[23]

The ethical crises of culture revolve, and have always revolved, around participation, inclusion, and equality.[24] The problem with cultures is not culture but who is left out of equal participation and equal humanness in the culturally constructed categories of "human" and "we." It is clear that all societies and their cultures put identity boundaries on who is "we"—as in who is Canadian, Mexican, American, Chinese, Dutch, Peruvian, and so on. It is also clear that these identity boundaries also define who is "equal" to "us" and even who is "human" like "us" in society—as in African slaves, aboriginal and conquered peoples, homosexuals, women, ethnic and racial minoritized groups, et al. There are many human identities (i.e., many ways of being "human") and all of these ways of humanness are "equally equal" parts of who "we" are, as long as these ways and identities construct "humanness."[25] This allows us to affirm, furthermore, that no human culture and no historical configuration of culture (*because* these are human constructs and *because* of they are results of culture's internal struggles over hegemony and dominance) is ever absolute, permanent, exclusively good, sinless, necessary, or superior: cultures cannot be turned into idols, although humankind seems to have this inclination. All cultural constructions of "humanness" or of "we" are no more than components and struggles in the overall aim of all cultures and cultural constructions: meaningfulness—i.e., that life be meaningful.

The above reflections on culture are important to this book because Christianity's origin rests precisely on a subversive affirmation of *who counts as human*.[26] On this affirmation is built a vision of all-encompassing meaningfulness, i.e., that life is meaningful, but meaningful only if compassionate without limits, conditions, or exceptions.

The claims of humanness and meaningfulness (for oneself, for one's community, or for others) are ultimately coextensive with and indispensable for human life. These claims and this meaningfulness are the aim of all cultures. Furthermore, because we can only meaningfully affirm, experience, or explain reality (and everyone and everything in it) because of culture and the means created by culture, culture is another inescapable context for Christianity and for all Christian living, traditioning, and claim-making.[27] No encounter with the Mystery occurs outside of culture either, if humans say they have encountered or experienced God; therefore, no experience of revelation is possible outside of culture or without it.

Culture is simply inescapable.[28]

Globalization

Time and transience, history and culture are grounding contexts for and of all that is human. But there is a contemporary context that is increasingly affecting and molding who we are as humans today, and who we will be in the future, in manners unforeseen just two decades ago (and unforeseen still today). As such it also affects Christianity and all other religions. I am referring to what has come to be known as globalization.[29] It is reasonable to say that we live today in an increasingly and irreversibly globalizing and globalized world.[30]

We do not need in this volume an exhaustive analysis of globalization and its worldwide effects or a thorough presentation of most current studies on globalization. But I do need to summarize, in a few synthetic paragraphs, what I think globalization is, does, and tends to do, and to make a few suggestions as to what globalization might have to do with crafting contemporary theologies of traditioning.[31]

By "globalization" is meant here the theoretical paradigm that attempts to describe humanity's current stage, with special emphasis on the development of worldwide capitalism, as *the* new cultural context. There is no commonly agreed-upon definition of globalization, but most scholars indicate that globalization at least refers to "the increasingly interconnected character of the political, economic, and social life of the peoples on this planet."[32] Globalization became evident after the 1970s, initially in the economic arena, with the growth of truly transnational corporations. More concretely, globalization has become the extension of the effects of western modernity and postmodernity to the entire world, accompanied by a compression of time and space brought about by the internet and other new communication technologies.

Has globalization brought benefits? The answer clearly depends on the answerer's location. For most of us across the First World and among some groups in the rest of the world, the advances in technology and science are beneficial. So are many of the global emphases on human rights, democratization, and expansion of public education as well as a measurable increase in overall quality of life.[33] As an academic working in a First World university and participating in a First World society, I am the first one to admit that globalization has benefited me and my family.[34] I suspect that most First World theologians can say the same. However, it would be morally repulsive if we used ourselves and the benefits we have received as the criteria by which to judge globalization.

Globalization's benefits to us, and to many like us, have come with the price tag of the increased impoverishment and marginalization of millions of human beings across most of the world. Globalization's beneficial byproducts have come at a high and morally unacceptable human cost. Consequently, theologians have to be very careful in their choice of philosophical, social scientific, and economic dialogue partners, because we could naïvely be contributing (and probably are contributing) to the ideological legitimation for the misery of millions of human beings, even if only by incorporating the theoretical, philosophical constructs of the First World academy without a rigorous ethical analysis of their implications and consequences for the rest of the planet[35]—and by dismissing as unimportant to our scholarship the realities and experiences (and scholarship!) of humanity's vast majority.

For us in the First World, and for some hegemonic groups across the Third World, globalization can be easily identified or confused with *our* societies' progress, technological advances, and other advantages. In other words, because we are the beneficiaries of globalization, we can fall into the trap of thinking that our own perceptions and analyses of globalization (and the analytic tools we have developed within and for our First World contexts) are sufficient and adequate to understand globalization. But globalization is global, and this means that the other two-thirds of the planet are affected by globalization too, though not in the frequently beneficial manner experienced by and in the First World.[36]

To understand globalization adequately, therefore, we need to incorporate into our analysis the experiences and data on globalization in and from the Third World. We need to do so not through the unquestioned application of analytic tools developed for and within the First World, but precisely through an inter-cultural dialogue that must engage the application of theoretical tools developed for and *within* the Third World. We in the First World are not the only ones with rigorous and serious analyses of globalization, its premises, and its consequences, although the forces dominant in globalization have very successfully tried to silence most alternative views by making us (academics in the First World) consider the alternatives as marginally interesting, insufficiently rigorous, or applicable only among the peoples from whom these analyses come.

Once we start studying globalization from a more compre-hensive, global perspective, what else do we discover?

Globalization has brought a real decrease in the functions and power of nations and of national governments. The globalized economy has become de-territorialized.[37] Access to cultural and symbolic goods is now increasingly de-territorialized through de-territorialized means, as is the case with the internet and other virtual vehicles. Divisions among human groups are in-creasingly dependent on access to the internet and other similar means, and much less dependent on territories of residence or national citizenship.

Contemporary capitalism has become global, thereby surpass-ing the strictly national, international, or multinational. Territo-rial states (nations) no longer set enforceable limits or standards of production. Territorial states no longer have the determining power to control transnational corporations. If national govern-ments attempt to control standards or legal arrangements, the transnational corporations simply move somewhere else, thereby making governmental attempts at control increasingly meaning-less. Transnational corporations are no longer tied to a territory, a culture, or a nation. The consequences of this new reality are enormous for nation-states, for the labor market, for the very concept of nation, and for human cultures.[38]

The globalization of the economy is becoming the foundation of profound cultural changes across the world, given that corporate profits today depend in a significant way on the transnational corporations' ability to "place" their products globally, with the greatest speed and efficiency possible. It seems clear that profits today depend less on the manufacture of products and more on the efficient, fast, and successful distribution of these products. The consequences of this new situation for workers across the world also seem clear: labor is increasingly globalized, with transnational corporations going wherever they find better labor conditions, fewer restrictions, and greater possibilities for the successful distribution of their products. Therefore, national labor codes, created for the protection of workers, can actually lead to unemployment and lack of protection for the very workers the labor codes were intended to protect. On the other hand, for the transnational corporations, the ideal labor force is the one less protected but better trained in the contemporary, global means of production and distribution. The poor, on both counts, are left behind. In other words, the poor remain disposable even in the new world of globalization.

In the process of the de-territorialization of capital, it is not only economic strategies and institutions that becomes globalized; ideas, thought processes, and socio-cultural patterns of behavior are also globalized and de-territorialized. Breaking cultural, social, political, and ideological barriers which had been built over the centuries, the means of massive and instant communication have shaped, and continue to shape, a truly global mass culture. A whole universe of symbols and signs is now broadcast and distributed globally by modern means of communications, thereby defining anew the manner in which millions of persons throughout the world think, feel, desire, imagine, and act. Signs and symbols are increasingly disconnected from historical, religious, ethnic, national, or linguistic particularities, becoming de-territorialized and global as well.

There is little doubt that globalization has appropriated those elements of western modernity and postmodernity that serve its de-territorializing global project, although globalization should not be simply confused with the western world's historical stages usually referred to as "modernity" and "postmodernity."[39] Thus, for example, globalization emphasizes the very postmodern attitude that relativizes all claims to truth or to universal validity in order to bring down the cultural, political, or religious barriers that may stand in the way of the methods and activities of the transnational corporations. At the same time, globalization emphasizes the very "modern" and universalizing scientific and technological claims made by western societies, since the eighteenth century, in their quest to control knowledge and the creation of knowledge in the world—thereby denying scientific and technological legitimacy or equality to any scientific or technological alternative from outside the western world.[40]

The obvious success of the transnational, globalization model in some corners of the world has made the rest of the world (i.e., the vast majority of humans, deemed to be "not successful" or "disposable" by the standards of globalization) to wish for themselves the success they see elsewhere. Globalization, therefore, is a major force behind, and cause of, migration and immigration.[41]

It would be utterly naïve to think that the de-territorialization of the economy, of cultural imagination, and even of human identities, somehow follows or obeys the dynamics of equality, justice, or democracy. In fact, globalization seems to assume and enable the construction of new hierarchies of power and of new power structures across the world. What globalization brings is a new, asymmetric distribution of privileges and exclusions, of possibilities and of hopelessness, of freedoms and slaveries.[42]

During the last three millennia, asymmetric power relations in the world were organized so that the rich needed the poor, whether it was for the rich to save their souls through works of charity on behalf of the poor, or for them to exploit the poor through labor in order further to increase their wealth, or both. Now, in these globalized times, the poor seem to be increasingly unnecessary; they are becoming increasingly irrelevant and disposable. Wealth and capital grow without the work of the poor, among other reasons because the labor force needed in the globalized economy is a smaller and well trained labor force which, almost by definition, prevents the participation of the poor. Globalization is a new way of producing wealth, but it is also, and concomitantly, a new way of producing poverty.

Globalization is not something that occurs outside of us, somehow alienating us from a supposedly "true" religious, cultural, national, or personal essence. Globalization occurs within and among all of us as well as beyond us. In this sense one could say that globalization is always experienced locally.[43] Globalization has had an impact upon, and continues to affect, cultures, belief systems, and epistemologies: our ways of being, of thinking, of knowing, of acting, of relating, and of believing.[44]

Globalization presents and understands itself to be *the* viable model for humanity's present and future. This implies that, from globalization's perspective, no other model can been judged to be a viable alternative, neither within the First World nor anywhere else. Globalization, therefore, includes forces of homogenization, of worldwide standardization at every level (cultural, social, political, economic, religious), and thus globalization is inimical to true diversity and to respectful, meaningful dialogue.[45] Or, in other words, globalization represents the new imperial quest and legitimizing ideology of the dominant economic and political forces of today's world—no longer territorial states, as in the past, but transnational corporations and interests. And just as in the past, imperial quests mandate conquest and colonization of the weak for the benefit of the strong because, in the logic of globalization, the weak (or those perceived as weak by the dominant) have no viable right or possibility to determine their lives, to choose which economic configuration their societies should adopt, or to maintain and develop their cultural uniqueness.

The forces dominant in globalization have been busy promoting scholarship that would substantiate the "inevitability" of globalization and the "goodness" of its paradigm for humanity's future. Within the logic of globalization, all stress on uniqueness or diversity by specific human groups is either co-opted as a step toward de-territorialization, or castigated and decried as an illusion which brings division and tension to the "global village."

The question can be raised as to what all this talk about globalization has to do with theology, and specifically with the theology of traditioning. In answer, I would first point to the unavoidable ethical dimension and demands placed on all theology that claims to be Christian and on the theologians who craft it. I would also propose that all contemporary theologies pay close critical attention to the location from which they come.

In other words, no theology today can avoid the challenges of and the questions raised by globalization. More specifically, no theology of traditioning can avoid the ethical and epistemological questions raised by the choices made when theologians select analytic tools and dialogue partners. Whose understanding and experience of Christianity is being presented as "the tradition"? Whose world, whose social class, whose gender, whose race, whose sexual orientation, whose ethnic and cultural contexts, are assumed as "standard" or "necessary" among western Catholics worldwide?

I have no doubt that all theologians, myself included, reflect their own location in their theological constructs. What I am suggesting here, however, is that we in the First World cannot uncritically assume our location to be "typical" of or "necessary" in western Catholicism, especially when we are dealing with a subject like traditioning, which involves the identity and faith of the worldwide western Catholic community, *two-thirds of whose members are in the Third World and are not the beneficiaries of globalization*, and who consequently can and do experience Christianity, and therefore western Catholic identity and faith, in ways significantly different from western Catholics in the First World.[46]

Diversity

Diversity could be thought of as the other side of the coin of contemporary globalization, but it is as permanent as time. The universe's diversification began with time and will end with it. Evolution, geological and biological, is the setting and cause of diversity in our planet. Life as we know it (and as we can know it) is always lived diversely, and there is no way to avoid this conclusion. Consequently, human diversity is not mainly a byproduct of globalization or of other cultural or social developments; it is as formative of ourselves and our world as time is. Diversity is a given in human existence.[47]

Nevertheless, it does seem that as globalization encourages the forces of homogeneity and regards diversity as obstructionist, there is an equally strong centrifugal force at work. Peoples all across the planet are increasingly emphatic about their cultural distinctiveness, their unique histories, and their rights to both. The struggle of peoples on behalf of their right to be who they are is part of the contemporary struggle for freedom and self-determination, and thus of the struggle for real and effective democracy. Earth's peoples have always known themselves to be themselves, i.e., recognizably distinct, as their culturally constructed identities have molded them. What is perhaps more evident, but evidently not new, is the insistence and defense of human diversity and of the right to be distinct, i.e., to be ourselves as we identify ourselves, thereby refusing to allow an other to "name" our identity.

Diversity is emphasized today as much as, or perhaps more than, in the past, precisely because globalization is attempting to erase differences which the dominant interests it serves deem unimportant. Perhaps we are today more aware of the struggles for the rights of diversity, but this is arguably because the internet and other means of immediate communication have made it so. In any case, we cannot dismiss diversity as unimportant or as merely a temporary, backward, and inconvenient stage in global history. By and in the very affirmation of their right to be who *they* understand themselves to be, the powerless and dismissed discover their own power and their authority to name themselves and to construct their meaningful humanness beyond the colonizing (globalizing) norm which the powerful claim as universal.[48]

Diversity is an inescapable context of our human experience. Never has a human group existed that has been identical to another or without identity; the same has been true of individual humans. Geography, culture, history, and relentless needs to adapt and survive in nature have made sure that diversity was (as it still is) how humans experience their humanness and the context within which they name (i.e., identify) themselves as "we" and as "I."[49] Therefore, it is no exaggeration to say that our many culturally constructed understandings of humanness depend on diversity as an unavoidable context of all human experience.

More importantly, acknowledgement of diversity is a critical way to recognize the rights of those dismissed by globalization to their cultures, their histories, and their lives. It is a critical way of recognizing their right to name themselves, beyond, and sometimes against, the power of the dominant. The dismissed thereby affirm their right to be themselves as themselves, and not merely as appendices to the hegemonic (and ultimately tribal) story and logic of the dominant.

The right to be and name ourselves, and to be respected for who we are, is the right to diversity. The right to be and name ourselves is also the right to culturally construct our humanness and the meaningfulness implied in being "our selves."

Theologically, catholicity is the acknowledgement of diversity and of the right to be who we are as we have culturally constructed ourselves as meaningful identities. Western Catholicism, consequently, should reflect on its traditioning (of revelation and more) only diversely because western Catholicism only exists in plural cultural, human realities and can only tradition itself as plurally diverse.[50]

The "Unsayability" of the Ultimate Mystery
Beyond Our Knowing

To speak of God, or to make claims about what God is said to have revealed, is to make reference to a Mystery who is beyond all human knowing and all human explaining. What humans say or claim about God is what *humans* say or claim about God. None of this is new in western Catholic theology.[51]

To speak of God implies that we claim to have the means to understand "God" meaningfully. To speak of God implies that we think we can speak of the Unspeakable and have the means to do so. In all human claims or talk about God, we are also implying (and thereby claiming, too) the possibility of expanding our human ways of knowing, of saying, and of experiencing. Furthermore, to speak of God requires reason, for the statements about "God" need to be meaningful to the speakers. The issue arises, then, as to which are our human means to speak of the Unspeakable. Analogy, actions, and symbol can "say" of justice what laws and courts of laws cannot. Analogy, actions, and symbol can "say" of love what neurological studies cannot. Of course, we need laws and neurology, but neither can ever claim to be the only possible (or ethically the best) way of "saying" justice or love. Such a claim would be unreasonable.

I want to make sure we start this section by affirming that the Mystery we refer to as "God" is unsayable and unknowable: nothing we say about the Mystery is the Mystery, captures the Mystery, understands or defines the Mystery.[52] To think otherwise is idolatrous. This does not turn theology (or philosophy or everyday religious speech) into an exercise of muteness, but it does demand that we put non-idolatrous limits on our speaking about the Mystery and on the authority with which we invest our doctrinal claims.[53]

Can we, nevertheless, speak non-idolatrously about the Mystery?[54] I answer affirmatively, as a theologian who is very much aware of the cultural limitations and power uses of all human speech, including and especially religious speech. We can speak non-idolatrously as long as we pay close attention to the tools, interests, and social uses of our speech, limit the claims of our claims, and do not forget the inescapable contexts we have discussed in the preceding sections of this chapter.[55] We can speak, furthermore, keeping in mind that "truth" regarding the Mystery is only and at best *verosimilitud*.

Verosimilitud

Claims about the Ultimate Mystery, in western Catholicism, tend to imply a "truth." But how can we affirm as "true" anything about the Mystery that is beyond all human knowing, understanding, and defining? I suggest regarding such affirmations as *verosimilitud*.[56]

The Spanish (Castilian) noun *verosimilitud* is translated into English by most dictionaries as "plausibility." The translation is somewhat insufficient when one considers the use of *verosimilitud* in real, daily speech. *Verosimilitud* is more than "plausibility." It is plausible or "similar to truth" because it is "very close to truth" or "bears characteristics of the true." But is it "true?"[57] In its everyday use, *verosimilitud* stands for what "can be or is *regarded* as true," even when the user of the term realizes or suspects that *verosimilitud* is not simply coextensive with "truth." The relationship established by the claimant regarding the claim is the point here, not the truthfulness or facticity of the claim.[58] Furthermore, the contexts of the claimant and of the claim are what make the relationship and the claim itself reasonable or not because reason, *always*, is contextual. (Reason and truth are always contextual, culturally claimed, understood, and expressed).[59] Without context nothing human can be claimed as human.

We seem to forget some of the most obvious consequences of affirming what we claim regarding God. The first and perhaps most evident consequence is how self-contradictory the claims can be. If it is true that the Ultimate Mystery we call God is beyond all human understanding, then that must mean that God is not understandable or "sayable" even by our best claims. Thus, the most insightful depths of Christian doctrine must always be held up against the inherent temptation of all human knowledge toward self-idolatry. In other words, God is as God is, not as *we* understand God to be, and not even as we experience God to be. Can we then dare to speak in God's name? Or to doctrinify the experience of encounter we call revelation?

Nevertheless, we do reasonably *trust* that the One who inexplicably encountered us in the experience we call "revelation" is (*verosímilmente*) as our experience *trusts*. I believe, and not as an act of faith but as a conclusion to a reasoned process, that western Catholic Christianity can rationally and positively engage the logical and epistemological concerns raised by any claim regarding God and reasonably answer them.

However, I must insist that we not forget human contexts.[60] We cannot be "colonizing" about these concerns and about the ways in which they are discussed. We must not dismiss as pertinent here the fact that most of the logical and epistemological concerns regarding the reasonableness of God-talk come precisely from the cultural world of the intellectual elites of the world's dominant societies and their interest groups. One must be severely uninformed to think that there is no connection between the interests of these hegemonic contexts and the concerns they raise, especially in matters religious. On the other hand, what do two-thirds of humanity think and say, especially when they exercise *their* ways of thinking and saying, *their* logics, and *their* epistemologies? Will their concerns regarding God-talk be the same as those that come from the dominant who market themselves as universal?[61]

We cannot forget or downplay that all human reason is like our eyes: our eyes can see everything except themselves. The eyes can only see their reflection in something else or deduce their own existence by the resulting sight. Consequently, that in which the eyes see themselves reflected will significantly affect the eyes' deductions regarding themselves. Likewise, reason may supposedly reason it all except itself; it may see and assess the reasonableness of all except itself. Reason cannot prove its reasonableness except through a reflection of itself or by deducing itself from the resulting reasonable operation.

Who reasons, and where and why, are clearly relevant conditioning contexts, at times blinding and always inescapable, that will also significantly alter reason's observations and deductions.[62] Furthermore, reason or logic is not coextensive with human relationships, yet *it is precisely in relating* (within the contextually possible reason of the claimants) that the *verosimilitud* of claims regarding God and faith is established as reasonable.[63]

Verosimilitud is effective (and thus reasonable) only to the degree that it is *verosímil* in relation to real life as lived by the claimants within their culture and other unavoidable contexts.

Briefly, then, when we make claims about the Mystery, and about the revelation of the Mystery, in western Catholicism, we can only affirm *verosimilitud* for the claims. Not just because they might be plausible, but because the believers who make, believe, and tradition the claims, in their contexts, relate to them as true and claim them as *verosímil* because of the claims' *verosimilitud* in and to real life. Affirming more than this is playing with idolatry.[64]

Analogy

Giorgio Agamben, speaking of method and logic, reminds us that neither can separate itself from its context, just as there is no method or logic valid for every context.[65] The same, I think, applies to what may be claimed as *verosímil* or employed as analogy.[66] It seems useful to say that *verosimilitud* is what may be claimed, while analogy is the "wrapping" of what is claimed.

The renowned physicist John A. Wheeler argues that it is very possible that we contribute to the ongoing creation of the past as much as to that of the present and future. In fact, he suggests, what we observe might be contributing to the creation of physical reality. For Wheeler, the principles of quantum mechanics dictate severe limits on the certainty of our knowledge. Andrei Linde,

another well known physicist, flatly insists that the universe exists
only when there is an observer to say there is, because it makes no
sense to say that there is a universe if there is no one to observe
it and say "there is a universe."[67] For both Wheeler and Linde, the
universe "out there" is only real to the degree and in the manner
that we can observe and speak of it "within here."

Do these two eminent physicists not believe that there is a
universe? Of course they do. But their points are of extreme
importance: Can we claim the existence of something without
observation? But does not our observation create the existence
of something, at least as claim? Furthermore, will what we may
claim of something not be limited and shaped by the limits and
possibilities of *our* observation?[68]

How then can we speak of what we cannot directly observe
and yet exists, and not as object of our knowledge? How can we
make reasonable claims if what we know as real is what we create
by our meager knowledge? The reader will now understand why
we need to keep in mind the discussion on *verosimilitud*, and why
analogy is a way of saying what might not be sayable, because
observability is not required for the analogical.

The Greek term *analogia* originally meant "proportion." A
number of ancient Greek philosophers saw analogy as a kind
of relation grounded in shared characteristics; thus, analogous
objects could share an idea, a pattern, a regularity, an attribute,
an effect, or a function.[69] Although not all European medieval theologians would have agreed with him, Thomas Aquinas
viewed human statements about God as always non-literal: all
such statements, according to Aquinas, were only figurative or
analogical.[70] The influence of Scholastic thought cannot be ex-
aggerated in the later development of western God-talk, just as
the theological crises of the Reformations period also affected
later theological and philosophical discussions on truth and language in the west.[71]

If we may generalize, analogy means the bridging of similarity or resemblance, between two distinct objects of knowledge

or between two distinct affirmations, which allows the speaker to make a new claim of knowledge.[72] Analogy is often the way to speak of (and from within) an experience that is or is felt to be beyond defining.[73]

Analogy, consequently, has been and remains an indispensable tool for human knowing (scientific, quotidian, philosophical, or theological).[74] But because analogy, like metaphor, lies at the foundation of our knowledge and choices, how we explain it is less important than the fact that we cannot know or decide without it. Analogy (like metaphor, paradigm, and exemplar)[75] is a cultural product—contextual, perspectival, and inevitably transient, as are all products of human cultural construction.[76] Consequently, as cultural, analogy is also an instrument of the hegemonic struggles present in every society; it cannot be otherwise. Analogy, therefore, carries the weight of asymmetric power relations within its bridging of similarity and resemblance and in the new knowledge unveiled by this bridging. Analogy is thus a non-innocent ethical act.

After this very brief reflection on analogy, aware of the cultural and non-innocent dimensions of all analogies, can we affirm that we may yet "say" the "Unsayable"? Yes—as long as we are aware that all of our sayings are ours, that none is literal or symmetric, that all are analogical or metaphorical, and that all can only be acknowledged as *verosimilitudes*. Agamben said it very well: "The only true representation is one that also represents its distance from the truth."[77]

To be ethical, effective, and reasonable, an analogy must (at least) be *verosímil* and, in today's real world, intercultural. We will continue to discuss analogy as the arguments of this book unfold.

Optics

We live in a world of many cultures, each affirming its right to exist as a people's all-encompassing "meaningfulness" or "meaningful humanness." And yet this world is becoming increasingly globalized as well as extraordinarily interconnected thanks to the power of contemporary means of communication. No other period of human history has had worldwide access to so much information and to so much instant communication, while emphatically defending its right to diversity.

How do we approach all human "sayings" regarding the Ultimate Mystery, all speech regarding encounters with the Mystery, and all reflections that claim to be born from these encounters? How do we do theology in and for the world as the world is today?

To think interculturally has become a necessary task in theology. What do I mean here by "intercultural"?[78]

Intercultural Thought and Intercultural Dialogue

Scholars (mostly philosophers of culture and of education) from Europe, India and, Latin America have been at the forefront of this movement we now call "intercultural thought."[79] Today many others, including theologians, are theorizing about this unavoidable consequence of globalization. If we reflect carefully, however, we can observe that the demands of the intercultural have been with humankind as much and as long as the existence of diversity.

I have found the work of intercultural philosopher Raúl Fornet-Betancourt to be particularly insightful and rich as a dialogue partner for western Catholic theology.[80] I will be using Fornet-Betancourt's contributions in what follows, although I cannot and do not make him responsible for my synthesis of his thought or for my use of it.

First of all, we must understand that interculturality is not "inculturation."[81] The latter supposes a "canonical something" which exists independent of a culture and which can be poured or transmitted into other cultures. The "canonical something" supposed by inculturation assumes, furthermore, an interpretation or understanding possible only within, and from within, a dominant culture, because the "canonical something" does not interpret itself, and, therefore, does not understand or proclaim itself (or by itself) as canonical. For something in the process of inculturation to be considered canonical implies that someone in and from a specific cultural horizon (and thus, because of a set of interests proper to the cultural horizon of the one doing the determining) has determined that this something exists and that it is definitively canonical. Inculturation, consequently, includes the possibility—and historically the reality—of colonization. Inculturation thus understood[82] has little to do with the truth[83] which is discovered and which convinces. Rather, it has to do with the acceptance of someone else's proclamation, inevitably constructed from within the proclaimer's cultural perspective, that the "truth" being "brought" to me should or must convince me.

Instead of inculturation, we should perhaps speak of "inter-trans-culturation," whereby another witnesses to me, in an open inter-discursive dialogue, what he or she understands and lives as truth, and I, *within and from within my own cultural perspective*, will contrast and perhaps assume that truth, because *I have discovered it as truth* within and from within my cultural horizon. And I in turn, upon my discovery of truth as it is possible within and from within my cultural perspective, witness to the other, again in an open inter-discursive dialogue, what I have come to understand and live as truth, inviting the other to question and grow *in what that other person understands and lives as truth*. Thus we move the process into an ever-deepening and continuing dialogue where truth is discovered and affirmed, over and over, through mutual witnessing, contrasting dialogue, and non-colonizing reflection.

The discovery of what will come to be referred to as "truth," then, results from intercultural dialogue and contrast, and not from arguments and concepts born within a cultural horizon foreign to me and designed to convince me by pulling me away from my own cultural horizon.[84] The argument that truth, including the Gospel's truth, must critique cultures cannot be made to imply or provoke colonization; and such would be the implication if the understanding of truth which is offered for acceptance by

another (including the Gospel's truth) proceeds from a dominant culture (or a hegemonic group within a dominant culture)
which has access to my culture precisely because of their hegemony or dominance; this would be the case also when the
critique of culture is not the historically possible fruit of the
receiving culture's own possibilities.

Convivir (which in Spanish means "to live-with" and which is
exactly the same as the Latin *convivire*), is the necessary assumption or pre-condition for interculturality. *Convivir,* "to live-with,"
implies, among other things, that those who *conviven* are actually
present with and to one another for a sufficiently prolonged
period of time and, further, that their presence with and to one
another engages them with and in one another's daily lives in
ways that each considers sufficiently meaningful and sufficiently
mutually respectful.[85]

Truth is a cultural and intercultural constructive process. No
culture, and no cultural situation, may be considered as the definitive locus of truth or as the best vehicle for the expression of
truth.[86] Cultures only offer us the possibilities and instruments
for seeking after truth. Truth will only unveil itself to us if we
are willing (in intercultural dialogue) to risk contrasting our own
truth with the truth claims and truth expressions originating in
other cultures. Reality, and thus truth, is not monochrome or
monovalent; rather, reality, and thus truth, is plurichrome and
plurivalent. There are many versions of reality and, consequently,
many versions of truth.

It would be dangerous nonsense to assume, in today's globalized and globalizing world, that the truth claims of one religious,
ethnic, or national group are universally valid just because this
one group has (through its own cultural categories and assessment) discovered or affirmed something to be true.[87]

By "universal validity" I mean that a truth claim, from within
a specific culture (as all truth claims inescapably are), is presented
to and possibly imposed on the potential recipients because the
claim's birthing culture assumes *its* particular perspectives (i.e.,

its questions and themes, *its* answers and solutions, *its* practices and approaches) to be applicable to and correct for all other cultures. The claim to universal validity has usually accompanied the history of power and colonization and has been all too frequently legitimized by these. Unless a group acknowledges to itself and others that there are indeed other claims to truth, just as evidently true within and through other equally legitimate cultural categories, the group's claims to universal validity may be regarded either as an indication of human hubris or as a violation of other people's right to cultural self-determination.[88]

Only in intercultural dialogue, contrasting truth claims with one another, can there begin to appear what may be said to be a universally relevant truth claim. By "universal relevance" I mean that a truth claim may be *offered*, from within a specific culture or group, to others who may find the claim to be useful, suggestive, or even true, thereby opening for and within the recipients new perspectives—questions and themes, answers and solutions, practices and approaches—that had hitherto remained closed, unclear, or ignored. It might be possible to discover common threads and denominators with universal relevance among the truth claims, but the original claim does not present itself as necessarily applicable or correct or "true" for all possible recipients and in all possible cultural contexts. The recipients must consent to the relevance of the claim that is offered to them. Only in the contrasting intercultural dialogue necessary for the discovery of universally relevant claims can truth be acknowledged, and only then can truth unveil itself without the trappings of empire, imposition, or idolatry.

I realize that the concern for relativism immediately comes to mind. How do we avoid relativism in such intercultural dialogue? It seems to me that there is no limitless relativism involved in the contrasting intercultural dialogue which leads to universally relevant truth claims because, first and most obviously, there is no limitless number of cultures, cultural contexts, or truth claims. Secondly, the fear of relativism is itself a culturally constructed, grounded, legitimized fear.[89] A history of the cultural fear of relativism might unveil it as more intimately connected with power structures and hegemonic pretensions than we might care to admit. In other words, the cultural fear of relativism might be discovered to have less to do with truth itself and more to do with some groups' need to make universal validity claims, which have historically accompanied the exercise of dominant power.[90] Thirdly, it might be important to pluck our understanding of truth from the prison of concepts, seeking it instead in our "inter-comprehension" with others, i.e., with others' lives, others' historical realities, and so on.[91] It might be important to let others, and to let truth itself, be "un-defined" for us (within our own cultural perspective), letting their alterity communicate with us as alterity and, therefore, without necessarily cleanly fitting within our cultural categories. This "in-definition" has nothing to do with relativism; on the contrary, it is the humble acceptance of our own cultural limitation and a critique to our own cultural inclination to intellectual self-idolatry. No culture owns *the* truth.

Truth, because it only exists culturally for humankind, is and must always be polyphonic, because cultures, across the world and within each culture, are polyphonic.[92] The music produced by a symphonic orchestra is not the result of a single instrument or of a single musician. The music produced by an orchestra results only when each instrument and each musician plays its, his, or her part, with the tonalities and expertise required for each part, and only when they all play together as an ensemble may we then hear the fullness of the symphonic composition played by the orchestra. In addition, no one orchestra can ever claim to have the definitive and exclusive interpretation of a given composition. Indeed, no composition could ever claim to be the definitive musical creation. Does this imply relativism? Not at all, because there are, at any point in history, a limited number of instruments, a limited number of musicians, a limited number of compositions, and a limited number of orchestras; there is a limited number of musical notes; there is a limited human auditive organ. Therefore, the admission of diversity, of particularities, and of limitation and contingency, does not necessarily imply relentless relativism. Rather, what we might culturally fear or label as relativism might in fact be no more than necessary and inevitable pluralism, which is a condition for the possibility of community, and indeed for catholicity itself.

One important intercultural concern is how to integrate the diversity of the world into each cultural particularity. This is different from, indeed the opposite of, the attempt to integrate the culturally particular into some sort of human universality. The postmodern emphasis on cultural particularity[93] seems to have little future in the world of globalization because cultural particularities, seen from many postmodern perspectives, appear to close themselves off thoroughly from the world's diversity, instead of seeking to integrate diversity into the cultural particularities.[94] Some postmodern perspectives presume that diversities need not dialogue in mutually challenging, critiquing, and enriching ways. Confronted with the contemporary difficulty of making universally valid claims, many postmodern philosophical views on particularities (proposed, not surprisingly, within the dominant First World) seem to have chosen to enclose themselves within their particular cultural worlds, giving up on the need[95] for intercultural dialogue which might unveil universally relevant truth, while philosophically legitimizing this closing off as the intellectually honest and best option. There sometimes seems to be an implied universally valid truth claim made on behalf of postmodernism's denial of universally valid claims!

It seems to me that First World postmodernism can become an attempt at ethically justifying self-sufficiency and the silencing of the voices of the non-dominant others, especially when the others might challenge either First World self-sufficiency, its particular cultural hubris, its silence in the face of situations of injustice, or the asymmetric power structures of globalization which clearly benefit many of the First World proponents of postmodernity.[96] It also seems to me, more importantly, that postmodern proposals are largely lacking in analyses of their own ethical responsibilities in today's globalized and globalizing world.[97] Many of the postmodern views on particularity can become an enclosed circle, risking sterility.

What is arguably and ethically needed is a radical critique of each cultural particularity's self-sufficiency, as well as a radical and critical openness to the others who question and challenge our cultural particularity toward solidarity with them. This is the case even and especially when there is no benefit to be obtained for our own particularity in and through that solidarity.[98] This seems to be the ethical way to avoid our drowning in First World cultural specificity as well as to avoid moral deafness at the crucifixion of the majority of humans in the globalized world.

Contemporary First World postmodernism, by arguing that its views are the best philosophical explanations for and in today's globalized world, is but refashioning and preserving the same, old, and tired First World colonial mentality which in past centuries set itself up as the world's standard and silenced most alternative voices.[99] The alternative to First World postmodern approaches is not, however, the return to what has been called "foundationalism."[100] The alternative, I suggest, is intercultural dialogue, which can acknowledge and accept much of postmodernism's critique while refusing to share postmodernism's inclination to sterile particularisms or its uncritical and ideological legitimation (by omission) of the First World's interests.

There are no multiple particularities and there is not one evident human universality. Rather, there are multiple historical, cultural, human universalities which can encounter one another, which can challenge one another, and which through intercultural dialogue might engage in the process of unveiling universally relevant truth.[101] Each one of the multiple universalities acts as the platform from which a way of thought is opened and launched in the world, opening and launching each universality into dialogue with other universalities and truth processes.

Our own historical, cultural universality is but the first point of reference from which to know and say what is ours, insofar as it is our concrete life and thought universe. But it is also our first point of reference in learning and perceiving the contingency of our knowing and saying. This discovery of self-contingency is a *sine qua non* condition for critiquing our own historical, cultural universality, thereby avoiding the self-idolatry of our historical, cultural universe. By acknowledging the contingency of our universality (and of its knowing, living, and saying) we open our universality to the possibility, indeed to the need, for dialogue, for learning from other historical and cultural universalities, and for allowing our universality to be called to solidarity with others. Dialogue with others and self-critique are not and cannot be merely options or possibilities, although they most certainly are those as well. Dialogue and self-critique should be recognized as life *needs*, without which any cultural, historical universality simply withers into self-idolatry and ultimate meaninglessness.

Consequently, intercultural dialogue is the opposite of Eurocentric dominant provincialism, whereby the dominant western cultures decree and define their own universality as the only "universally valid" universality. Intercultural dialogue does not engage in Eurocentric postmodernism's underlying colonial proposal as the best philosophical standard for the globalized world. (Postmodernism publicly claims to propose the exact opposite.)

Intercultural dialogue does not assume or propose any culture, any universality, or any philosophical or theological current as the best way (in any sense) for the world.[102] Indeed, intercultural dialogue assumes itself to be also in need of critique, as it too acknowledges itself contingent. It holds (while remaining radically open to correction) that the process of "contrasting" conversation, where all is risked in and for the sake of truth-searching dialogue, is capable of determining or clarifying what the intercultural dialogue should be and how it should be carried out. In consequence, it also holds that only through the contrasting and difficult process of unveiling universally relevant truth will universally relevant truth be unveiled without imposition, without colonization, and with the utmost respect for all who engage in this search.

There seems to be a need in theology (as there appears to be in philosophy and in the social sciences) to multiply and broaden the sources.[103] This does not simply mean that we have to add to the list of sources the names and contributions of other "objects of study" we might have set aside in the past, although this addition might prove important as well.[104] By multiplying and broadening the sources of theology I mean that the voices of other—previously unheard or silenced—theologizing subjects must be heard and considered on an equal basis with the voices of the Eurocentric theologians. In other words, the theologizing subjects from non-dominant communities must be positively and actively acknowledged as being also at the theological table (at the *convivencia*) and as always having been there, though mostly unheard and disregarded, as bearers of perspectives, alternatives, universalities, logic, and truth, *and* as theologizing subjects who might challenge and critique that which Eurocentric theology has assumed to be self-evident.[105]

Intercultural thought requires that we learn to think in new ways. We need to think in new "con-vocative" and "re-perspectivizing" ways. In other words, interculturality invites us to go beyond attempts at "enriching" Eurocentric perspectives by somehow incorporating the contributions of others, because this enrichment approach would ultimately leave our assumptions and methods untouched and uncritiqued, since it would be through them that we enrich what already is.

The "new" in the new way of thinking is found in risking our assumptions and methods by contrasting them with the assumptions and methods of others, and through this contrasting *dialogue* be willing to give up some or many of our own assumptions and methods and to acquire new ones. We are thus called to learn to see ourselves, our cultural universalities, our histories, and our lives, as well as our theological assumptions and methods,

in the new light offered us by those who are culturally different from us. Consequently, we *re*-perspectivize our theology as
a result of our accepting the *con*-vocation of others; this "convocation" is no more and no less a dialogue of many voices, all
equal, all heard, all respected, all critiqued, and all challenged. The
new way of interculturally thinking theology (and of thinking
all thought) is thus polyphonic, as it will ultimately lead us to
see our theology, as well as our cultures and history, as "respective," as inescapably bound and related to and with others. It thus
negates the temptation to self-enclosing idolatry and culturally
feared relativism.

It should be apparent that any serious intercultural dialogue
relies on there being conditions for dialogue.[106] This should be
obvious from what I have been discussing above. The conditions for dialogue I am referring to include the political, economic, social, gender, and other dimensions of life which contextualize any intercultural exchange today. Therefore, before
any serious conversation can occur, those invited (and inviting)
to dialogue must acknowledge and face the issues and consequences provoked among them by these dimensions of life as
well as the conditions for or against equality which these may
imply for intercultural dialogue. Once again, I recall that western Catholic theology (and indeed, all of Christianity) occurs
only in this world as this world exists. Today a de-contextualized dialogue (or one which does not begin by acknowledging
and facing the dimensions which impinge on its credibility as
honestly searching for shared truth) is an ideological exercise
which can only benefit those who are favored by globalization
and dominance.[107]

I must make one other important note on cultures. All human cultures are primarily the historically and ecologically possible means and ways through which a people construct and
unveil themselves (to themselves, and secondarily to others) as
meaningfully human, constructing the meaning of "human" in
this same process.[108] The values, meanings, and goals of cultures,

which define the human communities that construct them, have effective impact upon the social organization of the contextual-material universes that these communities affirm as their own because they *are* in these universes.

Even the most marginalized cultures are still vehicles of meaningful interpretations of life and reality for the communities that construct and claim them. And it is within and from within this meaningfulness that human communities create and speak their logic, their perspectives, and their sense of life, and engage in the quest for truth. It is within and from within this meaningfulness too that human communities universalize their interpretive universes. Thus true universality is not the de-contextualization of thought or concepts, as globalization and Eurocentric modernity might lead some to believe, but the dialogue that engages the human communities' meaningful vehicles of meaningful interpretations of themselves and their worlds (i.e., their cultures), acknowledging each and every one of them as human and potentially relevant—thereby suggesting that *there is a "human" condition which, although constructed and defined in and by every particular universality, can (but by contrasting dialogue) be effectively acknowledged as possessing universally relevant elements or description.*[109]

As I stressed earlier in this chapter, because the intercultural view of culture is historical, it presupposes that no culture is a monolithic block, as if a culture were the naïve or simple development of a single tradition that grew without conflict or contradiction. Rather, every culture bears witness to an internal history of conflict and struggle for the determination and control of its values, meanings, logic, and overall contour. The internal history of struggle for inner cultural hegemony is also part of the global intercultural dialogue, as that internal history remembers other silenced traditions and marginalized life experiences. Each and every human culture could have turned out differently, but if cultures exhibit their current values, meanings, and logic, it is because of the struggles for internal hegemony that they historically endured and which provided for the present outcomes.[110] The sacralization of cultures (given every culture's internal history and inescapable particularity) would itself contradict intercultural dialogue.

Effective Analogy

We discussed above that analogy is a bridging of believed (experienced, perceived) similarities or resemblances, between distinct objects of knowledge or between distinct affirmations, which allows the speaker to make a new claim of knowledge—as poetry does.

Analogy is often the way to speak of (and from within) an experience that is or is felt to be beyond defining. Analogy, consequently, can be a human way of saying the otherwise unsayable. Because of this, it is a way of speaking of the unsayable Mystery. But given the world of globalization and diversity, given too what we have learned of history, culture, and intercultural thinking, and (more importantly) given that most humans in our world are treated as disposable, we have to ask, ethically and methodologically, whether any analogy is theologically (and ethically) acceptable.

Analogy claims to unveil new knowledge by its bridging of similarities. But when this knowledge refers to the Mystery, what can be known? What can be similar? And what can be claimed as "true"? Analogy can only be a tool for saying the Unsayable, but analogy can never pretend ever really to say it.[111]

For western Catholic theology, not all analogies of the Mystery can be said to unveil *verosímil* knowledge of the Mystery.[112] Because for western Catholicism, as for all other strands within Christianity, the Mystery is neither theory nor doctrine.

The Ultimate Mystery, western Catholics claim, self-donated and thereby revealed itself in a Galilean Jewish peasant: Jesus, a day laborer from a village named Nazareth—in other words, a historical person is the revelation of God. Consequently, only those analogies that *effectively* unveil new insights (i.e., new knowledge) about the God revealed (i.e., self-donated) *in* Jesus of Nazareth can be, within western Catholicism, "effective" analogies. These effective analogies, in turn, limit the *verosimilitud* of all other western Catholic (and of all other Christian) claims—which leads us to conclude that not all that is claimed or said (by Christians) about the Mystery is *verosímil* ("true"). Only that is *verosímil* which can be affirmed of and because of the peasant Jesus of Nazareth; and yet, not all that can or must be affirmed is equally effective as analogy, because not all was of equal importance to Jesus or in his life.

We must also keep in mind that all analogies—including all effective analogies—are always contextualized in history and culture, "said" intelligibly within their various internal conflicts and power asymmetries (which, consequently and inescapably, limits the intelligibility of each analogy to the specific contexts within which it is employed) and are never literal or symmetric with regards to the Mystery. In today's world, furthermore, effective analogies must also be interculturally effective by being intelligibly "sayable" and by unveiling new knowledge within contrasting dialogues that may yield universally relevant claims.[113]

Analogies evidently respond to, and are employed as tools by, the various "speakers" within societies and cultures, and especially as tools of internally conflictive struggles for social and cultural hegemony. Hence, analogies are not and cannot be sufficiently understood if studied only by or from one side (especially the dominant or colonizing side) of their power contexts. In most societies the "speakers" who mostly control the conversation are not representative of the disposable majority. The majority, however, do have *their* analogies with which they challenge and critique the universal validity pretensions of the dominant's analogies. The dominant expect to analogically claim *their* reality and logic and the hegemonic *status quo* as analogy of the Mystery.

The analogies of the disposable majority, rarely (if ever) heard or regarded as equal among the hegemonic "speakers," are, nevertheless, potentially subversive of dominance by proposing a different hope for the future.[114] The disposable majority also claim *their* reality and logic and hope as analogy of the Mystery.

The differing and possibly contradicting claims of analogies, when understood within the real daily-life contexts of hegemonic dominance and power asymmetries, raise important questions on the *verosimilitud* of the claims, and on the criteria required to discern the more "effective" analogy. No analogy of the Mystery is ever culture-neutral, power-neutral, history-neutral, gender-neutral, or bias-neutral, if it is a human analogy.

The demands of *verosimilitud* weigh on effective analogies: because the latter must reasonably appear to be "close to truth," which in our case specifically means that a Christian *verosímil* "effective" analogy of the Mystery must represent its distance from hegemony's self-idolatry by representing the scandalously subversive message and life of Jesus the peasant.

III

Theological Elements

The Judaism of Jesus' day,[1] in rural Galilee as elsewhere, was viewed as an oddity by most non-Jews. Perhaps the oddest element, in the eyes of outsiders, was the strict monotheism that was reflected in Judaism's anti-idolatrous attitude.[2] Christianity inherited from Jesus and his earliest followers its anti-idolatrous stance.[3]

It might seem odd that we should begin this new chapter by discussing idolatry and anti-idolatry. However, the reader will soon note my insistence on the need for an *anti*-idolatrous attitude and perspective (which is clearly more than *non*-idolatrous or aniconic) as together we reflect on revelation, on the Christian proclamation of a subversive hope, and on what faith expects and doctrine might accomplish. If Christianity claims to tradition Jesus and his message, then we must deal with the fact that Christian traditioning cannot escape from the radical anti-idolatry of Jesus' message.

Idolatry and Anti-Idolatry

Idolatry is not reducible to the idea that a human-made artifact (the "idol") is thought to be divine. Idolatry is much more.

The human-made artifact is not just—for example—the sculpted "religious" image that some simply (or simplistically) might address as "God." Human-made also are persons or groups of persons, texts, historical moments, social formations, economic structures, political systems, national identities, religious expressions, and polities, and a very long list of etceteras. The idol, therefore, is not merely a simple or single human-made religious artifact but anything or anyone who claims to be, or is related with, as absolute, as final, as permanent, and, therefore, as God.

The idol claims to be the absolute presence, or the absolute analogy, or the final historical moment, or the ultimate symbol, or the only ethically possible behavior, or the permanent affirmation, or the only true doctrine. Consequently, the idol will lead to the claim that there is no need for further hope, no need for further quests, no need for further reflection or discernment, and no need for another *kairos*.[4] What will be, already is. Consequently, the idol requires repetition, obedience, and stability; questioning, hope, and change are its opposites. But the idol's diametrical opposite is compassion, because compassion is not afraid of doubt, vulnerability, or unexpected possibilities and futures. In fact, compassion is profoundly subversive of all non-compassionate presents (and of all the justifications and expressions—socially, communally, or individually created—of these presents).

Idolatry is not, therefore, just a philosophical or theological option that affirms as divine what or who is not God. It is, most dangerously, the human attitude that demands complete obedience toward the present or the past, and in that demand the divinization of what or who is not the Ultimate Mystery.[5] This obedience further commands the sacrifice of humans and their humanness to the idol, regardless of who or what the idol is. In fact, it seems that idolatry is best described not by what or who is the idol but as the dehumanizing relationships that demand ever increasing (and unquestioning) obedience and immobility and ever increasing sacrifices (of self, of hope, of future, of the humanness of others, and thus of all compassion) on the altar of the non-divine. Idolatry, therefore, is not mainly "religious."

In the Hebrew Scriptures, the "first commandment" is first because it is the reason and cause of Israel as a people.[6] The first commandment is not just an affirmation of monotheism. It is an affirmation of the covenantal relationship between God and

Israel, an affirmation often repeated in the Hebrew Bible. More important, however, is that the reason for the covenantal relationship is found in who and how the God of Israel *is and acts*, and not in Israel's understanding or merit: "I am the Lord your God, who brought you out of the land of Egypt, out of the house of slavery" (Ex. 20:2). This is why Israel will have no other God (the first commandment): *because* only the God of Israel is a liberating God, who frees slaves from their chains and who leads them to freedom. Or so did Israel hope.[7]

The first of the Decalogue commandments establishes that the only valid covenantal relationship is with the God of freedom and justice,[8] with the God who can make of the liberation of slaves an unexpected *kairos*. Hence the God of Israel is also the God of future and hope, who dares to break the enslaving power of empires. This implies and requires that no one, in the name of that God, may then enslave, deny justice, or trample on freedom and equality. To claim participation in the covenantal relationship with the God of Israel implied that the people of Israel would strive to establish a society of justice, equality and freedom—a reflection of how God is and acts. To do otherwise was not only to dishonor the one God, but to deny God. Because it was not possible to worship the God of Israel while enslaving or abusing the people of Israel (who existed as a people precisely because they understood themselves to belong to *that* God)—at least, it could not be justified by appealing to the Torah, because to worship while denying God in real life was idolatry (because the "God" invoked in worship could not be God). Biblical Israel and the early Church were anti-idolatrous in their attitude and expectations, and they knew why.[9]

We have already discussed that the "will of God," in the Galilean Jewish village context of Jesus' day, was often misunderstood by those who attempted to doctrinify and codify Torah, effectively reducing the Torah to compliance with ritual and purity requirements and with proper tithing. Jesus proposed a different, radical interpretation of Torah, wherein a compassionate way of life out-weighed all other demands and practice—doctrinal and ritual.[10] Jesus' radical stance was subversively anti-idolatrous and entirely committed to a life of compassion because he understood the "will of God" to be radically compassionate, as expressed in To-rah, and because he understood God's compassion to be the ul-timate cause for subverting all systems of dominance over the poor and vulnerable.

To understand compassion as *the* will of God, above anyone or anything that could claim any religious value or importance, is to stand against the idols that religious persons sometimes make of their explanations and of their practices, thereby turning their own explanations and practices into *the* criteria by which to measure commitment to God and God's will, instead of find-ing in compassion the ultimate criterion. According to Jesus, compassion and justice are immensely more crucial than ritual, obedience, doctrine, purity, or tithing, compassion being *the* cri-terion by which to measure the sincerity and reality of human commitment to God and God's will.[11] The God of Jesus does not demand the sacrifice of our humanness, but instead expects from us a radical commitment to be compassionate toward all, without limits, without exceptions, without conditions. Anything else is to misunderstand or adulterate the message of Jesus and the one whom he called *Abba*.

The Christian struggle against the idol, therefore, is not his-torically or theologically a consequence of some later doctrinal reflection. It has been and it is an integral part of Christianity's roots, assumed and emphasized by Jesus and the earliest Chris-tian communities as indispensable and evident part of their faith and thought. Therefore the Christian struggle against the idol is indispensable for Christianity.

As I mentioned earlier, idolatry and anti-idolatry are con-trasting perspectives from which to experience, to hear, to un-derstand (as humans can), and to live and speak (again, as hu-mans can and do) revelation. Consequently, the several contexts discussed in the preceding chapter are inescapable here too, since our humanness is always contextual. Idolatry and anti-idolatry, therefore, are also inevitably cultural, historical, and in all other ways contextual.

Furthermore, what we experience and what we claim regarding revelation will also and always occur in time, and thus will always be contingent and transient, because they are ours. Yet they can still be *verosímil*.

Once again, it is fruitful to keep in mind Agamben's dictum, "The only true representation is one that also represents its distance from the truth."[12] As I noted earlier in these pages, Augustine of Hippo also warned us against misrepresenting our contextualized and contingent understandings: "*Si comprehendis, non est Deus*."[13] The revealing Mystery is not bound by culture or time, but the human hearers of the revealing Mystery are. To think otherwise is to play with idolatry. Christianity is not about Christianity, just as the message of Jesus was not about Jesus or about establishing a new religion. Therefore, to pretend that *our* explanations of the Mystery and of the Mystery's revelation can be timeless, a-cultural or a-historical is to turn them into idols.

Christianity is for humans and by humans. This does not contradict revelation at all, but deeply respects it: to acknowledge that Christianity is for and by humans is to assume their humanness very seriously. Indeed, without humanness there is no Reign of God. This also means that Christianity does not become its own idol.

This insight is inescapable in Christianity, and yet we seem to dismiss its consequences in and throughout all that is Christian. The first of these consequences is Christianity's anti-*self*-idolatry. Which then demands a rethinking of ecumenism, of interreligious dialogues, and of ecclesiastically immodest self-understandings. The defense of "our" understanding is not the difficulty here, but the disregard for doctrinal modesty and anti-*self*-idolatry when discerning and defending "our" denominational or religious "truths." If "we" are the only ones to possess complete truth or complete understanding of the truth, have we not made an idol of that "we" which, obviously, is only human?

Christian anti-idolatry demands a never-ending ecumenical and interreligious dialogue, accompanied by modesty in all claims Christians might make to exclusivity or definitiveness. Furthermore, reception of God's revelation cannot happen or be claimed unless it accompanies and respects the non-Christian. This the case because Jesus was not Christian—and because, evidently, revelation is not the property of the religiously Christian or of the culturally western.

Anti-idolatry requires interculturality.[14] Christian catholicity has to be intercultural[15] or catholicity becomes an unsubstantiated claim interpreted and instrumentalized for the continued dominance of the culturally tribal, instead of a mark or sign of those who are the catholic (small "c") People of God.

Humanity's reason and its logics, cultures, histories, languages, symbols, images, texts, performances, and stories are not absolute or ultimate. They certainly are not *the* absolute or *the* Ultimate. Obviously, the same can and must be said of human religions, prayers, doctrines, and institutions: they are neither *the* absolute nor *the* Ultimate.

The Ultimate Mystery alone is absolute, and the human inclination to absolutize, whatever its good or bad motivation, that which is sacred to humans, has never granted and will never grant absoluteness to the humanly-regarded or humanly-understood sacred. Only the Ultimate Mystery is *the* absolute, and yet . . . who can fully know and understand the Mystery or what it might mean to affirm that it is *the* absolute? *Verosimilitud* and analogy are not absoluteness.

There seems to be a western cultural inclination to view the West's discussions, theories, reflections, and expressions of the Mystery as "best" or "definitive." There also seems to be a connection between this western inclination and colonization, and between this western logic and its all-too-frequent dismissal of the logic of the non-western. The western attempts at tribalization of the Mystery, and the subsequent claims of this perspective as "the definitive truth," cannot avoid playing with self-idolatry. The Ultimate Mystery alone is *the* absolute, and the dominant tribalization cannot make it otherwise.

Must we then only be silent before the Ultimate Mystery? Yes and no. Yes, because the Mystery is beyond all knowing and saying. No, because it is possible *modestly* (and more *verosímilmente*) to realize that all we can say about the Mystery is necessarily limited, cultural, perspectival, transient, neither definitive nor absolute, and *for us*. Whatever we say of God is or might be meaningful only for us, because whatever its meaning might be for the Ultimate Mystery itself is not available to us. We can speak of God non-idolatrously as long as we understand that all we say about God is not "God" and that it is meaningful only for us.

Consequently for Christians, when we sincerely and rightly claim that Jesus of Nazareth is both the revealer and the revelation of God, are we not really saying that he is *the* "revealing hermeneutic," *the* "effective analogy" of and about all Christian understandings of God? I am not saying that God is not like Jesus revealed for us. What I am saying is that we have no way of knowing whether God is or is not like Jesus revealed, except through Jesus as revealer and revelation, and this obviously assumes faith—which is also human, and thus cultural, historical, and inescapably contextual.[16]

Because God is unsayable, the "sayability" of God is inescapably human. But because all humans and all that is human are cultural, and because all cultures display (in each of their present-day manifestations) specific configurations of human meaningfulness(es) resulting from internal asymmetric power struggles to name and construct cultural identities, all cultures then have silenced or downplayed other ways of "saying" the unsayable Mystery within the cultures. Consequently, every "saying" regarding God carries and displays in itself (i.e., every affirmation about God has re-inscribed in itself) the dynamics of cultural and social bias and of power asymmetries, either to subvert the bias and the dominance or to reaffirm them.

Every "saying" regarding God or God's revelation, therefore, can be questioned for disguised or hidden bias, and for its option—subversion or affirmation—vis-à-vis the bias. Human, cultural "sayings" regarding God or God's revelation are tainted by androcentric, racist, ethnocentric, heterosexist, classist, and other blind spots, even when the option is the subversion of bias, and even when the proponents of the "sayings" have ethically chosen to distance themselves from the bias. This also applies to every doctrine because doctrines are "sayings" regarding God and God's revelation, albeit as results of internal conversations within Christianity.

It is idolatrous to claim that the human analogy, the metaphor, the poetry, or the symbol capture or exhaust all the Mystery is. The analogy (and the metaphor, the poetry, the symbol) might capture and exhaust what humans can rightly say or experience of the Mystery, but not what and who the Ultimate Mystery is.

The above discussion does not deny the possibility or the affirmation of there having been a revelation as long as by "revelation" we do not mean an event or experience nearly coextensive with doctrines, statements, "truths," or institutions. Specifically and very emphatically here, there is no denial of the possibility of revelation as long as by "revelation" we mean first and foremost the *self*-donation of the Mystery (before any and all doctrinification) and the *experience* of such self-donation. The reception of revelation follows the experience of (and acknowledgement of the experience as) revelation.

Revelation

To affirm that God has revealed Godself,[17] as Christianity claims, is somehow to presuppose an experience. It is to claim a definitive *kairos*. But it is also (and this is very relevant here) to affirm that revelation is God's *self*-revelation. These sentences, however, are more complex than they might appear at first.[18]

Revelation is God's self-revelation in God's scandalous self-donation. Hence, the revelatory *kairos* is also the scandalous *kenosis*.[19]

Revelation is neither theory nor doctrine,[20] and yet it is not only experience. Revelation, furthermore, is a cultural and historical dialogical moment between the Mystery and humans. To claim that revelation has occurred is to affirm that a kairotic experience of the Ultimate Mystery has occurred. These two moments (the kairotic experience and the affirmation, which require human understanding in order to be named "revelation") are always contextualized; they are inseparable if the claim that revelation has occurred is to be non-idolatrous. And yet, no matter how correctly and insightful our reflections on revelation might be,[21] all *Christian* reflection on *Christian* revelation must ground itself in Jesus of Nazareth. He stands as *the reason* for the claims, but also as *the limit* to what may be claimed, as Christian revelation. To claim Jesus as revelation is to affirm the subversive "break up" of human certainties and of all socio-cultural constructs and meaningfulness(es), because of the unexpected and scandalous kairotic and kenotic *self*-donation of the Mystery in a "disposable" and insignificant human life. To claim Jesus as revelation is to announce the death of our power-centered notions of God (which often disguise themselves under the veil of pious faith).

It is very pertinent here to recall E. Jüngel's insightful argument that if today people can experience, think, "say," and understand love and compassion, then they *can* also experience, think, "say," and understand God—as long as by "God" is meant the God who self-reveals and self-donates as love and compassion.[22] Jüngel's argument, reasonable and insightful as it is, is still insufficient in this real world of cultures, histories, and biases.

Revelation is experience—an experience of encounter *and* of human self-unveiling. In, through, and triggered by the experience, we unveil realities and depths within ourselves (and within humanness) that would normally have remained hidden to us. In, through, and triggered by the experience we unveil a depth of (our) meaningfulness, and we come to "understand" what our lives and the life of our world are about. The unveiling experience, however, is the consequent side of the encounter experienced—an encounter with the Mystery that, regardless of intensity, is limited, cultural, historical, transient, and contextual.

The Ultimate Mystery is not bound by culture, history, or any context. We are. And so is the incarnate revelation of the Mystery—which is the only revelation of the Mystery to which we have access (i.e., the one that becomes part of our world, even when "breaking it up").[23] And consequently, so are *all* of our experiences—including the experience we call revelation, because *we* experience, recognize, and name it "revelation." In revelation we encounter whom *we* name as "Someone," and who unexpectedly crosses the paths of our lives.[24]

This "crossing," disruptive and self-donating, allows *us* to experience, and later to attempt to name or say. But the encounter is as fleeting and ungraspable as time, except in its consequences: the human self-unveilings I mentioned above, as well as the certainty that "Someone" had crossed the path of our life. And the "bet of life" that this encounter requires.

Without experiencing the Mystery's "crossings" in our lives there would not be revelation for us. First, because the very affirmation that "the Mystery is" would be no more than a theoretical possibility, without any existential grounding, if the claim were not part and consequence of experience.[25] And second, because what we come to unveil in the experience will have importance or authority for us *because* it was experienced. In other words, if (in our experience of the Mystery) our unveiling of the depths of our meaningfulness drives us to transform our lives and thereafter to make claims, the transformation and the claims will have importance or "authority" for us only because they were first "confirmed" by the experience.[26] No other authority could thereafter have a role greater than the mnemonic. Consequently, if in our lives "God" is no more than doctrine or claim, then for us there is no God. And without God there is no possibility of revelation.

What Christians call "revelation," however, is not simply reducible to the experience of (encounter with) the Ultimate Mystery.

It is *in* and *because* of *their* experience of the Mystery that some humans can come to "dis-cover" for and in themselves— as the deepest meaningfulness possible in their lives—the God who *is* compassion, as announced in the message of the Reign of (that) God proclaimed twenty centuries ago by an executed Jewish peasant from Galilee. These are the Christians.[27]

It is *in* and *because* of *their* experience of the Mystery that some humans can come (always analogically) to name the Mystery as the God who *is* compassion, and who self-reveals and self-donates as compassion (and thus as compassionate) to all, without limits, without conditions, and without exceptions.

It is *in* and *because* of *their* experience of the Mystery that some humans can come to believe that the God who is compassion is really transforming this world.

Therefore, it is *in* and *because* of *their* experience of the Mystery that some humans can come to share the subversive hope inherent and inescapable in the (above) claims regarding the compassion of God and the God of compassion—claims made by Jesus of Nazareth.

That which is "dis-covered" *in* and *because* of the experience of the self-donating, compassionate Mystery is that which some humans find inescapably and subversively resonating in the life and message of Jesus of Nazareth. And vice versa.

At a later stage, this "dis-covered" content might demand that it be "said" through doctrines, creeds, and other claims. This is legitimate as long as these never substitute for or replace Jesus' message and God's self-donation as limitless and conditionless compassion, and as long as creeds and doctrines do not claim more than their exclusively analogical character allows.

Christians are those who harbor the subversive *hope* that Jesus was right—about God being compassion, and about this compassionate God's transformation of this world. And they do not just harbor hope: they bet their lives for the hope (i.e., *faith*).[28] Without the revelatory experience this hope and this faith could be no more than narcissistic claims.

We must also deduce, from our discussion of revelation as experience, that the human encounter with the Ultimate Mystery (and the unveiling "dis-covery" implicated therein) is not ethically neutral for and among humans. Because compassion is not ethically neutral, and neither is the transformation of this world according to the will of the God who is compassion. In fact, compassion is ethically and very subversively militant.

Christians have always insisted that there is a certain "knowable" content to revelation.[29] But if revelation is to be understood, as Christians claim, as having a knowable content, then this content cannot contradict or dismiss the experience of the God who is compassion. This is the case because—unavoidably—the contents of what Christians regard as revelation cannot contradict or dismiss Jesus' proclamation of the dawning Reign of God, that is, the Reign of the God who *is* compassion.[30]

Jesus did not preach Jesus. Jesus announced the dawn of the Reign of God. This we know.[31] Consequently, if Jesus announced the dawning of the Reign of God, and if he is held by Christians to be *the* revealer, can any subsequent Christian reflection on revelation dismiss or downplay what we know to have been the core message of Jesus of Nazareth? Obviously not.

Jesus spoke of the impending dawn of the Reign of God. In his day and context the expression "Reign of God" was known and his announcement that the Reign was dawning was neither innocent nor naïve: he must have known what his contemporaries were hearing and understanding as he publicly spoke and acted. Jesus' message and actions did not occur in a cultural or historical vacuum. His context allows us (as it did his contemporaries) to understand what he said and did and why these words and actions led to his trial and execution. Jesus' message was subversive within his context.

The core message of Jesus of Nazareth explicitly announced that God was transforming this world, in its structures of asymmetric power and wealth, *and* in its understandings of what religion is, to make this world a different world that reflects the compassionate will of God—because God is compassionate. This new world according to the compassion of God is to be constructed by radically living a life of compassion toward all, but especially toward the sinners, the impure, and the poor, i.e., the disposables of the world built by and for the dominant and the legitimizing pious. No doctrine, no religious practice, no power relation, no obligation (no matter how "holy" it might be) can stand in the way of this radical new world and this radical new way of being human, because this is God's will and because this is how God acts in order to be faithful to God's own promises. For proclaiming this, and for credibly acting on this proclamation in his own life,[32] Jesus of Nazareth was executed by the Romans. Christian claims of his resurrection are clearly referring to his having spoken and acted according to the will of God. In other words, God agreed with Jesus regarding the Reign of God and the God of the Reign, and raised him in order to demonstrate agreement.[33] And because Jesus was right about the Reign and about God, to be a Christian meant that one committed one's life to Reign-building, trusting the compassion of God.[34]

Revelation's contents, therefore, are not doctrines but the extraordinarily scandalous and dangerous (yet somehow reasonable) subversive hope that a Galilean peasant was right when he announced that God had begun to transform this world of asymmetric power and inhuman dominance into a radically new world (a "new creation") where justice, equality, inclusion, and especially compassion would reign.[35]

It is only as a *subsequent* (and reasonable) moment of clarification that in Christianity's history some understandings of the consequences of, or assumptions in, the aforementioned contents of revelation came to be broadly accepted as important or necessary in order to preserve, clarify or express (the aforementioned core contents of) revelation. This is the birth of doctrine—at its best a human, reasonable, and inevitably contextual effort. Consequently, it is reasonable to claim that the purpose of doctrine (and its proper role) is to give (cultural, historical, contextual) expression to the internal conversations among Christians about their hope.

Affirming the message of Jesus as true, and encountering the Mystery whom Jesus identified as God-who-is-compassion, are the two sides of revelation. Inseparably. Without either of these, there is no Christian revelation. Both are solely the Mystery's initiative. The experience confirms the message and the message becomes real and challenging in the experience. But is any of this reasonably credible?

Christians, of course, will affirm its reasonable credibility. Others would simply dismiss or scoff at the very possibility of a revelation.[36] I am not the first to reply that the subversive hope at the very core of Christian revelation, and the life-bet we call faith, are jointly the ground of Christianity's credibility in today's world.[37]

Revelation has content: the core message of Jesus. But how can we claim that it is God's *self*-revelation too? God is certainly experienced as *self*-donating by those whose paths of life are unexpectedly "crossed" by the Mystery. But this is not sufficient as an answer to the question in this paragraph—because, although the experience is certainly personal, the self-donation of the Mystery is not only for the personal benefit of those experientially engaged as individuals.[38]

The *self*-donation of the Ultimate Mystery, as experienced and understood in and because of revelation, is for all of humankind. Christians affirm that God has donated *Godself* in Jesus of Nazareth, for the benefit of all. We certainly have no access to God's inner life or ultimate intentions, except for the glimpses of God that unexpectedly cross our paths—we experience and understand them, we who are inescapably human, cultural, historical, transient, perspectival, gendered, sexually oriented, and more, and whose claims regarding these glimpses of the Mystery are and will always be (at best) analogical, contextual, and limited.

Our glimpses of the Mystery are not and cannot be absolute, and neither can our experiences or doctrinal claims regarding them. Consequently, the Christian affirmations regarding God's self-donation in Jesus are *the Christian affirmations* regarding God's self-donation in Jesus.[39] This does not call into question their *verosimilitud*, but it confronts our self-idolatries.

Nevertheless. . . .

- When the Ultimate Mystery unexpectedly crosses our paths, and reveals glimpses of Godself (which are not coextensive with whatever experiences or understandings of those glimpses we might have), we may arguably affirm that the Mystery has self-donated or self-revealed. And if the Mystery who self-donated is experienced and understood as compassionate toward all, without limits, conditions or exceptions, then the possibility of Christian revelation unexpectedly arises.

- If then, upon hearing[40] that a Galilean peasant announced that the God of Abraham is compassion and cares for all humans with equal compassion (without limits, without conditions, and without exceptions), we may therein hear of the Mystery we have experienced as self-donating compassion. We may come to realize that the God we experienced is the God of Jesus.

- And if we further hear that this Galilean Jewish peasant also and more emphatically announced that this God has begun to transform the world according to God's compassionate will ("the Reign of God is dawning") and that a human life according to God's will is a life lived for a compassion that imitates God's compassion, then we may come to realize that we are being called to Christian faith. This call is not to the affirmation of a creed[41] or an intimate sensation of being saved,[42] but a challenge to bet one's life for compassion and for a world transformed by compassion.

How can we say that Jesus *is* the revelation of God? That he becomes the revealer for those who accept the challenge of the call to faith is not the issue here. The question is whether we may affirm him as the revelation of God.

The historical Jesus did not preach himself. He arguably did not regard himself as anything but a human being—with an extraordinary and urgent message, but a human being. Everyone around him regarded him as only human. Self-perception and the perception of others are obviously important, at least for reasonable historical claims, but they are not and cannot be assumed to be the only criteria of what is reasonable or of what may be reasonably claimed.[43]

In his humanness Jesus *is* God's *self*-revelation—and *that* is what most Christians claim. Therefore, God's self-revelation is found in the human life and reality of a Jewish peasant from a small village in rural Galilee. It is found in one of the disposables of his day—politically, economically, socially and religiously disposable. Jesus was an unimportant individual from among the mostly unimportant of rural Galilee, in Roman-occupied Palestine, and in the eyes of the powerful and the pious of his day. Jesus was insignificant in his day and for his day, as the immense majority of his contemporaries were insignificant in Palestine and elsewhere, and as the immense majority of all of humankind before and after him. He was easily condemned and promptly tortured and executed by the powerful of his day as soon as he became a nuisance for them.

However, this specific, insignificant, and disposable human being *is* the revelation of Godself: *this* is what most Christians shockingly claim. Can they indeed claim this?

What, according to Christianity, is God revealing about God—what glimpses of the Ultimate Mystery—in the historical Jesus? In Jesus God is revealing what I have been recalling and repeating all along: that God is compassionate toward *all*, without limits, without conditions, and without exceptions, *and* that this God is intervening in this world in order to transform it according to God's compassionate will. In other words, what God reveals about God in Jesus is not different from Jesus' core message.

But there is more here. *Jesus*, and not just his message, is said to be the revelation of God. His words are corroborated and explained by his life. His message about the Reign of God and the God of the Reign was lived in his human life, and more densely in his willingness to die for what he held to be true, most important, and most decisive for humankind. This insignificant peasant bet his life on *his* firm hope that God was as he experienced, and that God had begun to transform this world into a new human reality built on compassion.

The execution of Jesus was his greatest failure, and yet it was for him the greatest act of generosity. In his worst moment of human insignificance he bet his hope and his life. He was most human, then, and most courageous, in his disposable weakness at the hands of the dominant. In this scandalously baffling contradiction Christians claim to discover the definitive self-donation (and, therefore, the self-revelation) of God.

Hope

I just stated above that Jesus of Nazareth bet his life on his hope that God was as he experienced, and that God had begun to transform this world into a new human reality built on compassion.[44] Since the birth of Christianity, hope has been held to be inseparable from faith and love and indispensable in Christian life, both individually and communally (see 1 Cor. 13).[45]

Hope, in our reflection,[46] is far from an unreasonable optimism. It is grounded in the discovery that the ultimate meaning and definition of our humanness is compassion—a humanness that, for Christians, is reflection of who and how God is (*imago Dei*). Furthermore, this discovery occurs always contextualized in this world—in its realities, cultures, histories, and asymmetric power relations. Thus the affirmation of compassion as the ultimate meaning and expectation of humankind is cleared-eye in this world; there is no naïveté here, where most of humanity is treated as disposable by the dominant. There is no romanticizing of compassion, because compassion is only compassion when lived and perceived as compassionate *in its consequences*. The world in which we live is outright cruel toward most human beings and abusive toward most other living creatures. To speak of or affirm compassion and justice in this world, therefore, is to bet for what most human beings do not experience in their daily worlds, and yet are what most humans rationally understand as desperate necessity: compassion and justice. No romanticizing here.

Hope is "irascible passion,"[47] pursuing a different world that *can* exist but still does not. Hope leads to the acting and the living that make the "should be" become. Hope is not a dream, but the affirmation that a different way of being *can* be constructed (by constructing it) in wide-awake reality. And in our real world, hope is not compassion but the "passion" that makes us see the logic and the need of living compassionately, while leading us there. Compassion is not the hope. That a world of compassion *can* be built—that is the hope.

To hope without actually constructing the hoped-for is not the hope I am discussing here. To hope is to live in a certain way, with commitments and risks, in this world. That is why St. Paul could (in 1 Cor. 13) claim that hope is inseparable from love and faith. That is why this hope is neither irrational nor naïve. This hope is very subversive.[48]

We have already discussed that the message of the Reign of God and of the God of the Reign—as announced by Jesus—is inherently subversive of the structures, the power asymmetries, and the economic and political interests that have succeeded and been dominant in the world that God's initiative is dismantling. There is no escaping this conclusion except by adulterating the message. To believe that Jesus spoke the truth in reference to the Reign of God and the God of the Reign, is necessarily to conclude that the current world is not according to God's will.

What is revealed by and in Jesus of Nazareth contradicts this world (as this world has been constructed and organized by its economic, political, cultural, and religious beneficiaries) and subverts it. What is revealed by and in Jesus not only proposes, but announces that God is really transforming the world. The subversion of the status quo, therefore, has begun.

Christians claim that, in the executed Jewish peasant Jesus of Nazareth, God revealed all of this. Furthermore, Jesus faced his death in the hope that this was true and actually happening, and Christians bet their lives (and many continue to bet their lives) on the same hope. Their hope, as did Jesus' hope, leads them to *do now* the "hoped-for." But note that I am using the plural—they, their—because the hope is, explicitly and necessarily, a shared, communal hope.

Ultimately, then, revelation is the hope—a radically subversive hope—in the *verosimilitud* of the Reign of God and of the God of the Reign, as announced by Jesus of Nazareth. It is also the hope that even if there were no God and no Reign, there undoubtedly would be and is compassion—worth committing to, and worth betting one's life for, in the construction of a world of dignity, justice, equality, and inclusion for all.[49]

Faith

In this reflection, as just above, I have referred to Christians "betting their lives" for–staking their lives on—the hope that what Jesus announced of the Reign of God and of the God of the Reign is actually so. That "bet of life" is faith.[50]

Consequently, faith is not about the mind's or even the heart's assent to ecclesial doctrines,[51] although I admit that this assent might follow faith. It is very difficult today to present the results of doctrine as any more than cultural representations of the hope.[52] It is also very difficult to claim for doctrines an evident clarity that—at least in western Catholicism—cannot and is not claimed for the biblical texts. Texts may be assented to if understood, but they are only understood after contextual interpretation (the text's and the reader's). And even then what is understood, and thus what may be assented to, is probably not coextensive in intention or in meaning with the original author's. It is, of course, still impossible to claim more even for Jesus' message of the Reign of God and of the God of the Reign. Because what we have are early Christian texts, reasonably reliable as they might be.

If faith, then, is the "bet of life" for the hope that Jesus was right (regarding God and God's transformation of this world), how can the message be announced today without fear of distortion? In other words, how can Christianity be proclaimed without inviting—in the best of cases—to a faith response in what is no more than an empty dream? Responsible short answer: There is no such guarantee, and there has never been, because of context (cultural, historical), of God-talk, of hermeneutics, of transience, and more, as we have been discussing throughout the present and preceding chapters. The guarantee for the hope, really, is only the *verosimilitud* of the hope.[53] And because faith rests exclusively on the hope, this too (therefore) is the only guarantee for Christian faith.

The "Christian faith"—certainly in western Catholicism—has *always* been "the faith of the Church." The potential confusion with this latter expression, however, arose from its centuries-long hijacking by the ordained (specifically since the eleventh and twelfth centuries),[54] in their concerted effort to reinterpret the use of the expression "the faith of the Church" to mean "the faith of the episcopate" or even the faith of a particular bishop. The reinterpretation of "Church," unfortunately, followed the same path, timeframe, and purpose. Nevertheless, it is historically evident that in western Catholicism the understanding that the "Church" is the entire "People of God" has never been forgotten,[55] as well as the consequent affirmation that "the faith of the Church" is "the faith of the People of God."[56]

That the Christian faith is the faith of the People of God

also points to its plural, communal dimension. Every generation has *heard of* Jesus and his message from preceding generations. After the first disciples, contemporaries of Jesus, all other generations, including ours, have relied on the witness of preceding communities to tradition the hope (regarding Jesus and his message) to them. The response to this announced hope has always, therefore, relied on the faith (i.e., the shared bet for the hope) of earlier communities. Faith, consequently, is inescapably plural, communal, historical, cultural, and certainly not just individual. The faith of the People of God relies on the faith of the People of God. Because it is dependent on communal, intergenerational, and intercultural witness (the bet for the hope) and announcement (the message of Jesus and the hope that he was right) to all succeeding generations. Today's Christians' hope, "hoped-for," and "bet-for" are all resting on the earliest and all succeeding Christian communities.[57]

This reliance—always cultural, historical, and contextual in every other way—requires the present's discernment and interpretation because, inevitably, the traditioning of the People of God across the centuries and across cultures has occurred (and continues to occur) in contexts, within the perspectival limitations and the transience of all human knowledge and understanding, and impacted by the dominant interests of every age. This discernment is intimately related to the role(s) of the *sensus fidelium*.[58]

The ecclesial discernment of the ecclesial hope and faith is always analogical and about the analogical to the degree that it is discernment about revelation. It is always historical and about the historical. It is also always cultural (and classed, gendered, raced, ethnic . . .) and about the cultural. And this discernment, in today's globalized, globalizing, and intensely diverse world,[59] must also be intercultural in order to be "catholic." This discernment, of course, is always communal and about the communal.

The Christian community's discernment about the Christian community's hope and faith, furthermore, often follows ecclesially established or shared criteria. Yet some of the important criteria of discernment are embedded in expressions of the *sensus fidelium*, and rarely explicitly formulated, except in doctrinal conceptualizations that, in themselves, cannot be more than transient cultural products. The *sensus fidelium*, nevertheless, often conveys its "sense of faith" through aphorisms that the People of God accept and repeat as wise and prudent (even if admittedly limited and incomplete) guides for discernment.[60] Among these wise and faith-full aphorisms there is one in Spanish: *dime con quién andas y te diré quién eres*—tell me with whom you walk and I will tell you who you are.[61]

A crucially important criterion for discernment is the insight that *andar con* or *caminar con* are indispensable[62] to understandably announce the hope (regarding Jesus and his message) and to witness understandably to it (by actually betting our lives for it). This is, precisely, the insight behind the Christian doctrine of the Incarnation: the compassionate solidarity of God definitively expresses itself in the divine self-donation as one who "walks with" the disposable of the Earth, to the extreme of crucifixion. *Kenosis*[63] is the outcome of, and the confrontation with, *kairos*. In other words, the *sensus fidelium* can discern (affirm or deny) if a "walking-with"—who *anda* with whom—is faith-full or not.

It is not enough, however, to discern who walks with whom, because perhaps as important is the discernment of the (power) relationship among those who walk together. The faith-full *andar* requires *kenosis*: without a compassionate life willing to risk and dare crucifixion there is no credible faith.[64]

Doctrine

The most crucial and the one indispensable "content" of revelation is the hope that Jesus of Nazareth was right when he announced the dawning of the Reign of God and when he insisted that the God of the Reign is totally compassionate towards all, without limits, conditions, or exceptions. And as we already saw, the affirmation of the reasonableness and *verosimilitud* of this hope is credible *only* when those making the affirmation *constatablemente* bet their lives for and on that hope.[65] In Christian theological terms: there is credible faith only when *kenosis* demonstrably follows *kairos*. What, then, is the role of doctrine?[66]

It is obvious that throughout its entire history, even in its earliest days, Christianity has not hesitated to explain itself. Nevertheless, the explanations were not all intended for the same conversation partners, nor were (or are) these explanations always expressed in the conceptual formulations we may now call doctrines.[67]

It seems clear that explanations were sometimes intended for intra-Christian contexts, while others were intended to justify Christianity among outsiders, and still others to proclaim kerygmatically (and for this purpose to explain) the hope of Christians. As we can deduce, these varied contexts and intents require distinctions.

If the proclamation of Christian hope is for the purpose of inviting others to join the movement of faith (as faith is understood here), then this goal will require explanations more socially analytic, more culturally critical, and more existentially *verosímil*. The role that doctrinal explanations might play herein is limited to and by the purpose: assent or agreement with these or those doctrines is not and cannot be made a condition for the betting of anyone's life (i.e., for faith). It is God who calls, and not our fine arguments. No ecclesial doctrine—and all Christian doctrines are ecclesial—can ethically justify one's dare of crucifixion. Only the subversive hope that is often at odds with human explanations can do so.

The apologetic purpose of many Christian explanations requires the understanding of and engagement with the challenger's culture and reasons. If the argument was made in certain terms and in specific contexts, then the Christian response must be in those same terms and address those same contexts. Otherwise, any apologetic—any defense—in favor of Christianity makes no logical sense as becomes a wasted effort. One defends (and an *apologia* is a defense) when and after there has been a challenge, and in response to a specific challenge. Apologetics is not an expression of an ecclesial *delirium persecutionis*.

A more fruitful way of understanding doctrine is to see it as "internal conversation." In other words, doctrine is *an* internal means to clarify and explain—in this moment, in this context, and among Christians—what the hope *they* share is about. Doctrine, however, cannot be perceived as coextensive with the hope, as equivalent to the faith, or as the content of revelation. It is internal conversation—analogical conversation that, at its best, serves Christians to better explain among and to themselves the importance, reasonableness, and *verosimilitud* of the hope on which they "bet their lives." As conversation, doctrine cannot be definitive; its inescapable transience cannot be ignored.

Doctrine helps Christians understand and affirm, as I said earlier, that revelation is the radically subversive hope announced by Jesus of Nazareth, and that even if there were no God and no Reign, there undoubtedly is compassion—worth committing to, and worth betting one's life for, in the construction of a world of justice and inclusion for all. But doctrine is not the hope, the life commitment, or the compassion. Doctrine neither saves nor changes the world. Doctrine, when it is what it should be, usefully clarifies and explains among those already committed to compassion because of their shared hope while, at worst, doctrine can become an idol on whose altar compassion and hope can be sacrificed for the sake of a sterile orthodoxy.

That is why a solely doctrinal announcement of Christianity is *not* an announcement of the Christian message. That is why engaging in persecutory behavior because of doctrinal disputes is not morally acceptable behavior among Christians.[68] The faith of the People of God has no need for doctrinal validation. Consequently, orthodoxy without a foundation and corroboration *in* demonstrable orthopraxis becomes an idol, because it pretends that correct "mental" assent is more important than *being compassionate*.[69] Our doctrines must catch up to compassion in order to be useful to Christians, because what is said *to help explain* revelation cannot then contradict or dispense with the self-revealing

God who *is* compassion, and because no doctrine or sum of doctrines can ever claim to *be* revelation as Jesus *is*.

Doctrine as internal conversation, furthermore, has its languages, and with these their various grammars, practices, and sounds.[70] However, there cannot be *one* doctrinal "language," limited to the literate and/or imposed by power asymmetries within the Church.[71] The insistence on doctrinal "monolinguism" cannot avoid being perceived as an act of colonization and, probably, of cultural idolatry. The catholicity of the People of God does not require that unity be confused with, or be adulterated by, imposed uniformity.

Nevertheless, doctrines have been crafted by Christians throughout their long religious history. And these doctrines have often served their purpose by clarifying and/or explaining among Christians what their shared hope and faith imply or demand. In this sense, doctrines are fruitful and useful—but as internal conversation.

Doctrines are developed in response to *internal* questions and in response to *internal* crises, as means to answers that may *contribute to unity and to lives of compassion*—hence, to clarifications of the faith of the Church (as "faith" is understood here). Doctrinal development is a slow, consensual process of clarification, coming to fruition in broadly accepted doctrine *as long as* it actually reflects the faith of the People of God. Doctrinal development is a consensual process of inter-discursive dialogue that *may* lead to *reception* of doctrine[72] beyond its birthing contextual and historical particularity.[73] A doctrine is truly "received" in and among diverse contexts, however, only when the power asymmetries and idols (including those still inscribed among Christians and their doctrines) begin to be named by the People of God and transformed by God's compassionate will. In other words, there is no "reception" except when the Reign of God begins to dawn *constatablemente*—which again means that only lived compassion is the measure of the validity or *verosimilitud* of a doctrine.[74]

Any discussion on the function and purpose of doctrine must—emphatically and inescapably *at its core*—reflect on and incorporate the *real* subjects who engage in this internal conversation. We must engage doctrine *from and among* the vast majority of the People of God.[75]

Any serious study of Christianity cannot avoid the importance played by the real faith of real people. In western Catholicism, the real Christianity of the immense majority of real persons and communities who self-identify as western Catholics has frequently been dismissed as, or been reduced to, no more than pious practices or simplistic credulity, often judged to border the magical or superstitious.[76] This dismissal or reduction is irresponsible and unjustified.

"Popular Catholicism,"[77] by this or any other label, *is* the way in which most western Catholic Christians are western Catholic Christians. It does not always agree and is not always coextensive with a western Catholicism that most ecclesial leaders and scholars assume to be "the" western Catholic tradition. This realization must make a serious impact on our reflection.[78]

Although the ordained suppose that they define western Catholic tradition and practice for all who self-identify within it, the sociocultural, historical, and theological fact remains that people are Christian most frequently in the manners and on the assumptions they received from their families, friends, and local communities and only tangentially from the ordained and their institutions. This applies to doctrines too, as internal conversations among Christians (and not merely among the ordained).

Popular Catholicism belongs to—and expresses the Christian faith of—those treated as subaltern by the hegemonic in culture, in society and in the ecclesiastical institution(s). By its centuries-old history,[79] popular Catholicism may be characterized as an effort by the subaltern—as an evidently *hope-filled* effort—somehow to understand (and maneuver within) a social reality that appears too adverse or dangerous.

Furthermore, if the experience of God can only happen in culture, this also means that it can only occur in society. And just as culture imposes its epistemological, hermeneutical limits on the religious experience, so does society. The location of a religious individual or group in any society will also shape the language, symbols, and other idioms used by that individual or group in the process of interpreting religious and social experience—in other words, in the crafting of doctrines (as internal conversation among the Christian marginalized). Therefore, not only culture but social location makes possible the diverse doctrinal and other interpretations of the religious experiences of humankind.[80]

The above remarks might not seem too relevant to a theological reflection on doctrine fascinated by, and focused on, the written texts of ecclesiastical elites. But if we recall that in societies the social location of persons and groups, and the cultures and subcultures born in and from them, bear the mark of conflict, then we must begin to consider that the literate elites have not represented the vast majority of Christians throughout history, and arguably do not represent them even today. A theological reflection limited to what is contained in documents written by the hegemonic and for the use of the hegemonic, does not necessarily represent the internal conversations (i.e., doctrines) of the real People of God.[81]

Regardless of our identifying or naming the conflict, or not, in any contemporary society, it is not possible to believe in good conscience that the vast majority of humankind, as well as the vast majority of the People of God in humanity's midst, "chose" to become part of the marginalized in their respective societies, or "chose" to be disenfranchised in their respective ecclesial communities, or "chose" to become socially disposable and culturally insignificant. It is ethically impossible to argue that there is something "genetic" or "deliberately chosen" in the marginalized social place and status of most humans (and, among them, of most western Catholics). The fact, and it is unfortunately a fact,

that most human beings are at their societies' bottom as disposables in the service of the dominant few has a great deal to do
with ongoing social conflict. It also has a great deal to do with
the religious expressions and doctrinal internal conversations of
most Christians.[82] The experiences of God, culturally and soci-
etally available to the disposables, bear this mark as well.

The hegemonic epistemology in contemporary society has
managed to keep most western Catholics, and their popular Catholicism, "in their place" and out of sight. It is from this "place
of unimportance" that *they* claim to have experienced the God
of the Reign, to have heard the message of Jesus, and to have
bet their lives for the hope awakened by Jesus and his message.[83]

So, if our reflections are correct,[84] the saying of the God experienced by the people is (necessarily) culturally and socially contextualized in ways possible only to them, and expressed by *their*
analogical language, symbols, and understandings of the Mystery,
shaped by *their* culture, by *their* social location, and by the *conflict*
underlying much of our globalized and globalizing world and of
which most of the People of God have been victims.

Thus, the people's western Catholicism cannot be like the
western Catholicism of other Christians (including other western
Catholics) whose social location is different or hegemonic, who
might not be at the bottom of society's ladder, and/or who benefit from the current configuration of any society that treats most
of its members (including most western Catholic Christians) as
disposables. This does not contradict the Christian reality and
depth of the "insignificant" people's western Catholicism—not
any more than Jesus' peasant understanding and practice of the
religion of Israel contradicts his being Jewish.

Any individual or group in society may experience the
Mystery. Important differences among people and groups will,
however, be found in any claim to having encountered the
Mystery, on how the Mystery is analogically "said," on how the
experience is undergone and interpreted, and so on. Just as it
is impossible to conceive of the existence of an event without

some prior understanding that would allow it to be labeled as "existing," it is equally impossible to speak or conceive of an experience of God without the prior understandings provided by culture and social location. Therefore, the most important difference among individuals and groups in reference to experiences of God will be *which* interpretations and "sayings" about God and God's revelation are presented to the rest of society as "norm" or as "best," and how those interpretations or "sayings" are received. Power asymmetries will determine the social success of these interpretations and claims.

In other words, even if it may be true that God can be experienced by anyone or any group, and that God's revelation can and should be announced to everyone, the very instant an experience is perceived as "of God," the culture and social location of individuals and interest groups utilize hermeneutical tools made available by those persons' or groups' standing in society; thus they make any subsequent testimony or explanation of the experience or of revelation "acceptable" and "respectable" (or not) in society *in the same manner as and degree to which "acceptability" and "respectability" are given to the subculture and social location of that individual or group in their broader (and inescapably conflictive) culture and society.*

Religious subjects will interpret and attempt to remember, symbolize, and live by that which *they* experienced in the encounter with God. When this interpretation and these attempts are shared by others who also claim to have met God, there an internal conversation is born. And when an individual or group "pours" the experience of God and of God's revelation, and the internal conversation, into meaningful symbols, memories, explanations, and guidelines for living that can be shared by others in society, there the experience becomes socialized. But this socialization, obviously, is not the result of detached calculation.

In theological terms, there is Christianity *only* where the experience of God and the revelation of God have become subversively and *constatablemente* incarnate in the culture, history, and life of the believing people.

Among other consequences, this implies that the western Catholicism of hegemonic groups and their allies in any society will express itself through the symbols, doctrines, and lifestyles of hegemony, and will claim the authority bestowed it by hegemony, which evidently are *not* those of the western Catholic sub-altern (disposable, marginalized) groups in that same society. The doctrinal orthodoxy of the hegemonic, however, might actually be deemed heterodox and literally "dis-graceful" when "heard" among hegemony's victims.

If it is true that western Catholicism must incarnate in the social and historical realities of its communities, then there cannot be one single way of being western Catholic—not even within each of the denominational strands that form and shape western Catholicism. The different ways will reflect the conflicts, the social locations, the economic classes, the biases and marginalizations, and all the other realities that are part and parcel of human societies.

If communities of the disposables are discriminated against, are the objects of dominant racism and bigotry, and are the victims of injustice—as they certainly are—then *their* Christianity cannot possibly be understood without further prejudice unless *their* conflicts and suffering are admitted as truly and inescapably shaping their experience of God, their understandings of revelation, their claims, their explanations, and their doctrines. And by the same token, to the degree that other western Catholics have benefited by participation in, or by access to, the hegemonic groups and ideologies (whose byproduct has been the marginalization of most of their fellow humans, including most of their fellow Christians), to that degree their Catholicism is shaped in the likeness of society's victors.

The religion of the hegemonic participates in *their* dominant power, social location, and culture, often doctrinally legitimizing the marginalization of others, while also veiling the eyes and consciences of the dominant so that they not see what they do to others. The religion of the dominant (including its doctrines, its liturgies, and its institutions) will be inevitably shaped by their hegemonic abuse and bias, and will typically claim to be the norm.

If hegemony in society is dependent on a given group's ability to persuade other groups within that society that *it* is the best qualified to lead, then this persuasion requires the creation and distribution of explanations, of symbols, of justifications, and of "objective analyses" of reality that effectively legitimize (often by veiling their purpose) the leading group's pretensions. In other words, it will religiously produce *legitimizing doctrines*.

To the degree that the other groups in society (especially the subaltern disposable) accept the validity of the explanations and justifications, and to the degree that they assume the symbols of the dominant, the hegemony of the latter is secured. Given the presence of conflict within modern societies, the creation and dissemination of a dominant group's reasons for hegemony (including its religious doctrines) do not happen without some form of coercion. And yet, no subaltern acceptance of the reasons for hegemony is ever complete or without some doubt.

The dominant group within sociocultural hegemony will attempt to present its hegemonic role and its explanations as necessary and, when this role and this explanation are expressed through its religious categories and its doctrines, the dominant group will affirm that *these* are divinely sanctioned and willed, "revealed" as *the* truth or as close to truth as possible. After all, there is no better argument in favor of a particular group's hegemony (and hence, in favor of a particular social formation) than to spread the belief that it is divinely established or sanctioned. Obviously, there can be no possible appeal beyond God's decision. The sad stories of Christianity's role in the justification of African slavery and in the legitimation of the doctrine of Manifest Destiny are clear examples of this, at the cost of millions of destroyed lives. Furthermore, the reasons in favor of a group's hegemony are created and disseminated not only in the direction of the disposable subaltern but also toward the very interior of the dominant group: this group's members have to be convinced of their "right" to hegemony and of their "moral rectitude" and of other groups' "inferiority" or "disposability."[85]

However, and as I noted above, the process of creating and disseminating the explanations (doctrines) and symbols that result in the (divine) legitimation of the hegemony of a group in society is never a completely successful process. Those who benefit from hegemony as well as those who (as disposable subalterns) internalize hegemony's reasons are always left with some margin of doubt or suspicion. Doctrines may be taught, repeated, and explained, but not totally believed.

Further, it seems the legitimizing process suggests to both dominant and subaltern groups that to harbor a doubt is not desirable, and that guilt should be felt in response to "doctrinal hesitation."

This doubt or suspicion is all too frequently sensed but not reflected upon theoretically by the subaltern or marginalized, because the doubt or suspicion is symbolized rather than explained. It can externalize itself through behaviors deemed unsettling or unacceptable by the dominant or it can be sensed through the (often quiet) disregard or anonymous subversion of ecclesiastical, social, and cultural norms, of exclusivist doctrinal orthodoxy, and of canonical decisions. It is present in the refusal to yield to legitimation of hegemony and injustice, often without full awareness of the reason for this refusal. And it is always proof that the legitimation of one group's dominance in society or ecclesiastical institution(s) has not fully succeeded.

When the doubt is allowed to become conscious and when unspoken suspicion becomes spoken, the result is a confrontation with reality that profoundly and unequivocally calls into question the explanations and justifications of hegemony, *including its doctrinal explanations.* The same western Catholicism that acted as accomplice in the legitimating process can become the source and channel of blunt, explicit challenge to the hegemonic groups in society and in ecclesiastical institutions and in their explanations, doctrines, and practices.

In other words, popular Catholicism, as the people's real Catholicism, can be either liberating or alienating. It will play these roles to the degree that it either confronts social reality or escapes into a self-created, self-deluding, and therefore false world. The experience of doubt will lead to either role only insofar as the perceived needs and interests of the people are served by and through either role, and (crucially among most western Catholics) to the degree that liberation or alienation are explained and understood—through the doctrinal internal conversations of the marginalized—as being God's will. In contemporary societies there does not seem to be room for credible intermediate options that appeal to some sort of social neutrality: it's either submit or subvert. And *doctrines will serve as "internal conversation" explanations to justify one or another option* among the "disposable" vast majority of western Catholic Christians.

What of revelation needs explaining (i.e., doctrine) in the hegemonic segment of society might not be regarded as important in the same society's subaltern segments, and vice versa. Doctrine, therefore, is crafted not in a social or cultural vacuum (as a merely theoretical "religious" exercise devoid of real-life consequences). Doctrine is constructed within, and in response to, the conflictive struggles for hegemony, and as means of internal conversations among Christians, either to religiously justify and explain submission to a hegemonic social configuration or to religiously justify and explain the subversion of the very same hegemonic configuration.

Consequently, when we consider the subjects and contexts of doctrine-making, we unveil doctrine's legitimizing and subversive roles. Much more importantly, when we confront these roles with the most central "content" of revelation (the daring hope that Jesus was right when he announced that the Reign of God is dawning and that the God of the Reign is compassion towards all) we can only conclude that *the only ethical role, purpose and option for Christian doctrine is to explain (always as internal conversation among Christians) the "bet for the hope" that will subvert all hegemonies.*

The episcopate, at least in western Catholic Christianity,[86] has an important role in the discernment of doctrine and even in the proposal of doctrines—again, understanding doctrines, at their best, contextually as internal conversation about revelation and faith, for the subversion of all human hegemonies, as required by the Reign of God and the God of the Reign. The episcopate has a literally "extra ordinary" role, and by the expression "extra ordinary" I mean to say that it is neither exclusive, conclusive, nor ordinary, and certainly not sufficient by itself.[87]

Any doctrine, as we have seen, is internal conversation, to clarify or explain what among Christians might be questioned. Doctrines, therefore, are potentially valid and useful Christian attempts at better understanding or better clarifying the hope and faith of the entire People of God—who alone, as the entire People, are the Church. The episcopate's discernment is not about clarifications of the bishops' hope or faith, but of the hope and faith of the entire People of God whom the bishops serve.[88] Consequently, without the Church there would not be an episcopate. Hence, the "extra ordinary" role of bishops in the discernment of doctrine is not sufficient by itself. But the episcopate does have an important role in the discernment. The process of doctrinal discernment is certainly the responsibility of the entire Church, but historically the bishops have often led the discernment to a conclusion, although rarely initiated it.

Ecumenical councils and regional synods, as ecclesial contexts for resolution of questions or disputes, are historical examples of the role of bishops in the discernment of doctrines. Christian history cannot explain much of its own development without the doctrinal contributions of councils and synods. Yet no conciliar creed or synodal decision would be remembered or have had any positive effect unless the People of God had "received" it as *its* explanation to *its* questions.

The "extra ordinary" role of the episcopate, therefore, is one of proposing to the rest of the Church clarifications of the faith of the entire Church, and the entire Church, in the exercise of its "sense of faith," will (or will not) "receive" and thereby confirm the proposed result of the bishops' discernment. This role of the episcopate should necessarily include a clear discernment as to the effect and consequences of any episcopal proposal in the conflictive contexts of hegemony and dominance—a discernment, unfortunately, in which the bishops have historically often failed. It has not been uncommon for episcopally proposed doctrines to become a legitimizing strategy of power asymmetries.[89]

This has been the historical process, but have we ever considered the historical exercise of the *sensus fidelium* in the reception (or rejection) of episcopally proposed doctrines, within and among the vast marginalized majority of the People of God? What have the majority of the People of God understood *they* were "receiving"? What are the theological, dogmatic consequences of these issues? And, much more importantly, what are the consequences for the real life of the real People of God?

Unfortunately, to commence here the conversation that might lead us to answers to these questions would take us away from the present focus of our reflection. Nevertheless, these questions must be dealt with in a future study of traditioning.

Doctrine, therefore has a role: to explain and sustain, among Christians, in each of their historical and cultural contexts, the Christian understanding of God's self-donation and self-revelation through and in an executed Jewish Galilean peasant.

Christian doctrine has the role of explaining and sustaining the effective, real subversion of all human hegemonies and of all human self-idolatries, because Christians hope in the truthfulness of Jesus' message that the God who is compassion is, already, drastically transforming the world according to God's compassionate will.

Christian doctrine has the role of explaining and sustaining the daring bet of human lives in the effective, real subversion of all hegemonies, because of the Christian hope.

What Christian doctrine cannot be is an idol.

Christian doctrine becomes an idol when it effectively attempts to reduce revelation, the hope, and the faith to itself, i.e., to doctrinal affirmations or explanations, crafted by humans in contexts and for purposes not reflective of the core message of Jesus.

It becomes an idol (or, more precisely, an idolatrous agent of the self-idolatrous hegemonic) when it turns itself into the object of obedience or when it claims to possess sufficient and definitive truth. Or when it becomes a weapon at the service of power. The doctrinification of the subversive hope of the Reign of God, and its consequences, is the idolatry that has often seduced some among the People of God—and made a mockery of the crucified.

Christian doctrine becomes an idol when it blocks the "hearing" of God's self-revelation, as it does when it displaces the subversive, compassionate hope through the doctrinification of the crucifixion and through the domestication of the crucified.

It becomes an idol when it robs the cross of the cry and the anguish and the desolation of the crucified and of all the crucified, by reducing it to spectacle or doctrinal sentences. It becomes an idol when it calms our consciences and allows us to ignore all the crucified women and men among us.

IV

Traditioning:
A Theological Proposal

> *We proclaim a crucified Messiah: a stumbling block . . . and*
> *foolishness . . . But the foolishness of God is wiser than*
> *human wisdom, and the weakness of God is stronger than*
> *human strength.*
>
> *1 Corinthians 1:23, 25*

Doctrine, at best, is analogical of revelation.[1] If revelation is God's
self-donation (and thus God's *self*-revelation), then no doctrine
can ever pretend to be more than an abysmally insufficient analogy,[2] or a mere (and just as abysmally insufficient) representation
that may be true only to the degree that it explicitly acknowledges and represents its distance from the truth, that is, from the
Ultimate Mystery who is beyond human understanding.[3] Either
that or doctrine becomes an idol by claiming to be the truth or
the definitive conveyer of the truth.

Christian doctrines, to some degree, assume hope—the hope
that they still support and help understand *verosímilmente* the subversive hope of the Reign. But doctrinification, the turning of
doctrine into the definitive measure or object of faith, requires
the end of hope. Doctrinification assumes its definitiveness by
not acknowledging its own unavoidable transience as a human
construct.[4]

The traditioning of revelation is not the traditioning of
doctrinal truths. Traditioning is about the hope and the faith

and, consequently, about the Reign of God and the God of the Reign. It is also, inescapably, about that Galilean Jewish peasant who announced the dawn of the Reign.

Kairos in Lo Cotidiano

Western Catholics, as do all human persons and communities, exist only in their daily realities, in their historical and cultural *cotidianos*.[5] These *cotidianos* act as the epistemological and hermeneutical "locations of interlocution" *from which* human persons and communities construct knowledge and understand the (experienced) real in manners meaningful to them,[6] and *onto which* come from others the knowledge and understanding of what is real for them.[7] This dual function ("dual direction") of each respective *cotidiano* is important for our understanding of traditioning.

Although we might refer to *lo cotidiano* in the singular, indicating by the expression daily life as it is really lived and experienced, the fact remains that there is no single experience or living of daily life that is experienced and lived in the same way or in the same contexts by all humans. We all live our daily lives within our specific contexts, thereby granting our personal and communal *cotidianos* their perspectival characteristics[8] as "particular universalities."

What is *lo cotidiano*? This Spanish expression is not merely coextensive with "daily life." It is the real life that is lived, lived and experienced, by real people, in the everyday. Reality cannot be experienced except in daily life: this is *lo cotidiano*. It is only in daily life that we experience and live life.[9]

This is so obvious that it seems strange for theologians to look for great philosophical principles in order to ground the starting point of their theological constructs. *Lo cotidiano* is where we should go for our theological starting point.

In people's *cotidianos*, it should honestly be recognized, we find messiness and struggle and the unfair fight for (unfair) survival; we find racism, ethnocentrism, oppression, misunderstanding, colonial agendas, attempts at suppression, domestic violence, gender stereotypes, homophobia and heterosexism, and other very real and deeply unethical and unacceptable behaviors. Nevertheless, it is in *lo cotidiano* that we also find the goodness, the resilience, the courage, the dignity, the beauty, the wisdom, and the extraordinary strengths of everyday people.

Lo cotidiano is daily life as it is experienced and lived by real people, but it is not just the raw data or the raw facts of daily life. *Lo cotidiano* is also the "knowing" and the "understanding" of daily reality.[10] It is important to note that *lo cotidiano* is not lived as a linear sequence (from a beginning to an end) but as *moments* that only later are granted meaning, significance, connections, and cultural-historical location from within *lo cotidiano* itself; the perspectival lenses thus created will serve further to weave the moments into a meaningfulness they did not originally demand or display.[11]

As we live and experience daily life, *in* daily life, we are not aware of it (and we do not experience it) as more than transient moments, some important and others not, but moments nevertheless. It is only later, and always as another moment within *lo cotidiano*, that we might discover or grant meaning and connection to the moments of our daily lives.

Lo cotidiano is the opposite of the "museumification" of daily life or experience. Museumification may be understood as the turning of a living reality (in this case, daily life as it is lived and experienced) into an ideal, or more precisely, ideological, "representation" of itself, as if it were an artifact.[12] This demands, therefore, that we keep in mind that to theorize about *lo cotidiano* is not *lo cotidiano*, yet it is a moment within the real lived daily life of the theorizer(s)—a moment that only later, and to serve various interests, might acquire meaning and justification (or not). Furthermore, and of crucial importance here, the museumification of daily life involves and requires the "ordering of the artifacts," i.e., choosing among the moments, in daily life thus "re-presented." This ordering or choosing inescapably re-inscribes hegemony's power asymmetries.[13] The re-presentation and ordering of the lived moments of daily life as artifact(s) would then claim to be real life, and its chosen moments to be the only ones worth remembering as significant.[14]

Kairos, as we have already seen in preceding chapters, is the moment of breakthrough, of crisis, of "break up" and, thus, of opportunity. It is surely a moment within *lo cotidiano*, a moment that only later will acquire or be granted meaning and significance, or not. It is the *outcome* of the kairotic moment (unexpected as the moment emerges in real daily life) that will bestow on it significance or irrelevance—assuming, of course, that the opportunity was seized.[15]

A very frequent western notion of history sees history always marching forward toward an ever more wonderful future—typically a future that is the result or the development of our present, in spite of all difficulties, somehow marvelously assuming and reaffirming the history-building protagonic importance of the world's dominant. Invariably, also, humankind is portrayed as the unstoppable builder of this ever-better future. This frequent view of history, however, seems to be the museumification of history, with its concomitant ideological re-presentation and re-ordering of the meaning(s) granted to the moments of daily life, and thereby the reinscribing of hegemonic power asymmetries in "history" and its outcomes.

More importantly, however, this frequent view of history stands in sharp contrast to the real daily life experienced by the vast majority of humankind. This museumified history diametrically contradicts the Christian hope-filled assertion that the self-donation of God occurred scandalously in a moment of *kairos*, a moment of crisis and "break up" of all human hegemonies, logics, and futures. The grand narratives of human history are neither salvific nor humanizing—except in the expectations of their hegemonic beneficiaries—because they museumify real life into ideologically re-presented artifacts, re-ordered to serve the dynamics of hegemony's self-idolatry.

God's revelatory *kairos* stands as the very opposite—as a moment of opportunity to understand and to act in drastically different ways,[16] because *whom and what* God reveals as

God's definitive self-donation are *whom and what* the dominant historical narrative regards as irrelevant and disposable.[17]
In other words, Christianity claims that every (Christian) understanding of revelation has to acknowledge that *at its core*
stand the real lives of the disposable and the insignificant (the
crucified) of every historical and cultural context. In fact, its
core *is* an executed Jewish peasant who dared to hope that
God was transforming the world according to God's compassionate will.

If a *kairos* becomes significant and meaningful—indeed, if it
comes to be regarded as *the* defining moment of the self-donation (and hence, of the *self*-revelation) of the Ultimate Mystery—
that *kairos* must be accessible to all humans and as the kairotic
moment in each of their respective *cotidianos*.[18]

Consequently, no doctrinal affirmation can conceivably access the *cotidianos* of humankind, because doctrines are unavoidably cultural and culture-specific, and are therefore "conditioning
fences." At best, doctrine can be (as I have discussed earlier) analogical internal conversation that attempts better to understand,
but it cannot pretend to *be* the revelatory *kairos* or the opportunity this kairos breaks open for humankind. God's revelation
is not reducible to a good argument or addressed only to those
who belong to a culturally favored group.

Most of humankind, in the past and at present, is formed by
"disposable" and "insignificant" peoples and persons—disposable
and insignificant according to the beneficiaries of the dominant
power asymmetries.[19]

If there are universal human experiences, one of them undoubtedly is the real daily-life experience of power asymmetries,
within all societies for the benefit of the few and the historical
and cultural "insignificance" of the many. This universal experience shapes and has shaped human understandings of what it
means to be human and the meanings of history and culture, as
it has molded—indeed infected—much that is religion.[20] This
universal human experience, therefore, is the opposite of the
Reign of God.

Because the "disposable" vast majority of human beings exist only in their daily realities—in their historical and cultural *cotidianos*—their *cotidianos* act as their "locations of interlocution." From these locations, the "unimportant" and "disposable" peoples of the Earth construct knowledge and understand their (experienced) reality in manners meaningful to them. For this, they do not wait for the approval of the dominant, the educated, or the pious. Their *cotidianos* are their starting point. It is in "insignificant" *cotidianos* that the revelatory reality-breaking *kairos* occurs and, Christians affirm, *did* historically occur.[21]

The personal kairotic moment, when we confront the decision to choose a drastically different direction for ourselves[22] (guided by compassion and justice) or continue to participate (as victims or victimizers) in this world of power asymmetries, is when, within each of our *cotidianos*, we are confronted with the challenge of a specific subversive hope: Was Jesus of Nazareth right when he said that God was transforming this world according to God's will? Was Jesus right when he claimed that God is compassionate towards all, without any limits, conditions or exceptions? Is Jesus of Nazareth, therefore, credible as bearer of this news? The only credible argument for the hope is not an argument but the Christians' demonstrable (*constatable*) bet of *their lives* for the hope—the hope they expect is subverting what the present world of asymmetries holds as self-evident and permanent. In other words, faith is the only credible reason for the hope, as the hope is the only reasonable justification for the risk of faith.[23]

How can such faith and such hope be traditioned in our globalized, globalizing, and intensely diverse world? What can traditioning be?

An "Effective Analogy"

The language of the hope is a crucial part of an answer to these questions, because all traditioning occurs as *logos spermatikos*[24] within the many human *cotidianos* and because all traditioning occurs as part of the Christian *paroikousa* ("homeless sojourn-ing") throughout history.[25] It is only God, however, who turns the human, ecclesial actions, and processes we call traditioning into the *kairos* that confronts us with its demands.

Today's western Catholic traditioning occurs among[26] two interlocutors who are very much intertwined (often to the point of identity) in contemporary societies and cultures and extraordi-narily interconnected: the already self-identifying western Cath-olic multitudes and the even larger segments of humanity that self-identify beyond the broad perimeters of western Catholi-cism. It cannot be denied that it is sometimes hard to distinguish one interlocutor from the other. Furthermore, it is of extreme importance here that immense majorities of both groups are re-garded (by the dominant in the globalized economy, in today's societies, and even within the Christian denominational bodies) as insignificant, unimportant, and/or disposable.

The language needed today for traditioning the hope and ex-plaining the faith[27] must be interculturally effective as well as under-standable for all who hear it. It must not adulterate the core message of Jesus of Nazareth, which was the reason for his hope and still is the reason for ours.[28] The language must also be anti-idol.

Benefiting now from the reflections in the preceding chap-ters, we can say that what is needed is an intercultural "effective analogy"—an analogy that can[29] "speak" within the experience of everyday life of the vast majority of humanity (Christians or not). It must be an analogy relevant to the *cotidianos* of most of the world, as most of the world is: poor, marginalized, non-European, non-white. Hence, we need a "universally relevant"[30] analogy that, without being less analogical or less cultural, is ef-fective interculturally by becoming "inter-discursive" among the often-conflicting segments within any one universally particular *cotidiano* and/or among and across several other universally par-ticular *cotidianos*.

The effective analogy I am suggesting here[31] must engage human (and therefore Christian) inter-discursive dialogues, in which what some understand and live as their meaningfulness (their *logos*)—in Christian traditioning's case, the hope embedded in Jesus' core message of the Reign of God and of the God of the Reign—is communicated to others within and from within these others' own cultural perspective.

The meaningfulness thus communicated must always be "live" (and by this I mean that meaningfulness is demonstrated in lived real life, and not as a theory), *as real lives that are lived compassionately*. Some persons might come to assume that meaningfulness (*logos*) as their own, but only because *they* have discovered it as meaningful (within and from within their own cultural horizon). They in turn, upon their discovery of the meaningfulness (*logos*) originally witnessed to them, will communicate to still others what they have come to understand and live as meaningfulness (*logos*), but again only in and as their real lives lived compassionately.

This process, which is traditioning, also invites the "speaking" and "hearing" others to question and grow in what they understand and live as ultimately meaningful, thereby moving the process into an ever-deepening and continuing dialogue where meaningfulness is discovered and affirmed, over and over, through mutual witnessing, contrasting dialogue, and non-colonizing reflection.

The discovery of what will come to be referred to as "meaningful," then, results from intercultural dialogue and contrast, and not from arguments and doctrinal concepts born within a cultural horizon foreign to most of humanity and often employed to convince the "unimportant" that in order to be "good" Christians they must move away from their own cultural horizon. The argument that hope and faith must critique (indeed, subvert) cultures cannot be made to imply or provoke colonization of those treated as insignificant by the dominant beneficiaries of this world.

Notice, nevertheless, that in this real-life dialogue within and from within human *cotidianos*, the ultimate message is about human life's meaningfulness. Notice too that the dialogue, if non-colonizing, can only be an occasion (a moment in *lo co-tidiano*) for "planting the seed of meaningfulness" (a *logos sper-matikos*)—in other words, for the *possibility* of there being a moment of *kairos* that, if seized, will then demand a kenotic life of compassion. Only in retrospect can we then claim this moment's traditioning character.

How then is meaningfulness expressed and understood in the dialogue? What common language is there for a non-colonizing intercultural dialogue? Western Catholicism claims that only an analogical expression is the language to announce the meaningfulness, because the meaningfulness witnessed to by the faith of Christians is the news that God is transforming this world and that God is compassionate towards all without limits, conditions, or exceptions. Obviously the analogy will only be effective if it can speak of a *credible* meaningfulness within the *cotidianos* of most of the world, insignificant and dismissed as they are.

This is why the crucified peasant that Christianity remembers is absolutely necessary to the credibility of the meaningfulness, because it is his execution that unveils the meaningfulness as a profoundly subversive hope, thereby inviting the bet of real life for the hope. Christian traditioning has the audacity to claim (credibly only in Christian living) that the Ultimate Mystery can be encountered in the execution (the act of injustice) inflicted on Jesus, and more precisely, *in those executed* by the act of power, Jesus of Nazareth *and* all others who are victims of power.[32]

This is Christianity's effective analogy of the Mystery it calls God: *in the victims of power we encounter the Ultimate Mystery and the most profound meaning of human life*, with the very subversive consequences implied by this analogy and this meaning. This effective analogy arises as possibility, of course, *because* of the crucifixion of Jesus, *because* of the continued crucifixions of multitudes of others like Jesus, and *because* of the subversive hope that the Ultimate Mystery has not turned away and cannot turn away.

Even if God did not exist, the transformation of the world into a new reality of compassion, justice, and inclusion remains the most extraordinary, meaningful, and subversive dare to humanity. Christians, of course, believe that by Jesus' cross God is credible, but not an omnipotent God, necessary by high philosophical argument or political expediency: rather, a God who self-reveals as compassion in the life and crucifixion of a peasant who dared risk it all for the hope that, if God is compassion, then God will transform the world for the benefit of those abused by the non-compassionate world.

A crucified peasant is an understandable analog, among and within the *cotidianos* of the immense majority of humanity. Peasants are still abused, denigrated, and executed by the powerful. That a peasant was executed resonates as real daily life in most of the world; it has for more than two millennia. That a peasant dared to dream of a daily world of compassion and justice also resonates as real daily hope in most of the world; it resonates very meaningfully and dangerously. That a peasant spoke of God as limitless and conditionless compassion toward the abused victims of the powerful again resonates as a real-life hope in most of the world, and as meaningful.[33] But is it credible?

Most humans will not answer by philosophical argument but by meaningful resonance with their own credible hope—in other words, by considering the *verosimilitud* between the executed peasant and his message on the one hand and their real-life condition and hope on the other. The crucified Jesus is effective analogy that can unveil and name the hope that is already in the lives and struggles of the vast majority of humankind. But only the grace of God can transform the analogy into the moment of *kairos* in *lo cotidiano* of human lives. Conviction and daily reality will grant credibility to the subsequent bet of life.

Most of this will make little sense to those who benefit from the present world of power asymmetries. It will seem equally senseless for those whose fear is greater than their hope for a really compassionate world. But it arguably makes meaningful sense, albeit always as dangerous hope, for most of humankind.

Nevertheless, the historical and cultural baggage of the institutions of Christianity are an obstacle to traditioning among Christians and beyond. The self-idolatry of many among the ordained, the learned, and the pious also seems a scandalous and heavy burden with which traditioning must critically contend. So, yes, historically and culturally there are, and there have always been, Christians who live as a great and obvious stumbling block to Christian traditioning.[34] Just as surely there have been, and are still, very many western Catholic Christians who will not hesitate to put compassion and the struggle for justice above all else, risking life and security for the sake of a better world for all.

The hope for another human world remains. It beckons for faith.

Of course, there are other honorable, plausible, and legitimate ways of understanding, expressing, and living the hope. Not only Christians know of compassion and justice and equality. Not only Christians hope for a new world where compassion, justice, and equality will reign, nor are Christians the only ones who can bet their lives for this new world. Not only Christians struggle for a world where all will be welcomed and regarded as equals in dignity and rights. The early Christians were fully aware of this too, and their answer remains valid today:[35] whoever is compassionate is acting according to the will of God and must consequently be welcome as partner in the shared hope and in the construction of a new world.[36]

The hope for another human world remains. Christian traditioning of the hope, therefore, is not for Christianity's gain.

Compassion

Throughout the present volume I have very often referred to compassion as the very center of Jesus' message regarding the Reign of God and the God of the Reign. Unquestionably, it is Christianity's most important commandment, and before it all else must yield—because God is compassion. Christian traditioning, furthermore, is only made credible by compassion that is *constatable*, demonstrable, lived, since it is the dawn of a new real world of real compassion that traditioning announces. The hope for this new world is made credible by the lived bet for it. Without its center in compassion, Christian traditioning would be eviscerated of its meaning.

But what is compassion? The original Latin meaning of the noun "compassion" is significant: "to endure with."[37] But if this is the meaning of compassion, then *with whom* we are to endure is more determining than *what* we are asked to endure, because the reality of the *who* determines the extent and demands of the *what*.

If we take seriously the reality of Jesus of Nazareth, and especially the reality of those whom he mainly addressed and with whom he lived (other villagers, often poor and landless, abused and dismissed by the powerful, the learned, and the pious of their day), then today's Christian traditioning cannot, in the name of Jesus, disregard the poor, the abused, and the insignificant of the twenty-first century. This is evident. As it is also evident that if those who benefit from power are addressed, the very credibility of traditioning demands that they hear of the dawning Reign of God (which will take away their power) from the location of poor, the abused, and the disposable (who will be the beneficiaries of the Reign).[38]

Christian traditioning is an unavoidable dimension of Christian compassion, as much as compassion is an unavoidable dimension of Christian traditioning. Without "enduring with" those most marginalized, ignored, and abused, there is no Christianity—there is the denial of God.

This sense of compassion as "enduring with" further justifies "the crucified Jesus" as the effective analogy of God and of the hope of the Reign.

With whom we are to endure, then, is determining of compassion, but it is not the difficult issue in traditioning, or in understanding what is meant by compassion, hard as it might be for those enamored of power or of the powerful. It is a different matter when we reflect on *what* "enduring with" the abused demands in the twenty-first century.

What do the disposable persons and peoples of today need (as conditions *sine qua non*) in order not just *to escape* marginalization and/or poverty, but *to construct* a new world where there will be no more hunger, no more injustice, no more exclusion, no more dominance of the few over the multitudes?[39] At least three (admittedly complex) inseparable and non-ending commitments are required.

Truthfulness

They, we, and all who would bet our lives for the hope that a new world is not only possible but in fact dawning, need to speak, think, and live truthfully.

There is the obvious need to speak truth to power,[40] but this in turn requires observation, reflection, and even study. Antonio Gramsci has spoken and written of the important contributions of those he called "organic intellectuals."[41] So have Jacques Rancière and others. However, besides the work of the committed intellectuals of whom these authors speak (and who might not necessarily be academics), much more important, is the *process of "unveiling" carried out by the people themselves*—precisely by those deemed too insignificant or incapable by the hegemonic. Paulo Freire's "pedagogy of the oppressed" immediately comes to mind,[42] but it is not his method that I have in mind here. The process of unveiling may be well assisted by organic intellectuals and their liberating methodologies, but the protagonic subjects must be the very populations that asymmetric hegemony has abused and dismissed.

The vast majority of humanity know how to see, how to think, how to figure out facts and connections; they know how to name reality and the unjust power relations that have constructed their reality, and they know how to communicate their reason and their thought, among themselves and to others who

would learn how to listen. The "disposables" are not theoretically paralyzed or devoid of rational explanations. Their thought
and reason, and their *logos*,[43] are expressed (as they can only be)
through *their* means.[44] This might further marginalize them in
the eyes of the powerful, the learned, or the pious (who cannot understand as significant any thoughts, reasons, or expressive
means other than their own) but in no way does it erase the
validity or truthfulness of the thought, the reason, and the *logos*
of the "insignificant" multitudes.

However, because the thought, reason, *logos*, and expressions of
the "disposable" are human, these are all, always and inescapably,
contextual, limited, and perspectival–with all that these contextualizations imply, as we have been discussing throughout this book.

Compassion in Christian traditioning, consequently, requires
that the traditioners, regardless of their social location, learn to
listen to, and understand, the thought, the reason, and the *logos*
of the "disposable." It requires that the traditioners not just listen
but become fluent in the languages that are the expressions of
the "disposable."

Nevertheless, the demand to listen and learn—congruent with
the hope to which the traditioners witness—must not be allowed
effectively to re-silence the "disposable" by making the traditioners
assume the role of "voice" for those whom hegemony has already
silenced (among the dominant). I repeat what I said above, that
the vast majority of humanity know how to see, how to think,
how to figure out facts and connections; they know how to name
reality and the unjust power relations that have constructed their
reality, and they know how to communicate their reason and their
thought. They do not need "voices" but allies, and listeners and
dialogue partners, as equals at the table, allies who will know not
to steal the people's own voice. Christians are not "the voice of the
poor"—unless they are the poor.

The processes of "unveiling" in which the insignificant vast
majority of the people in world (many of whom are Christian)
engage, should lead to truthful analyses and reflection on the

world's reality, but not just to analyses and reflection. Part of this truthfulness has to be the admission that all human understanding is contextual, perspectival, and therefore limited. The gauge of truthfulness is not merely the value or the rigor displayed by the people's insight on reality. A necessary gauge is the recognition (as a consequence of what we discussed earlier on *lo cotidiano* and on the many *cotidianos*) that all others, including other marginalized, "insignificant" peoples, also have their own (contextual, perspectival, limited) analyses and reflection. These demand a dialogue of the marginalized, among the marginalized, in the languages of the marginalized.

In other words, the acknowledgment and avoidance of cultural self-idolatry is part of truthfulness. Truthfulness also includes the acknowledgment and affirmation of the people's strengths unveiled for the construction of a new world of compassion, and of the inabilities and weaknesses that may become its obstacles. The seductions of the idol and its idolatries do not know the boundaries of marginalization.

Christian traditioners, most of whom are among those the world marginalizes as disposable, are, because of their hope that Jesus was right, bound by truthfulness. Their committed participation in the unveiling process can significantly contribute to this dimension of compassion.

Solidarity

There can be no compassion, no "enduring with," unless there is demonstrable solidarity among those who endure with each other, a solidarity that, in our world, demands that it be for, from, and among the marginalized multitudes of Earth. Solidarity is not assistencialism.[45] It is the discovery, the effective affirmation, and the shared pursuit of common bonds, of common hopes, of common interests, among those who would be solidarious with each other.

The crucifixion of Jesus analogically (and for Christians, definitively) expresses God's solidarity with humanity. In one executed peasant, Christian hope discovers that God shares with humanity—and most of humanity shares with God—a common bond, a common hope, a common interest in the construction of a human world truly without injustice, exclusion, or oppression. A new world without crucifixions.

As God is solidarious with humans, who are abysmally unlike God, so humans should be solidarious with each other and, especially with those not like them—most especially with those *most unlike* them.

As Jesus did not try to save his life by re-interpreting or softening the explicitly subversive consequences of his message and hope, neither can Christian traditioners. To be solidarious, in this world, is a real and serious risk that can (and will) bring consequences for those who would dare "endure with" the marginalized. Solidarity is not a theory or a pious emotion without consequences.

The unveiled and pursued common bonds, hope, and interests that are solidarity should also confront the well-attested human inclination to benefit from the other. The struggle for a new world of justice, inclusion, and equality cannot bring about new injustices, exclusions, or inequalities. Too many human experiments have failed for this reason. All human experiments face the inclination to self-benefit at others' expense.

Grace

All human efforts at constructing a new world will fail unless the new world is the Reign *of* God. By this I only mean that our human efforts will never be enough to fully create the new hoped-for world—not if we are the sole builders, our tools the sole tools, and our plans the sole plans. After all, humans are responsible (by cowardice or malice) for crafting the reality of cruel power asymmetries and dominance that have sacrificed and still sacrifice most of humankind. "The master's tools will not dismantle the master's house."[46]

I stated in the Introduction to this book that every Christian theology of traditioning will inevitably come to recognize that traditioning will not become *kairos* without the grace of God. And so here we are.

In western Catholic theologies, this recognition is commonplace because by "grace" is typically understood the presence and life of the compassionate God. Because God *is*, always and everywhere, so is God's compassion. Therefore, every instance of solidarity, of truthfulness, of subversive hope for a world of justice, and every bet of human life for that new world, is an instance of God's grace,[47] even if we might not be aware of it, and even if we cannot name God.[48] In the best western Catholic theologies of grace, what is indispensable is neither the knowing nor the naming, but the being and the living.

Without the grace of God there will be no Reign of God. Consequently, without the grace of God there would not be the compassion that can and will transform this world according to the will of God. With God's grace, however, *all* human acts and committed lives of compassion become "sacraments" subverting this world into the Reign, whether they know and name it or not.

The Mission of the People Of God

The mission of the Church is to tradition the hope that Jesus of Nazareth was right regarding the dawning of the Reign of God and the God of the Reign.

The mission of the People of God, therefore, is for the People *constatablemente* to bet their lives for that hope, in each of their many *cotidianos,* understanding that their hope is subversive of all of the world's structures and systems, and of all securities and certainties, that construct and reinscribe asymmetric power relations among humans. (These power relations provoke the marginalization of the vast majority of humanity, treated now as "disposable" by those who benefit from the structures and systems and who craft the securities and the certainties.)[49]

Christian traditioning, we must acknowledge after all the discussions reflected in this book, has historically been an exercise of subversive memory and hope as well as an exercise of rein-scribing power asymmetries. Traditioning has demonstrated moments of grace (betting for compassion, for justice and liberty) as well as moments of idolatry (betting for dehumanization, for inequality and marginalization).

So, as we conclude this stage in our joint unending *paroikousa*, what can we say is Christian traditioning?[50]

1. The People of God are given their identity by their shared hope and by their shared faith—their bet for the hope.

2. Their identity will be meaningful to the degree that their hope is expressed and lived *constatablemente* in their daily and risky faith.

3. Their hope and faith will be credible if they truly and demonstrably live compassionately and as builders of a compassionate world.

4. Their compassion will be real and credible if it is truthful and solidarious and as long as it is not self-idolatrous or reinscribing of power asymmetries.

5. Their compassion will not be an agent of the idol or of renewed dominance as long as it is gauged by the marginalized disposables themselves, in each of their *cotidianos*, as risk-taking "enduring with" them.

6. The disposables of the world will be able to gauge compassion if, *constatablemente*, this compassion empowers and liberates and subverts the real world in ways that they—the disposables—recognize and need.

7. The disposables will understand the hope that sustains the faith (the lived bet) of Christians if the language of the hope is not doctrinified.

8. The language of the hope will not be doctrinified as long as it is analogical and recalls its inescapable transience and intensely diverse contextualizations.

9. The globalized and globalizing contexts of all of today's humankind—not just of the wealth-producing

economy that benefits mostly the few, but also of the poverty and marginalization of the vast majority—require an intercultural language for saying the hope and proposing the faith.

10. For most of the real world, the most effective intercultural language for the hope is the effective analogy that is the crucified peasant Jesus.

11. This is the most effective intercultural language because it witnesses to the reality of the disposable majorities of the world by remembering the execution of one like them.

12. This remembrance, however, is subversive memory—subversive of the structures and justifications of marginalization and disposable status that the dominant want to impose on the majority of humankind.

13. It is subversive memory because this one executed Galilean peasant is said (by Christian traditioners) to have been right when he announced that the God of Israel was radically transforming this world according to God's will.

14. According to Christian memory of Jesus, the will of God is as God is: compassion toward all, without limits, without conditions, and without exceptions.

15. Consequently, compassion like God's is the *sine qua non* for anyone who comes to share in the hope that Jesus was right about God and about God's transformation of the world.

16. Because demonstrable, lived compassion is so central (because God has so revealed in God's self-donation in Jesus), nothing else can claim to be more important or more demanding among Christians or in Christian traditioning.

17. Because compassion is not a commitment only possible among Christians, all who *constatablemente* live by and share this commitment are fellow-builders and witnesses of the Reign of God, even when they might not agree on the "name" of God. Because it is the

being and the doing, and not the knowing, that signals the presence of the God who is always beyond all human knowing.

18. It is only the grace of God, in a totally contextual moment of *kairos*, that can break open the possibility of human recognition of the hope of Jesus, the hope shared and witnessed by Christian traditioning.

19. It is only the grace of God, in totally contextual ways, that can entice the foolishness of betting our lives for the hope.

20. It is always in concrete, contextual *cotidianos* that the fools may be identified, as a People, not by what they claim or doctrinally explain but by the subversive hope that has led them demonstrably to bet their lives together for a world built on compassion, justice, and dignity for all. This is the Church.

◆ ◆ ◆ ◆

Now we proceed to more conversations and more risk-taking. We move on to new or renewed locations of interlocution and to new or renewed struggles for the future. In real life and about real life, in our respective *cotidianos*, with all those who are just as foolish as we are, fueled by the hope and the faith many of us share, and because of our commitment to build a world worthy of the dignity we claim.

I have not said in the preceding pages all that perhaps needed saying, and I have not unpacked all that could have been unpacked. The book ends as the book began, as a moment in a *cotidiano*, shared by many.

Notes

Introduction

[1] The reader will note that only in the last chapter will I briefly discuss my understanding of "compassion."

[2] I will, in a moment, refer to the western Catholic perspective I assume in this book. However, at the very start, I want the reader to understand that just as by "western Catholic" I do not mean any particular denomination, by "Christian" and "Christians" I do not mean denominations other than western Catholic. Furthermore, and more importantly, as I will explain in Chapters Three and Four, *self-identifying* as Christian is not and has never been regarded as coextensive with *being* Christian. If readers remember instances of documented Christian hypocrisy, they should know that this author is also aware of many such instances and is equally ashamed of and disgusted by them. However, I will not surrender the labels "Catholic" or "Christian" because these have been sullied by those who claim to be "Catholic" or "Christian" but whose lives suggest they are not, or because the labels have been misused by those who should be better informed.

[3] If revelation, in fact, had a content beyond the experience of the Mystery and the hope to which it gives rise. As the volume develops, the reader will note the "unpacking" and development of these introductory paragraphs as well as of many of their assumptions, terms, and premises. Of course, I recognize, at times painfully, that there has been much more in Christian history than the subversive hope to which I am referring.

[4] See P. Freire, *Pedagogia do oprimido* (Rio de Janeiro: Paz e Terra, 2011; originally published in 1968); English translation: *Pedagogy of the Oppressed* (New York: Seabury Press, 1973). Freire demonstrates that education—and traditioning is an educational process—cannot be the transmission of an established "deposit" of knowledge, practices, and understandings. If it were, and Freire says that oppressive education is, it would be a "banking" pedagogy, where a "deposit" is merely transmitted ("banked") from the learned to the unlearned, while the latter forever remain dependent on those who determine, construct, and transmit the "deposit." Christian traditioning, consequently, is terribly cheapened and ethically threatened by such colonizing and dehumanizing approach and understanding.

[5] It is obvious that this is a book of theology, which means that prior reflections have occurred, and arguments have been made and dealt with, regarding the

reasonable possibility (or not) of the Mystery we call "God," the reasonable possibility of revelation, and the rationality and conditions of religious God-language. In a subsequent chapter we will further discuss some of these issues.

    [6] All reflection and thought occur from and within specific social and cultural perspectives, and the same is true of all scholarly methodologies. The present volume is no exception. Nevertheless, there is no apologetic intent herein on behalf of western Catholicism. Facts (demographic, historical, and other) will suffice to reasonably justify the legitimate importance of this conversation's perspective within Christian theology. I will reflect more at length on perspectives and contexts later in the book. I will elaborate in the next note on my definition of "western Catholicism."

    [7] In the present volume, every time the term "Catholic" appears, it will always and only mean what will be explained in the first chapter about the expression "western Catholic." Therefore, and I insist, nowhere in this volume will the term "Catholic" ever be coextensive with or identical to "Roman Catholic." See O. Espín, "Catholic Tradition," in *An Introductory Dictionary of Theology and Religious Studies*, ed. O. Espín and J. Nickoloff (Collegeville, MN: Michael Glazier, 2007), 212. The contents of that dictionary entry will be much expanded, and in a few important ways superseded, by the discussion in Chapter One.

    [8] Again, understanding "western Catholicism" as explained in Chapter One.

    [9] See, for example, F. X. Clooney, ed., *The New Comparative Theology: Interreligious Insights from the Next Generation* (London: T&T Clark, 2010).

    [10] See C. Bell, *Who Owns Tradition? Religion and the Messiness of History*, 2001 Bannan Institute Lecture (Santa Clara, CA: Santa Clara University, 2001).

    [11] One cannot help recalling Hans-Georg Gadamer's argument in his *Wahrheit und Methode* (Tübingen: J. C. B. Mohr/Paul Siebeck, 1975).

    [12] In Chapter Two, and at other points throughout the book, I will discuss "culture" as well as "interculturality" at length.

    [13] And therefore, to the degree that revelation can be claimed by humans as "revelation."

    [14] I use the neologism "culturalness" to indicate and underline the cultural nature or character of human life.

    [15] I prefer the more immediate "unsayable" to the more abstract "ineffable" and will use it throughout most of the book.

    [16] However, as we will see later, not all analogies are "effective" analogies for expressing the Christian understanding of the Mystery.

    [17] "Available" does not mean "employed," because even today many theologians still seem to consider cultural and intercultural analyses of only tangential interest to their theologies. Today cultural and intercultural (and other) analyses are available to, but unfortunately still not significantly employed by, many theologians.

    [18] An expression which often, and factually, refers to the vast majority of humanity in its condition as persons, peoples, and nations marginalized by those who think of themselves as "First World" (or as "First World 'wannabes'"), with the cultural and ideological baggage the categories "first" or "developed" (and "third" or "underdeveloped") imply in the minds of the dominant and in their use of the terms.

¹⁹ I use "Church," capitalized, to mean the entire People of God, whereas "churches" are "denominations," unless "Church" is part of the official name of a denomination, e.g., the Episcopal Church, the Church of the Brethren, the Independent Church of the Philippines.

²⁰ Y. Congar, *Tradition and Traditions: An Historical and a Theological Essay* (New York: Macmillan, 1967). This book remains, in my view, the best history of western Catholic theologies of Tradition. Unfortunately, it does not focus, in any significantly sustained way, on the processes of traditioning outside of western Europe and the Mediterranean basin, a seriously flawed methodological assumption and limitation, especially when one remembers Congar's otherwise broad Catholic perspective.

²¹ Throughout this book, much will be explained and discussed about the people's daily religion. More specifically, the people's daily religion will be understood as *the everyday religion of everyday self-identified members* ("church goers" or not) *of the overall western Catholic tradition*. No other "popular" religion is considered here.

²² See O. Espín, *The Faith of the People: Theological Reflections on Popular Catholicism* (Maryknoll: Orbis, 1997) and some of my other books, as well as numerous articles and chapters. A more complete bibliography can be found at http://www.latinobiliography.org.

²³ Throughout this volume, the term "ecclesiastical" will only refer to matters of denominational polity and politics and to institutional processes within the churches. On the other hand, the term "ecclesial" will always be used to refer to the Church as the People of God and to all elements that pertain to its mission, its communal experience, and its various dimensions. However, it must be clear to the reader that what is "ecclesial," as well as that which is "ecclesiastical," is always cultural, historical, and social, existing only in cultures, histories, and societies, resulting from and engaged with and in them.

²⁴ D. Tracy's lifelong work (together with the work of other eminent scholars like P. Ricoeur, G. Gutiérrez, L. and C. Boff, P. Freire, G. Agamben, B. Sarlo, J. C. Scannone, H.-G. Gadamer, and others) has demonstrated the inevitable and inescapable cultural, interpretive, and historical character of transmission. From a vast and distinguished body of work, see especially (but certainly not only) D. Tracy, *Plurality and Ambiguity: Hermeneutics, Religion, Hope* (San Francisco: Harper and Row, 1987).

²⁵ Yves Congar has said as much in *Tradition and Traditions*, 296.

²⁶ We will see in Chapter Three that faith is much more than what it might appear I am suggesting here. Yes, it has to be reasonable, but not for purposes of assenting to logical argument. Faith is the wager or "bet of life."

²⁷ The expectation and role of reason within theology are clearly ancient within western Catholicism. Many of western Christianity's greatest minds have stood for reason against all sorts of fundamentalisms and fanaticisms. Their appeals to reason and rationality in theology and in the development of doctrine are well documented. That is why recent crises (unresolved as of this writing) within a number of western Catholic and other Christian denominational communities seem to me to be expressions of biblical and/or ecclesiastical fundamentalism's renewed assault against reason and rationality in theology and Church. If past history is an indication

of the possible resolution of these contemporary crises, fundamentalism's assault will once again be defused and marginalized within theology, churches, and society, but never permanently defeated because fear (religious and social) is a very successful social control tool. In other words, fear-bred insecurity breeds fundamentalism and its corollary, intolerance, and supports the manipulation of believers under various guises and for various agendas. The fearful need for security and certainty always wants to overcome adult faith. The *deus ex machina* also wants to be the *deus ex timore*.

²⁸ See O. Espín, "Method in Theology," in *An Introductory Dictionary of Theology and Religious Studies*, 863–67.

²⁹ By "Latino/a" (in this book and elsewhere) is meant *only* the *United States* populations and communities of Latin American origins and ancestry. "Latino/a" is, therefore, *not* equal to or co-extensive with "Latin American." "Hispanic" is *still* a colonizing term which I prefer not to use as synonym of "Latino/a." Occasionally, "Latino/a" and "Latina/o" (equally employed and so written to signify gender inclusion) might be rendered as "Latin@" (also to signify inclusion); the pronunciation of these inclusive but difficult spellings, interestingly, are the easier *latinoa* or *latinao*.

³⁰ The Latino/a manner(s) of doing theology (although much more complex than suggested here) is usually called *teología de*—or *en*—*conjunto*, a descriptive phrase originally coined by theologian Arturo Bañuelas. It would be inappropriate and false to suggest that the present volume represents all or most Latino/a theology, but it is accurate to see it as an expression of *teología de conjunto*. For a brief introductory ecumenical overview of Latino/a theology, see E. D. Aponte, "Hispanic/Latino Theology," in *Global Dictionary of Theology*, ed. W. A. Dyrness, V. M. Kärkkäinen, and J. F. Martínez (Downers Grove, IL: InterVarsity Press, 2008), 397–400 as well as O. Espín, "Latino Theology(-ies)," in *An Introductory Dictionary of Theology and Religious Studies*, 753–54 and O. Espín and M. Díaz, eds., *From the Heart of Our People: Latino/a Explorations in Catholic Systematic Theology* (Maryknoll: Orbis, 1999). See also the very insightful C. Nanko-Fernández, *Theologizing en Espanglish* (Maryknoll: Orbis, 2010).

³¹ In Latino/a theological perspective and method, theology is not "books talking with books." Latino/a theology is a critical (and self-critical) disciplined reflection, born of questions *really* raised by, and *really* grounded in, *real-life* issues of *real* communities, brought to engage the claims of Christian revelation and faith, and of theology, by professional theologians *who are part of those real-life communities*. Because of this, Latino/a theology implicates, locates, and engages the theologian communally and socially, and its final goal is not primarily understanding but transformation (of the real-life issues and contexts of the communities). Understanding, therefore, is one moment, arguably indispensable and critical, in the quest for transformation. In its methodological approach Latino/a theology is not unique in the history of western theology, and it does not claim to stand alone in dealing with questions and issues of real and specific cultural communities. There is much more to Latino/a theological methodology (e.g., theologizing *en conjunto*). For further study I refer the reader to the bibliography in the preceding note and also, especially, to the ACHTUS-

sponsored online bibliography on Latino/a theology and related fields, accessible, as noted above in n. 22, at http://www.latinobibliography.org.

[32] The reader and I know that many are the guises under which gender, ethnic, cultural, racial, and heterosexist privilege and prejudice hide themselves. Even among scholars.

[33] See J. L. González, *Mañana: Christian Theology from a Hispanic Perspective* (Nashville: Abingdon, 1990), 52.

Chapter I

[1] This first chapter will clarify terms and topics, but this is not the only chapter where these terms and topics will be discussed and "unpacked." For the fuller view of each of the terms and topics in this book, the reader is encouraged to bring to the succeeding three chapters the clarifications in this first one, and vice versa. This is important for a full understanding of the arguments in this work.

[2] Anyone familiar with New Testament scholarly studies is very much aware of the meaning and importance of the statements just made. There have been, by 2013, several "waves" in the quest for the historical Jesus. I am not committed to any one of these waves nor to any one author. But we cannot ignore or dismiss the scholarly movement that seeks to reconstruct what can be known about the historical Jesus. It is crucial for a credible theology, as well as for a historically credible Christianity (and not a credulous version of it), that the basic traits and contexts of the life and message of Jesus of Nazareth be historically established (or at least solidly approximated), employing the usual scholarly methods that discern and support contemporary scholarly assertions regarding the life traits and contexts of many of antiquity's historical figures, as well as texts from antiquity that claim to reflect a historical figure's thought and life. However, we do need to keep in mind the caution wisely (and scientifically) argued by S. Arbersman in *The Half-Life of Facts: Why Everything We Know Has an Expiration Date* (New York: Current/Penguin, 2012).

[3] In Chapter Two I will be discussing the meaning of the notion of "history," and in that discussion I hope to make clear that I do not understand history apart from meaningfulness, a meaningfulness granted culturally to some "dead" events by humans who mine their past in order to find meaning for and in their present. I affirm this because all historical constructs (i.e., all "history") exist for the benefit of present interests. This is one reason, I will argue, why history is never innocent and why it is always a cultural construct for and by the present. The brief discussion of the historical Jesus' life and message in this first chapter in no way contradicts what I will discuss in the second chapter regarding history; in fact, it confirms it. The present-day interests served by any history are not in themselves exclusive; yes, some interests can be hegemonic and serving the dominant, while some interests can be subversive of dominance and of the claims and assumptions of the hegemonic. Hegemony and subversion are both human interests. Histories are culturally crafted and traditioned for one or the other, or both.

⁴ It is important to realize that this opening part of Chapter One is not, and cannot be, a thorough or complete examination of Jesus' context, message, and actions, and it is not (theologically speaking) a christology. The bibliography on each and all of these topics is vast. I refer the reader to the literature, especially to the publications cited in this note. The purpose of this opening part is to present my understanding of Jesus' message and its meaning within his context. The reader should also know that in this section, as well as elsewhere in the present volume, when I refer to the "historical" Jesus' message and actions, I follow mainly the work of W. R. Herzog, who in turn is in conversation with J. D. Crossan, J. P. Meier, B. J. Malina, J. C. Scott, and others, whose works I have also used here. I have further incorporated insights from publications by C. Bravo, R. Schnackenburg, H. Echegaray, M. Fraijó, C. Mesters, D. E. Oakman, R. Horsley and J. H. Yoder. This section on the historical Jesus' message and actions, therefore, is dependent on the following works: W. R. Herzog, *Prophet and Teacher: An Introduction to the Historical Jesus* (Louisville: Westminster/John Knox, 2005); Herzog, *Parables as Subversive Speech: Jesus as Pedagogue of the Oppressed* (Louisville: Westminster/John Knox, 1994); Herzog, *Jesus, Justice, and the Reign of God* (Louisville: Westminster/John Knox, 2000); J. D. Crossan, *Jesus: A Revolutionary Biography* (San Francisco: HarperCollins, 1994); Crossan, *The Historical Jesus: The Life of a Mediterranean Jewish Peasant* (San Francisco: HarperCollins, 1992); J. P. Meier, *A Marginal Jew: Rethinking the Historical Jesus*, vols. 1 and 2 (New York: Doubleday, 1991, 1994); R. Horsley, *Jesus and the Spiral of Violence: Popular Jewish Resistance* (Minneapolis: Augsburg Fortress, 1993); Horsley, *Jesus and Empire: The Kingdom of God and the New World Order* (Minneapolis: Fortress, 2002); Horsley, *Jesus and the Powers: Conflict, Covenant, and the Hope of the Poor* (Minneapolis: Fortress, 2010); Horsley, *Galilee: History, Politics, People* (Valley Forge: Trinity Press International, 1995); Horsley, *Archaeology, History and Society in Galilee: The Social Context of Jesus and the Rabbis* (Valley Forge: Trinity Press International, 1996); Horsley, *Bandits, Prophets and Messiahs: Popular Movements at the Time of Jesus* (London: T&T Clark, 1999); W. Stegemann, B. J. Malina, and G. Theissen, eds., *The Social Setting of Jesus and the Gospels* (Minneapolis: Fortress, 2002); B. J. Malina, *The Social World of Jesus and the Gospels* (New York: Routledge, 1996); B. J. Malina and J. H. Neyrey, *Calling Jesus Names: The Social Value of Labels in Matthew* (Sonoma: Polebridge, 1988); Malina, *The New Testament World: Insights from Cultural Anthropology* (Louisville: Westminster/John Knox, 2001); Malina, *The Social Science Commentary on the Synoptics* (Minneapolis: Augsburg, 2002); M. Fraijó, *Jesús y los marginados* (Madrid: Cristiandad, 1985); C. Bravo, *Galilea, año 30: Historia de un conflicto* (Mexico City: Centro de Reflexión Teológica, 1989); H. Echegaray, *La práctica de Jesús* (Lima: CEP, 1980); R. Schnackenburg, *Reino y Reinado de Dios: Estudio bíblico-teológico* (Madrid: Ediciones Fax, 1974); J. H. Yoder, *The Politics of Jesus* (Grand Rapids: Eerdmans, 1994); and D. E. Oakman, *The Political Aims of Jesus* (Minneapolis: Fortress, 2012). Useful reference tools on Jesus and the earliest apostolic generation—their historical, economic, political, cultural, and religious contexts—are the articles by a distinguished list of specialists in *Handbook of Early Christianity: Social Science Approaches*, ed. A. J. Blasi, J. Duhaime, and P.-A. Turcotte (Walnut Creek, CA: Altamira, 2002). Also important

here are two books by J. C. Scott, *Weapons of the Weak: Everyday Forms of Peasant Resistance* (New Haven: Yale University Press, 1986), and *Domination and the Arts of Resistance* (New Haven: Yale University Press, 1990). I will refrain from repeating all the above mentioned sources at every turn, and generally refer the reader to them for what follows on Jesus, his context, and his message.

⁵ For an understanding of Torah in Judaism, see A. J. Avery-Peck, "Torah," in *An Introductory Dictionary of Theology and Religious Studies*, ed. O. Espín and J. Nickoloff, (Collegeville: Michael Glazier, 2007), 1387.

⁶ Herzog, *Prophet and Teacher*, 173–212. See also J. C. Scott, "Protest and Profanation: Agrarian Revolt and the Little Tradition," pt. 1, *Theory and Society* 4, no. 1 (1977): 1–38, and "Protest and Profanation," pt. 2, *Theory and Society* 4, no. 2 (1977): 211–46; F. Krantz, ed., *History from Below: Studies in Popular Protest and Popular Ideology* (Montreal: Concordia University Press, 1985); and A. Gramsci, *Os intelectuais e a organização da cultura*, 3rd ed. (Rio de Janeiro: Editora Civilização Brasileira, 1979).

⁷ A. J. Saldarini, *Pharisees, Scribes and Sadducees in Palestinian Society* (Grand Rapids: Eerdmans, 2001).

⁸ Herzog, *Parables as Subversive Speech*.

⁹ Herzog, *Prophet and Teacher*, 125–52 and Crossan, *Jesus: A Revolutionary Biography*.

¹⁰ Oakman, *The Political Aims of Jesus*, 79–130.

¹¹ "The problem is not the Torah but those who judge in its name while denying its meaning and purpose" (Herzog, *Prophet and Teacher*, 144). It is useful to recall Deuteronomy 27:19's curse: "Cursed be anyone who deprives the alien, the orphan, and the widow of justice."

¹² In Spanish here I would say *constatablemente*. *Constatablemente* is the adverb derived from the verb *constatar* and is much stronger and more proof-demanding than the mere "observable."

¹³ Herzog, *Prophet and Teacher*, 99–124.

¹⁴ The Greek term *stauros*, usually translated as "cross," was more generically used to describe an instrument of execution that included a "standing pole," which is the original meaning of *stauros*. By extension, and commonly enough in Koiné Greek, the term was applied to the object frequently employed in Roman executions of political subversives.

¹⁵ See M. A. Beavis, *Jesus and Utopia: Looking for the Kingdom of God in the Roman World* (Minneapolis: Augsburg Fortress, 2006).

¹⁶ See Horsley, *Jesus and Empire* and Schnackenburg, *Reino y Reinado de Dios*.

¹⁷ See Herzog, *Prophet and Teacher*, 1–42, where the author offers a very good summary of the contemporary historical and cultural studies. See also the bibliography cited in n. 4 above.

¹⁸ Jesus' Galilean Jewish peasant listeners must have actually thought that he was right, that his radical interpretation of Torah reflected the faith of the people, and that this was good news on which it was worth betting one's life. If what Jesus was saying and doing had not attracted a significant following among Galilean peasants (the abused backbone of Palestine's economy at the time), his message would not

have worried the religious elites in Jerusalem or the Herodians in Galilee, or led the Romans to execute him.

[19] M. Borg, "Why Was Jesus Killed?" in *The Meaning of Jesus: Two Visions*, ed. M. Borg and N. T. Wright (San Francisco: HarperCollins, 1999), 91.

[20] "It is impossible to write a history of Jesus without producing theology about him. . . . We cannot turn the figure of Jesus into theology without turning him into history and telling the story of his life and fate. Without this, faith has no history." J. Sobrino, *Jesus the Liberator: A Historical-Theological View* (Maryknoll: Orbis, 1993), 60, 63. See also Crossan, *The Historical Jesus*, 395–416.

[21] It is important to add that, within Christianity, the hope that Jesus was right rests on the deeper and prior hope that God, and God alone, is the initiator of the hope announced by Jesus and of all hope. In other words, neither Jesus of Nazareth nor the early Christians "figured it out." The initiative is God's, who then grounds the further claims to there having been "revelation" in, as, to, and through Jesus. I will further discuss the notion and claims of revelation below and in Chapter Three.

[22] Hope, to be Christian and therefore subversive, must be effective and reasonable. It cannot be grounded in wishful dreaming and it cannot be reduced to an optimistic attitude. I will discuss reasonable hope in Chapter Three,

[23] Perhaps this, not the emphases on later development of Christian rituals, polities, or doctrines, is the most important justification and contribution for Christian participation in meaningful and potentially fruitful interreligious dialogue.

[24] The list of this world's "disposables" remains scandalously long. In Jesus' day it might have been the sinners, the impure, the slaves, and others, depending on whose "list" we refer to; the disposables of the Romans included the Jews themselves, and very many more. Over the twenty centuries of Christian history the lists seem to have increased, or maybe we are more aware of more lists. Among most Christians there have always been disposables (so treated and judged, in direct contradiction of Jesus' message), e.g., African slaves and their descendants, women (especially those who are not of European descent), gays, lesbians, and transgender persons, native Americans and aboriginal populations across the world, medieval serfs and nineteenth century industrial workers, Muslims and Jews, and everyone who is not "Christian like us." Evidently and equally scandalously, non-Christians (including atheists and agnostics) very often have their equally long lists of disposables.

[25] I will say more in Chapters Two and Four on the meaning of the expression "effective analogy." At this point I also want to emphasize that it is obvious Jesus of Nazareth said and did more than the few summarizing paragraphs here might suggest. I do not want to "reduce" Jesus, but I do not want to "amplify" him either beyond what the best historical data will allow. Later Christian doctrinal developments, legitimate as they might be, are just that—Christian *developments*—and cannot be claimed either to have come from Jesus' lips or to have been strictly contemporary with him (geographically, culturally, socially, historically, or religiously).

[26] "Leap of faith" is an expression borrowed from S. Kierkegaard, but not necessarily here with all the various meanings given to the expression by Kierkegaard.

[27] "We," because Christianity is really and only communal. Individualism was

very foreign in Jesus' context and within Jesus' message, and remains foreign among most human cultures today. "We," also, because this writer should be regarded as Christian.

[28] Here it is obvious that one needs to recall G. Gutiérrez, *El Dios de la vida* (Lima: CEP, 1989) and J. Sobrino, *El principio misericordia* (San Salvador: UCA, 1992).

[29] Other important points about traditioning will be raised throughout this book. Let me also refer here to what is evident to any student of the western theologies of tradition: that within western Catholicism there have been myriad discussions of "tradition," its authority, and its role in Christianity. Most of these discussions, however, resulted from the sixteenth century Reformations and their aftermath. Y. Congar (in his *Tradition and Traditions,* see n. 32 below) claims that in western Europe the first explicitly systematic and comprehensive theology of tradition (first published in 1549) was written by the Spanish bishop, theologian, and reformer Martín Pérez de Ayala, soon to be drowned out by the multisided shouts of the (Lutheran, Calvinist, Anglican, and Roman) reformers, although some of the theological apologists (e.g., P. Melanchthon and M. Cano) also contributed works important for the history of the theology of tradition. Today's theologians, less concerned with denominational apologetics and more serious about ecumenism, have also given us much to think about traditioning and its contents. I am not disregarding this conversation (¡al *contrario!*) but tradition*ing,* with its emphases on process and context, has not really been part of the discussion, which has focused mostly on contents, authority, and related topics. For important bibliographic contributions to the contemporary conversations, see P.-B. Smit, *Tradition in Dialogue: The Understanding of Tradition in the International Dialogues of the Anglican Communion* (Amsterdam: Vu University Press, 2013); J. C. Skillrud, J. F. Stafford, and D. F. Martensen, eds., *Scripture and Tradition: Lutherans and Catholics in Dialogue* (Minneapolis: Augsburg, 1995); and D. Thorsen, *The Wesleyan Quadrilateral: Scripture, Tradition, Reason and Experience as a Model of Evangelical Theology* (Lexington, KY: Emeth, 2005). Obviously, many distinguished authors within these and other ecclesial strands under the broad umbrella of "western Catholicism" have produced, over the past few centuries (and especially during the second half of the twentieth century) numerous and important studies on tradition. Outside of western Catholicism (but still within western Christianity), an indispensable text is D. T. Irvin's *Christian Histories, Christian Traditioning: Rendering Accounts* (Maryknoll: Orbis, 1998).

[30] See O. Espín, "Tradition (in Christianity)," in *Introductory Dictionary of Theology and Religious Studies*, 1390–95 and "Tradition and Traditions," in ibid., 1395.

[31] In Chapter Three I will discuss at length what I mean by revelation and why I have just stated that subversive hope is its core and ground—indeed, its ultimate content.

[32] See Y. Congar, *Tradition and Traditions: An Historical and a Theological Essay* (New York: Macmillan, 1967), 237–56.

[33] See O. Espín, "Reception of Doctrines," in *Introductory Dictionary of Theology and Religious Studies*, 1133–34.

[34] See Congar, *Tradition and Traditions*, 237–56.

[35] Congar's insight is crucial: "Tradition is not primarily to be defined by a particular material object, but by the act of transmission, and its content is simply *id quod traditum est, id quod traditur.*" In *Tradition and Traditions*, 296. Italics in the original.

[36] I will say more later on the difficulties of "inculturation," as I suggest (following R. Fornet-Betancourt) that "inter-culturation" might be the only way for evangelization to face up to its temptation to colonize in the name of God.

[37] See Congar, *Tradition and Traditions*, 296–306.

[38] On the *depositum fidei*, see R. P. Carbine, "Deposit of Faith," in *Introductory Dictionary of Theology and Religious Studies*, 331–32 and N. C. Ring, "Deposit of Faith," in *New Dictionary of Theology*, ed. J. Komonchak, M. Collins, and D. A. Lane (Wilmington: Michael Glazier, 1987), 277–79. See also A. E. McGrath, *A Scientific Theology*, vol. 3, *Theory* (London: T&T Clark, 2007), esp. 143–51.

[39] For example, see R. Bauckham and B. Drewery, eds., *Scripture, Tradition and Reason* (Edinburgh: T&T Clark, 1988) and especially A. C. Thiselton, *The Hermeneutics of Doctrine* (Grand Rapids: Eerdmans, 2007).

[40] See 1 Cor. 11:23, 1 Tim. 6:20, 2 Tim. 1:14, and others. The very existence of the gospel texts, and of the other New Testament writings, is a very strong indication that for the apostolic generations there were contents (memories, practices, teachings) and parameters that needed to be faithfully followed and transmitted. From those contents these generations did not hesitate to derive further practices and teachings. (See, for example, Acts 15 and its account of the early Christian community's decision to welcome Gentiles into Christianity without requiring them first to convert to Judaism.)

[41] See Congar, *Tradition and Traditions*, 196–208.

[42] See Vatican II's *Dei Verbum* (Dogmatic Constitution on Divine Revelation), in *The Documents of Vatican II*, ed. W. A. Abbott (New York: America Press, 1966), 111–28.

[43] I have already insisted, in the Introduction, that by the expression "western Catholicism" I do not mean here (or ever!) "Roman Catholicism." I also want to make it very clear that the descriptive sections that follow on western Catholicism reflect *my* understanding of this significant way of being Christian. Therefore, I am not suggesting that the following description and understanding of western Catholicism is doctrinally necessary or accepted by all western Catholic communities. Nevertheless, I do think that very many western Catholics would see their Christianity reflected in it.

[44] During a conversation in January 2010, my University of San Diego colleague, Prof. Susie Babka, suggested that I think about the following: "The western Catholic tradition is *more* debate, intuition, ethical nuance, experience and wisdom, symbol and analogy, etc., and *less* exact doctrines or commandments, precise definitions, specific liturgical rubrics, clearly delineated canonical relations, etc. How 'we do' being Christian is much more crucial to what we mean by the expression 'western Catholic' than any conceptual definition." Professor Babka's suggestion led me to shape several sections of this book in the manner they here appear. I am very grateful to her.

⁴⁵ Of course, readers might also have other means of transportation in mind, or maybe uniquely located cities. These do not compromise my example but only increase the purpose of its employ here.

⁴⁶ Obviously, the same needs to be seriously considered when reflecting, inter-religiously, on the Mystery Christians call "God."

⁴⁷ The term "denomination" refers to a religious group *qua* socially identifiable, organized group. It might refer to the shared beliefs, rituals, leadership, and other characteristics of this group, but "denomination" is, emphatically, a *social-scientific* identification term. "Church" (although today frequently confused with "denomination" in daily and even in scholarly usage) is a *theological* term that refers to the faith-justified constitutive elements of the communities of Christians. Although neither term can be separated from the other today, it is important that we keep the distinction in mind. In some western Catholic denominations, discussions of the "denominational" are usually engaged under the terms "ecclesiastical" and (less frequently and more inaccurately) "canonical."

⁴⁸ Maps, however, are not always trustworthy. Nevertheless, they remain valuable and important tools to organize and thereby understand a territory, even when one acknowledges the maps' margins of error. We use religious affiliation statistics here exclusively as maps may be used. See O. Maduro, *Mapas para la fiesta: Reflexiones sobre la crisis y el conocimiento* (Buenos Aires: Centro Nueva Tierra, 1993) and W. Mignolo, *The Darker Side of the Renaissance: Literacy, Territoriality and Colonization*, 2nd ed. (Ann Arbor: University of Michigan Press, 2003).

⁴⁹ I will very shortly begin to discuss the elements that, taken together, describe western Catholicism. It will be evident, as that discussion progresses, *that no one denomination is the sole or main representative of western Catholicism.* During the first millennium of Christianity there were no "denominations," just geographically and culturally (and hence liturgically) distinct manners of being Christian. Today, however, Christians do not identify mainly (if at all) through the labels of the first millennium. Today, unfortunately, we might need to appeal to denominational labels in order to "map" what I mean here under the umbrella term "western Catholicism." So, for this one time only, and again insisting on the inadequacy of denominational tags (as maps) to chart accurately the broad territory of western Catholicism, let me include the following demographic, religious-affiliation statistics. The reader will thereby know which denominations I think may be placed today under the "western Catholic" umbrella. All figures are to be read as statistical approximations, and all were correct as of 2011. There were, in 2011, some 2.1 billion Christians in the world. Of this number, 1.9 billion were Roman Catholic (source: Center for Applied Research in the Apostolate [CARA], Georgetown University, Washington, DC, 2012). There were 80 million Anglicans (source: Anglican Communion Office, London, 2012). There were 75 million Lutherans (source: World Lutheran Communion Office, Geneva, 2012). There are six million members of the Philippine Independent Church—also known as the *Malayang Simbahan ng Pilipinas* and as the *Iglesia Filipina Independiente* (source: Office of the *Obispo Máximo*, Manila, 2012). And then there is a somewhat diffuse movement of small denominations, usually jointly called "Old

Catholic," approximately 150,000 Christians throughout the world (sources: World Council of Churches, Geneva, 2012 and J. Visser, "The Old Catholic Churches of the Union of Utrecht," *International Journal for the Study of the Christian Church* 3, no.1 [2003]). The 25,000 members of the Polish National Church worldwide are not "officially" members of the Old Catholic movement, yet they remain heirs of its episcopate, which suggests that there are other small ecclesial communities that might include themselves under the "western Catholic" banner and yet not appear on any statistical "map" of denominations. One large group of Christians is heir to the insights and contributions of John and Charles Wesley, but are Methodists to be included under the "western Catholic" umbrella? One could argue that they should be. There were 85 million Methodists in the world in 2011 (source: World Methodist Council, 2012).

[50] The expressions "Third World" and "First World," as we recall, are part of the heritage of the Cold War, which extended approximately from 1945 to 1990, and in which the adversaries never went directly to armed conflict against each other (although they did through several "delegated wars," fought by their surrogates). The Cold War labels, as we also remember, were uncritically used by all: politicians, "regular folk," academics, et al. According to these uncritical and inaccurate labels, there was a "First World" identified with the capitalist countries that were economically "developed," wealthy and technologically advanced, and democratically participatory, where freedom and the rights of all were protected and promoted. There also was a "Second World" identified with the countries officially guided by communist principles, which had centralized economies, lived with little or no democratic participation, and were under a centralized, ideologically monolithic single party. The "Third World" was formed by all other countries on Earth, identified as economically and culturally poor countries, "underdeveloped," in need of profound social reform, of just distribution of wealth, and of real democratic participation, and which were so weak that they had little to contribute to knowledge, to history, to science, and so on. These evidently false and ethically questionable labels nevertheless suggest how Eurocentric dominance, regardless of ideological label or position, can marginalize most of humanity, turning most human communities and their nations into spectators of Eurocentric-led and Eurocentric-defined conflicts—for Eurocentric gain. Furthermore, the Cold War and its labels are also indicative of the fact that *"European" is not coextensive or synonymous with "Eurocentric."* Unfortunately, we still have not crafted better tags to map (in matters of justice, of participation, and of distribution of wealth) the world's population. So I will use "First World" and "Third World" in this book, aware that these labels are still inaccurate and questionable, although today less inclined to ideological manipulation than during the Cold War.

[51] This is in addition to the "western" history and connections already discussed above. We recall again that "western Catholicism" echoes the first Christian millennium.

[52] If revelation is, ultimately, the self-revelation and self-donation of God—which consequently means that it cannot ever be interpreted as expressing or "containing" anything that conflicts with the God revealed—revelation also means that

the humans who experience and encounter the God revealed and donated cannot be called to the revelatory event as anything else but human. And humans are cultural, historical, contextualized, and perspectival. Revelation, then, is the most "authentic" divine/human event for both God and humans, and inescapably asymmetrical.

[53] This is also the case because, as we have seen, Jesus' message was not about the eternal salvation of a few but about the radical transformation of this world according to the compassionate will of God (i.e., according to the divine "self" revealed and donated).

[54] "People of God" and also "Pilgrim People of God" are umbrella terms to identify Christians as one community (i.e., one "people" who are "of God"). The emphasis, however, is not merely or mainly possessive ("of" God) but testimonial and "faith-full"— i.e., it points to those who have bet for, and thereby in their lives witness to, the subversive hope that Jesus was right when he announced the transformation of this world into a world of compassion as being God's will, as beginning to occur, and as reflecting the very self of God.

[55] We will see later, and as consequence of what I have just stated, that faith is the other side of hope. This perspective understands Christian faith as a subversive commitment that implicates the Christian's entire life. The wager or "bet" for the "hope" is faith! Thereby we also discover in God's revelation the origin of faith and of hope.

[56] I will later discuss the Christian notion of grace within the context of faith and hope.

[57] The indispensable centrality and foundational role, in Christianity's faith and hope, belongs to revelation as God's *self*-donation. The reasonable hope that God *is* compassion, and that *this* God has begun to transform *this* world according to the divine compassionate will, is the ground on which Christianity rests. This was Jesus' proclamation and what led to his execution, and this is the ultimate meaning of the Christian claim that he was raised from death. The People of God, as I have stated above, are those who bet on this subversive hope—that Jesus was right. The New Testament then plays a role as indispensable witness to Jesus and, at bottom, to God's self-donation in and through Jesus. But the New Testament is not the revelation of God; Jesus is! The People of God composed, collected, and trusted the texts now in the New Testament in their role as "hermeneut" of Jesus, an inescapable role we will discuss later.

[58] It is too easy for specialists (theological or ministerial) to argue wonderful theories regarding the reading and interpretation of New Testament texts while ignoring the illiteracy of most Christians. The methodological assumptions of the literate, and the implied power asymmetries, are very questionable in a universe of illiteracy. Furthermore, the dominant literate elites of any historical period act as the main legitimizing force behind the assumption that the written texts (and also their written, learned, or "authoritative" interpretations) are "obviously" superior to the People's "faith-full" and "simple" response to God's self-revelation, thereby (unacceptably but factually) reinscribing social power asymmetries among the People of God.

[59] This, as we will see later, is a powerful idolatrous inclination within the history of Christianity and its tendency to doctrinify the subversive hope at the core of Christianity.

[60] And as a Christian, so does this author. But not naïvely, uncritically, or in a decontextualized manner.

[61] When we look at the real-life religion of most western Catholic Christians, today as well as over the past twenty centuries, we see that this order of precedence (i.e., revelation preceding texts and interpretations) more accurately describes what is and has been held by real-life western Catholics. This is also a sound theological understanding for the relationship between revelation and Scripture as well as between traditioning and Scripture.

[62] Much more on this in later chapters.

[63] The variations within and among the Christian canons of the Hebrew Scriptures are an obvious indication that the reception of the Hebrew Scriptures into the Christian Bible was not an authoritative decision but a consensual, popular (i.e., communal) process that held validity even for non-Jewish Christians too after they became the vast demographic majority within Christianity. Early attempts to rid Christianity of Judaism's scriptural heritage, as in the case of Marcion, repeatedly failed among Christians, and not because of learned theological or doctrinal arguments or without the assumption of other interests. See R. Fuller, "Old Testament," in *Introductory Dictionary of Theology and Religious Studies*, 976 and G. Macy, "Marcionism," in ibid., 819.

[64] See, in this chapter, the first section on Jesus and his context.

[65] Recognizer of truth that is done and lived and not just asserted. More on this in upcoming chapters.

[66] In my estimation, the best and most comprehensive study of the *sensus fidelium* from a (I intentionally use the indefinite article) western Catholic perspective is D. J. Finucane, *Sensus Fidelium: The Use of a Concept in the Post-Vatican II Era* (Washington, DC: International Scholars Publications, 1996). Despite its subtitle, Finucane's volume is a historical and theological *tour de force* covering much of Christian history. See also O. Rush, *The Eyes of Faith: The Sense of the Faithful and the Church's Reception of Revelation* (Washington, DC: CUA Press, 2009); O. Espín, *The Faith of the People: Theological Reflections on Popular Catholicism* (Maryknoll: Orbis, 1997), and Espín, "Sensus Fidelium/Sensus Fidei," in *Introductory Dictionary of Theology and Religious Studies*, 1252–56.

[67] But have the whole People of God bet their lives on the subversive hope and message proclaimed by Jesus? Which is another way of asking, as a consequence, if we can honestly, reasonably, and *constatablemente* assume that because someone is baptized into the People of God they are, *ipso facto*, committed and "faith-full." In other words, have they *bet their lives on the subversive hope*? I raise the question, but this is not the place to search for an answer. Nevertheless, the point I want to make has to do with the consensus of and within the entire People of God (i.e., the *sensus fidelium*, itself a plural expression) vis-à-vis claims that give the ordained exclusive or superior rights over revelation, doctrine, or truth. The entire People of God, not only or mainly the ordained, received revelation and are responsible for traditioning it.

[68] It is important to note that I am not referring here to individual interpretation of Scripture. The "People of God" is (are!), by definition, plural and communal.

[69] *All* human cultures, including the cultures of the pious, the learned, and the dominant, bear the inescapable wound and imprint of sinfulness. It is ethically disgusting to pretend that some are "more" or "less" sinful than others.

[70] See Espín, *The Faith of the People* as well as T. Bamat and J.-P. Wiest, eds., *Popular Catholicism in a World Church* (Maryknoll: Orbis, 1999). More later on "popular Catholicism."

[71] See W. Reiser, "Spirituality," in *Introductory Dictionary of Theology and Religious Studies*, 1318–19 and G. Cavazos-González, *Beyond Piety: The Christian Spiritual Life, Justice, and Liberation* (Eugene, OR: Wipf and Stock, 2010).

[72] For example, the apostle Paul reminded us that we only see "though a glass, opaquely" (1 Cor. 13). Paul also reminded us (ibid.) that we can have all the faith possible (even to move mountains!) but that without love that faith means nothing. In other words, as the letter of James and the first letter of John also tell us, if the "bet" for the hope of Christians is not factually translated and *constatablemente* perceived in and as compassionate lives, that faith (that "bet") is useless and dead—and false. The gospel of Matthew's parable of the last judgment (Matt. 25:31–46) is very clear on the sole (!) criterion for God's judgment: compassion toward the most disposable, i.e., "the least." Augustine of Hippo also wisely taught that "if you understand, it isn't God" (*si comprehendis, non est Deus*) in his Sermon 52.

[73] Much more on "effective analogy" in Chapters Two and Four.

[74] Because no human language, no human culture, no human logic could ever pretend (except as an act of idolatry) to have completely or absolutely understood or "said" the Mystery or anything regarding the Mystery. Truth, as we will see later, does not depend on or require such human *hubris* and idolatrous attitude.

[75] On liturgy, see M. Collins, "Liturgy," in *New Dictionary of Theology*, 591–601; D. Krouse, "Liturgy (in Christianity)" in *Introductory Dictionary of Theology and Religious Studies*, 777–78; R. C. D. Jasper, "Liturgies," in *The New Westminster Dictionary of Liturgy and Worship*, ed. J. G. Davies (Philadelphia: Westminster, 1986), 314–16; and the immediately following entries (ibid., 316–39, by several other authors) on liturgies among the Orthodox, Roman Catholic, Anglican, Baptist, Christian Church (Disciples of Christ), Congregationalist, Lutheran, Methodist, Old Catholic, Pentecostal, Reformed, and other churches.

[76] By "belief" and "believing," Prosper seems to have meant the doctrinal expressions (and the assertion of these doctrinal expressions) of the faith—certainly not faith itself. On Prosper of Aquitaine, see G. Macy, "Prosper of Aquitaine," in *Introductory Dictionary of Theology and Religious Studies*, 1095. On Prosper's phrase and theological consequences today, see O. Espín, "Whose *Lex Orandi*? Whose *Lex Credendi*?: Latino/a Catholicism as a Theological Challenge for Liturgy," in *Proceedings of the North American Academy of Liturgy* 36 (2006): 53–71. Prosper's phrase is in his *Capitula Caelestini*, in *Worship in the Early Church: An Anthology of Historical Sources*, vol. 3, ed. L. J. Johnson (Collegeville: Liturgical Press, 2009), 179. D. Van Slyke argues for rendering the phrase as *ut legem credendi lex statuat supplicandi*: see D. Van Slyke,

"*Lex orandi, lex credendi*: Liturgy as *locus theologicus* in the Fifth Century?" *Josephinum: Journal of Theology* 11, no. 2 (2004): 130–51. Both renderings (although certainly not *lex orandi lex credendi*) do seem to have been from Prosper, as he used both phrases in several of his own versions of the text of the *Capitula Caelestini*, using different titles for the several versions of the same text.

[77] One example is the Roman liturgical tradition. See J. A. Jungmann, *The Mass of the Roman Rite: Its Origins and Development* (New York: Benzinger, 1951; original in German). Another example is the Anglican liturgical tradition, more varied today than the Roman, but with equally deep apostolic and medieval origins. See G. J. Cuming, *A History of Anglican Liturgy* (New York: Macmillan, 1982). Other examples of western liturgical traditions could be mentioned.

[78] For the notion of the "marginalized" (as distinct from, and often opposed to, the often misleading and factually incorrect "minorities"), see C. Nanko-Fernández, "A Marginalized Majority? Hispanic Theologians and the Latino/a Presence in the U.S. Catholic Church," paper presented in the Hispanic/Latino Theology Section, *Proceedings of the Catholic Theological Society of America* 58 (2003): 147–48. Complete text of the paper courtesy of its author.

[79] Pilgrimages, processions, devotions, and other popular celebrations today have (as they historically have had) the power of convocation that few clergy-presided celebrations have, and when these do, they are usually associated with popular pilgrimages, processions, and devotions. I am not suggesting that clergy-presided liturgical celebrations are irrelevant or unimportant. What I am underlining is that we cannot understand or even describe the role of liturgy in western Catholicism if we exclude popular liturgies; these have been indispensable in western Catholic history. I would also argue that they stand at the origin of much we now regard as Christian liturgies. This is one enormously important (theological) reason for the (theological) study of popular Catholicism. See Espín, *Grace and Humanness: Theological Reflections Because of Culture* (Maryknoll: Orbis, 2007) as well as Espín, *The Faith of the People*. See also J. O'Callahan, *El cristianismo popular en el Egipto antiguo* (Madrid: Ediciones Cristiandad, 1975).

[80] On prayer, see W. Reiser, "Prayer," in *Introductory Dictionary of Theology and Religious Studies*, 1071–72 and J. M. Reese, "Prayer," in *New Dictionary of Theology*, 787–91. The literature on prayer covers two millennia of Christian history and reflection.

[81] Matt. 6: 9–13 and Luke 11:2–4.

[82] I mean "before" in the sense of "in the face of" (in Spanish, *ante*), not in the chronological sense (in Spanish, *antes*).

[83] I will expand on my use of "idol," "idolatry," and related terms in Chapter Three.

[84] See n. 12 above on the adverb *constatablemente*; *constatable* is the related adjective.

[85] Foreign and contrary. By "individualism" I do *not* mean the rights and responsibilities of each and all persons in community. By the term "individualism" I mean a western ideology, long developing, that (because it is ideology) most persons

and institutions in the western world take as "obvious." As ideology, individualism benefits dominant interests and, *veladamente*, unauthorizes solidarity. It ideologically presents itself as defender of individuals from the "tyranny" of community. See, for example, L. Dumont, *Essays on Individualism: Modern Ideology in Anthropological Perspective* (Chicago: University of Chicago Press, 1992) and S. Steven, *Individualism* (Essex: European Consortium for Political Research, 2008). Still important in any contemporary discussion of individualism is Antonio Gramsci's discussion on hegemony, ideology, and their roles in what he calls the historical block. See especially but not only, Gramsci's *Prison Notebooks* (New York: Columbia University Press, 2011), vols. 1–3.

[86] Therefore, "community" is inescapably historical and cultural too, but not reducible to the historical or cultural or sociological (institutional) or to any combination of these. There is a *magis* ("more") in the human communion that, for western Catholics (and others too), is an "effective analogy" of the trinitarian Mystery.

[87] There is historically and theologically a very important role for the episcopate, which on occasion includes decisions on orthodoxy. This is not what I am questioning. What is not acceptable is the episcopate, by itself and without the expressed consent of the People of God (i.e., the *sensus fidelium*) making such decisions and claiming these to be binding *because they* made it. It is the entire Church (i.e., the entire People of God) that has received revelation and is responsible for its proclamation, traditioning, and real-life witness. Therefore the People of God may not be dismissed from the process of determining what is or is not part of, or in agreement with, revelation (i.e., orthodoxy). Although not all in the People of God have the same contributing role, all have a contributing role in the mission of the Church. History does not allow us the *ingenuidad* of thinking that the episcopate has never been very wrong.

[88] As would the best current sociological theory. See M. A. Vásquez, *More than Belief: A Materialist Theory of Religion* (New York: Oxford University Press, 2011) and J. Jardines, *El cuerpo y lo otro: Introducción a una teoría general de la cultura* (Havana: Editorial de Ciencias Sociales, 2004), esp. 107–96, 229–76. On the most evident and grounding of all (western Catholic) ecclesiological assertions, that "the Church is the People of God," see "The Church," in *An Episcopal Dictionary of the Church*, ed. D. S. Armentrout and R. B. Slocum (New York: Church Publishing, 2000), 94; A. Antón, "Postconciliar Ecclesiology: Expectations, Results, and Prospects for the Future," in *Vatican II: Assessment and Perspectives; Twenty-Five Years After*, vol. 1, ed. R. Latourelle (New York: Paulist, 1988), 407–38 (esp. 416–20); "Church," in *The Oxford Dictionary of the Christian Church*, ed. F. L. Cross and E. A. Livingstone (Oxford: Oxford University Press, 1997), 343–46; E. Hill, "Church," in *The New Dictionary of Theology*, 185–201; O. Espín, "Church," in *Introductory Dictionary of Theology and Religious Studies*, 243–44; M. A. Hinsdale, "People of God," in ibid, 1025; and the Vatican II document *Lumen Gentium* ("Dogmatic Constitution on the Church"), in *Vatican Council II: The Conciliar and Post-Conciliar Documents*, ed. A. Flannery, rev. ed., (Collegeville: Liturgical Press, 1992), 350–440. I will say much more later in the book about this grounding ecclesiological assertion.

[89] See, e.g., Acts 2:4, 1 Cor. 10:17–21, 2 Cor. 13:14, and Phil. 2:1. See also F. M. Gillman, "Koinonia," in *Introductory Dictionary of Theology and Religious Studies*, 720.

[90] A theory is valid to the degree that it effectively explains what is real. But the real is not constituted *because* someone theorized its possibility. The real precedes the theoretical.

[91] The presence of the ministry of bishops did not establish western Catholicism and it has never been its key identifying mark. Furthermore, it is insufficient (for western Catholicism) that there be bishops; these, it is affirmed, *must* be "successors to the apostles," hence in "apostolic succession."

[92] This is not the place for an examination of the roles of the apostles according to the New Testament texts (some of these texts contemporaneous with, but others much later than, the apostolic generations), or the varied roles the apostles historically played during very early Christianity. It is clear that the term "apostles" was not used first (chronologically) to refer to the Twelve. Only later did the terminological confusion occur in reference to these two distinct groups. Paul, Apollos, Junia, Andronicus, and others are explicitly mentioned in the New Testament as apostles, but were evidently not among the Twelve (e.g., Rom. 16:7). Some scholars suspect that the very existence of the Twelve as a group distinct from the apostles is a New Testament theological development and not a historical fact. Nevertheless, the "apostles" (understood to include others not of the Twelve, e.g., Paul) were the only group that later generations claimed had left "successors." See J. D. Crossan, *The Birth of Christianity* (San Francisco: HarperCollins, 1998); R. Boisclair, "Apostle," in *Introductory Dictionary of Theology and Religious Studies*, 70–71; H. C. Kee, "Sociological Insights into the Development of Christian Leadership Roles and Community Formation," in *Handbook of Early Christianity: Social Science Approaches*, 337–60. It is historically evident that there were women (e.g., Junia) and men in the group of the apostles.

[93] See, for example, 2 Cor. 1:1 and 8:23; Acts 1:21–26 and 13:1–3; 1 Cor. 1:1, 9:1–5, 12:28, and 15:5–9; Rev. 18:20; Eph. 1:1, 2:20, 3:5, and 4:11; Rom. 1:1, 1:13, and 16:7; Gal. 1:1 and 1:19; Col. 1:1; 1 Tim. 1:2 and 2:7; 2 Tim. 1:2 and 1:11; and Titus 1:1. Even Jesus is called an apostle in Heb. 3:1. See also, for example, *Didaché* 11:3–6.

[94] It is very probable (and in many cases obvious) that the majority of bishops do not behave, and historically have not behaved, as the witnesses described in the text and as demanded of them by the Gospel. Neither have all Christians behaved as thoroughly committed to compassion and justice as their own message and ethics demand. It is clear, nevertheless, that throughout Christian history many bishops have been exemplars of the apostolic ministry, just as many Christians have been extraordinarily courageous in their compassion. Often, those who lived as the Gospel demands have been the victims of others who did not hesitate to use ecclesiastical or political authority to persecute, deny, or attempt to silence the subversive hope at the heart of Christianity. It is, nevertheless, a painfully necessary question to ask whether the failure of the majority (of bishops and of Christians) throughout history dismisses the continued validity of the subversive hope of Jesus—the executed Jewish peasant—and of those who would take him and the Reign of God seriously.

[95] See W. Kasper, *Theology and Church* (New York: Crossroad, 1989), 156–65; Kasper, "On the Church: A Friendly Reply to Cardinal Ratzinger," *America* 184, no.14 (April 23–30, 2001): 8–14; and especially Kasper, "Das Zweite Vatikanum weiterdenken: Die apostolische Sukzession im Bischofsamt als ökumenisches Problem," *Kerygma und Dogma* 44, no. 3 (1998): 207–18. It is true that, for many within western Catholicism, the "apostolic succession" has been frequently reduced to the ritual transfer of a power from one generation of bishops to another. The "apostolic succession" is *not* about a power or its repeated ritual transmission over the centuries. If the unbroken repetition of a liturgical, ritual gesture were coextensive with becoming a "successor to the apostles," then the "apostolic succession" thus understood would have lost its indispensable reference to the real, historical apostles and their courageous ministry in the early Church. See also A. Ehrhardt, *The Apostolic Succession in the First Two Centuries of the Church* (Eugene: Wipf & Stock, 2009; reprint of the 1953 edition); "Apostolic Succession," in *The Oxford Dictionary of the Christian Church*, 91; V. de Waal, "Apostolic Succession," in *The Westminster Dictionary of Christian Theology*, 35–36.

[96] See Gal. 5:6 and James 2:17. See also Augustine of Hippo, *Enchiridion*, 8.

[97] Until about 700–800 CE.

[98] See B. M. Metzger. *The Canon of the New Testament: Its Origin, Development and Significance* (New York: Oxford University Press, 1997); B. M. Metzger and B. D. Ehrman, *The Text of the New Testament: Its Transmission, Corruption and Restoration* (New York: Oxford University Press, 2005); H. de Lubac, *Scripture in the Tradition* (New York: Crossroad, 2001); L. D. Davis, *The First Seven Ecumenical Councils (325–787): Their History and Theology* (Collegeville: Liturgical Press, 1990); E. Vilanova, *Historia de la teología cristiana: De los orígenes al siglo XV* (Barcelona: Herder, 1987); J. Pelikan, *The Emergence of the Catholic Tradition (100–600)* (Chicago: University of Chicago Press, 1971); J. L. González, *A History of Christian Thought: From the Beginnings to the Council of Chalcedon* (Nashville: Abingdon, 1987); and, of course, Irenaeus of Lyon, *On the Apostolic Preaching* (Yonkers, NY: St. Vladimir's Seminary Press, 1997).

[99] See J. Pelikan, *Creeds and Confessions of Faith in the Christian Tradition*, vols. 1–4 (New Haven: Yale University Press, 2003–05), especially vol. 1, *Early Eastern and Medieval*. It is very relevant to the present volume that, historically, some of the conciliar creeds and doctrinal statements were in opposition to the reasoned views and arguments of the learned (and sometimes politically powerful) elites of their time. Therefore, the reasoned views and arguments of the learned are not, by themselves, sufficient to establish "truthful" doctrine or to call for "reception" by the People of God.

[100] Atrocities have been committed throughout history by many who thought of themselves as reasonable and as bearers of the rational. Consequently, to judge the "reason" of others is not necessarily an unbiased act: our generation is also a subject of atrocities. The victims of slavery, of androcentric bias, of religious persecution, of homophobic bigotry, of racist or xenophobic stereotyping, of the manipulation and abuse of the poor, and more, were (and are) invariably victimized by those

who thought of themselves as being "right" and their logic and arguments as being "correct" and "rational." Yet the atrocities were no less atrocious, and their victims' suffering no less real. It is ethically indispensable for human reason never to be thought of as anything but *human*, and consequently, as always perspectival, limited, and historically and culturally contextualized *and* wounded by sin. The greatness or importance of reason is not diminished by truthfully admitting its contextualized, wounded humanness.

[101] See J. L. González's excellent, three-volume *History of Christian Thought*, rev. ed., (Nashville: Abingdon, 1987); J. Pelikan's five-volume masterpiece, *The Christian Tradition: A History of the Development of Doctrine* (Chicago: University of Chicago Press, 1975–91); and A. C. Thiselton, *The Hermeneutics of Doctrine* (Grand Rapids: Eerdmans, 2007). Fanaticism has existed and continues to exist; but to claim that religious fanatics have been or are the western Catholic majority is, to be blunt, itself an act of the fanatical and not of the rational. Furthermore, the nineteenth century "faith vs. reason" dichotomy is exactly that: a nineteenth century thought moment that is neither normative nor valuable. As it is being argued in the present volume (and in thousands of volumes by others) western Catholic faith cannot be without its *also* being reasonable.

[102] More on reason and experience in the Chapter Two.

[103] Further discussion of *lo cotidiano* will occur in Chapter Four.

[104] This, it seems to me, is the meaning of the well-known theological dictum "grace builds on nature."

[105] In Latin, "more."

[106] See Acts 15; Gal. 3:27–29; Rom. 12:5; 1 Cor. 12:13; etc.

[107] I should clarify that although this book proposes and attempts to engage and justify an intercultural approach to traditioning and to the contents traditioned, it is obvious that neither this author nor any other author (or a group of authors) within western cultures, alone, can construct an actual intercultural theology of traditioning (not even experimentally) because the latter can only appear to be the result of a real-life intercultural process and dialogue, but can never be intercultural. A single-culture volume cannot ever be an intercultural process or dialogue. This book, therefore, is at best an intercultural proposal but it is not, and cannot be, the intercultural theology it proposes and invites.

[108] The crisis of Arianism reminds us that it was the faith and praying of real, everyday people that established the "orthodoxy" expressed at the first council of Nicaea—because most bishops were Arian. The Nicene Creed reflects the faith of the People of God. We could point to very many other instances in Christian history.

[109] What I have stated in this paragraph should help us understand that western Catholic ecclesiologists are dogmatically challenged by the continued ecclesiastical and theological identification of the Eurocentric with the "mainstream" or, worse, with western Catholicism itself. Furthermore, because historically most of the real People of God have been illiterate, there must be some serious reflection on the theological and ecclesiastical fixation on written texts,

including the biblical texts. Who is left out, then, by the insistence that reading is required for access to authority and leadership? Why, then, could all not read? Today, as literacy and further education increase among the real People of God, the *de facto* silencing of the vast majority will come to an end—and I am not referring here to denominational "canon laws" or other participatory procedural bodies. I am referring, explicitly, to a profound transformation in attitude towards the "other."

Chapter II

[1] Regardless of diverse recognized standards or venues across the centuries, theology has never constructed itself or fallen from the skies. *Humans* do theology, and that is my point.

[2] Colonization and dominance do not factually or ethically justify the claim of "universal relevance" often claimed by the Eurocentric on behalf of their theologies. See D. Chakrabarty, *Provincializing Europe: Postcolonial Thought and Historical Difference* (Princeton: Princeton University Press, 2000). Although Chakrabarty does not reflect on theology, his critique of Eurocentrism, and its thought patterns and colonizing assumptions, are relevant to theology in today's world.

[3] History and culture, of course, have always been contexts of theologizing—inevitably. But today it is arguable that there is a clearer, critical *awareness* of their molding roles, and of their importance as contexts of *all* theologizing and of all that is human.

[4] Needless to say, insights from I. Ellacuría are present here, especially from his *Filosofía de la realidad histórica* (San Salvador: UCA Editores, 1990), chap. 2, 3, 4 and 5 (but esp. chap. 4, sect. 3, and all of chap. 5); insights are present also from his *Escritos filosóficos* (San Salvador: UCA Editores, 1996–2001), esp. vols. 2 and 3, and *Escritos teológicos* (San Salvador: UCA Editores, 2000–02), esp. vol. 2, chap. 5, sect. 5.2 and 5.3. Nevertheless, my perspectives on history are not borrowed from Ellacuría and I consider myself far from some of his assertions regarding history and from many of his philosophical grounding reflections. For the best introduction to and summary of Ellacuría's philosophical thought in any language, by his most prominent disciple, intellectual heir, and successor, see H. Samour, *Voluntad de liberación: La filosofía de Ignacio Ellacuría* (Granada: Editorial Comares, 2003). Much of Ellacuría's thought was influenced or inspired by X. Zubiri's own. Regarding history, for example, see X. Zubiri, "La dimensión histórica del ser humano," *Realitas I* (of the Xavier Zubiri Seminar, 1972–1973): 11–69.

[5] See M. de Certeau, *L'Absent de l'histoire* (Paris: Mame, 1973); de Certeau, *L'Écriture de l'histoire* (Paris: Gallimard, 1975); and de Certeau, *La Possession de Loudun* (Paris: Gallimard, 1990; orig. 1970). "Objectivity" in history refers to events to the degree that these did occur in the past, but nevertheless it is an act of interested *subjectivity* (not of objectivity) to assign this or that importance or meaning to the events (or to choose to include these but not those events in our collective, cultural

memory). See P. Ricoeur, *Histoire et Vérité* (Paris: Le Seuil, 1955), 24–32 and of course Ricoeur, *Memory, History, Forgetting* (Chicago: University of Chicago Press, 2004), esp. 21–43, 68–92. See also P. Nora, "Comment on écrit l'histoire de France," in *Les Lieux de mémoire III*, ed. P. Nora (Paris: Gallimard, 1993), 24. It is interesting to contrast de Certeau's views on time and history with J. K. Campbell, M. O'Rourke, and H. S. Silverstein, eds., *Time and Identity* (Cambridge: MIT Press, 2010).

[6] I cannot exaggerate the richness of critical thought, or the important discussions on power asymmetries in the crafting of interested histories (given that *all* histories are interested and asymmetrical), that I have discovered, thanks to Prof. E. Ortega-Aponte, in the work of cultural philosopher B. Sarlo. I am particularly impressed by Sarlo's reflections in *Tiempo pasado: Cultura de la memoria y giro subjetivo* (Buenos Aires: Siglo XXI, 1996), *Tiempo presente* (Buenos Aires: Siglo XXI, 2001) and *Scenes from Postmodern Life* (Minneapolis: University of Minnesota Press, 2001). On Sarlo's thought, see R. Pistacchio Hernández, *Una perspectiva para ver: El intelectual crítico de Beatriz Sarlo* (Buenos Aires: Corregidor, 2006).

[7] See M. de Certeau, *La Faiblesse de croire* (Paris: Le Seuil, 1987). The reader should note that "objectivity" and interested subjectivity also apply to the contents of tradition in a similar way to history, as mentioned in a preceding note. Clearly, this section on history needs to be engaged together with the section on traditioning in Chapter One.

[8] Pretensions, because time and transience cannot be dismissed by hegemonic claims to objectivity. Objectivity does not and cannot cancel transience. Time and transience are the ultimate contextual antidotes to human pretensions to self-idolatry and absolute truth. Injustice is, therefore, a choice of the powerful, who (against transience) want to interpret unjust structures as inevitable, permanent, required by nature, or divinely imposed—because these structures benefit them. See M. de Certeau et al., "La Beauté du mort," *Politique Aujourd'hui* (Dec. 1970): 23. The reader will remember that Jesus of Nazareth subversively re-interpreted a shared tradition, against hegemonic interests that also purveyed themselves as definitive and true.

[9] Collectively and individually, in society and in religion. See Ellacuría, "Dimensión histórica del ser humano," part of the mimeographed text (and professorial notes) for the course *Persona y comunidad en Zubiri*, taught by Ellacuría at the Universidad Centroamericana "José Simeón Cañas" (San Salvador) in 1974; original of the text in the *Archivo Ignacio Ellacuría*, UCA, San Salvador. My thanks to Prof. Héctor Samour, head of the department of philosophy at the UCA and chief archivist of the *Archivo Ignacio Ellacuría*, for granting me access to the collections, as well as for his knowledge, guidance, and wisdom on Ellacuría's works and thought.

[10] And with the meaning of "human" all other human meanings, including religious ones.

[11] See P. Ricoeur, "La marque du passé," *Revue de métaphysique et de morale* 1 (1998): 31.

[12] See J. Rancière, *The Names of History: On the Poetics of Knowledge* (Minneapolis: University of Minnesota Press, 1994).

[13] Writing is an extraordinary aid to memory, but it can also become the poison of memory if it is turned into the idol that supplants or overthrows the memory of the poor. See Ricoeur, *Memory, History, Forgetting*, 96–119 and Ricoeur, *Essays in Hermeneutics,* vol. 2, *From Text to Action:* (Evanston: Northwestern University Press, 1991), 227–337.

[14] The affirmation of the memory of the poor as inescapable actor in the construction of history (with all that "history" implies and involves) is an extraordinarily important dimension of the Catholic Christian insistence on the power of Eucharistic remembrance.

[15] Remarkably relevant here is J, Baldwin's insight, "for a tradition expresses, after all, nothing more than the long and painful experience of a people; it comes out of the battle waged to maintain their integrity or, to put it more simply, out of their struggle to survive." See J. Baldwin, *Collected Essays* (New York: Library of America, 1998), 27–28. My thanks again to Prof. Elías Ortega-Aponte for directing me to Baldwin.

[16] See M. de Certeau, *L'Invention du possible*, vol. 1., *Arts de faire* (Paris: Folio-Gallimard, 1990), 131. This, again, is an insight of extraordinary importance implicated by and in every celebration of the Eucharist. Tradition and traditioning are like the living old cities of the world: many of their buildings survive from century to century, but the use of those buildings is always present and often different from the original one. What was once a family home might now, centuries later, be a restaurant or a storage facility, but its occupants are always and only in whichever is the building's present, preserving the same building because of its new (always present) use. The forms and experience of traditioning legitimize the truth claim (*verosimilitud*) of its content. More on this later in this book.

[17] This includes all experiences of and claims regarding revelation, prayer, doctrine, faith, etc., as well as all statements, configurations, understandings, and transmissions of them. Nothing religious, consequently, is ever a-cultural. The Mystery is not bound by culture, but we certainly are, as are all our experiences of and claims about the Mystery. I will return to this later.

[18] Indispensable is R. Fornet-Betancourt, "Tradición, cultura, interculturalidad: Apuntes para una comprensión intercultural de la cultura," text of the keynote paper presented by its author in September 2011, at the *XII Corredor das ideias do Cone Sul*, Universidade do Vale dos Sinos (Unisinos), São Leopoldo, RS, Brazil. See also the final chapter in J. Lezama Lima, *La expresión americana* (Mexico City: Fondo de Cultura Económica, 2010); M. de Certeau, *Heterologies: Discourse on the Other* (Minneapolis: University of Minnesota Press, 1986); and J. Rancière, *The Ignorant Schoolmaster: Five Lessons in Intellectual Emancipation* (Palo Alto: Stanford University Press, 1991).

[19] This is basically the same argument offered by the anthropologists who challenge any and all definitions of culture as "human culture" or the "culture of humans," leaving aside (they argue) the "animal cultures" or the "cultures of non-human animals." This is far from a settled issue among anthropologists, as debates continue on whether non-human animals have cultures (as all humans have, and on

this all anthropologists agree). Because this is an argument both recent and unsettled among anthropologists and others in broader cultural studies, I have opted to limit our discussions in this chapter and volume only to human cultures or the cultures of humans. The focus here is not on culture as much as on humans and the contexts of humanness. See E. Viveiros de Castro, "Cosmological Deixis and Amerindian Perspectivism," *Journal of the Royal Anthropological Institute* 4, no. 3 (1998): 469–88; T. Ingold, "Becoming Persons: Consciousness and Sociality in Human Evolution," *Cultural Dynamics* 4 (1991): 355–78; Ingold, ed., *Key Debates in Anthropology* (London: Routledge, 1996); Ingold, ed., *Human Worlds Are Culturally Constructed* (Manchester: Manchester University Press, 1991); and R. W. Lurz, *Mindreading Animals: The Debate Over What Animals Know about Other Minds* (Cambridge: MIT Press, 2011). See also J. G. Cantrill and C. L. Oravec, eds., *The Symbolic Earth: Discourse and Our Creation of the Environment* (Lexington: University Press of Kentucky, 1996). Nevertheless, and very crucially, see S. Harding, *Sciences from Below: Feminisms, Postcolonialities and Modernities* (Durham: Duke University Press, 2008).

[20] Necessarily keeping in mind what I have just said in the preceding two paragraphs, as well as the discussion on "western culture" in Chapter One. I am fully aware, therefore, that my reflections herein on culture are not ethically interest-neutral or innocent, as I am fully aware too that they are as perspectival and biased (in their specific ways), as are all other definitions or understandings of culture. My specific cultural milieu is acknowledgely western as Latino/a because this is who I am, but please note that I did not just write that I am western *and* Latino, as if there were an appended Latina/o perspective to a western canonical or mainstream one. I am saying that I am western *as* Latino/a, which means that I share in western culture as a member of a minoritized community in a western country—and this gives me a western cultural perspective not available to those outside of my minoritized community. This perspective is neither better nor worse, nor interest-neutral, but *it is western although not in a hegemonic way*. The western world has marginalized other communities too, by race, ethnicity, gender, sexual orientation, religion, and in other ways, thereby requiring that a real, factual understanding of any western culture inescapably include the perspectives of the marginalized—contrary to the dreams of the self-appointed dominant and *excluyente* perspectives. See J.-Ph. Deranty, ed., *Jacques Rancière: Key Concepts* (Durham: Acumen, 2010).

[21] On culture, see R. Kusch, *Obras completas* (Buenos Aires: Editorial Fundación Ross, 2000), vols. 1–3 (Kusch was one of Latin America's great theorists of culture); A. Jardines, *El cuerpo y lo otro: Introducción a una teoría general de la cultura* (Havana: Ed. de Ciencias Sociales, 2004); M. T. de la Garza, *Política de la memoria* (Barcelona: Anthropos, 2002); B. de Souza Santos, *Una epistemología del sur* (Buenos Aires: Siglo XXI, 2009); H. K. Bhabha, *The Location of Culture* (London: Routledge, 2004); D. Sobrevilla, ed., *Filosofía de la cultura* (Madrid: Trotta, 1998); B. Shore, *Culture in Mind: Cognition, Culture, and the Problem of Meaning* (New York: Oxford University Press, 1996); G. Yúdice, *The Expediency of Culture: Uses of Culture in the Global Era* (Durham: Duke University Press, 2003); J. Beverley, *Subalternity and Representation: Arguments in Cultural Theory* (Durham: Duke University Press, 1999); D. Swartz,

Culture and Power: The Sociology of Pierre Bourdieu (Chicago: University of Chicago Press, 1997); P. L. Berger and T. Luckmann, *The Social Construction of Reality* (New York: Doubleday, 1966); D. Ribeiro, *O Processo Civilizatório: Etapas da Evolução Sócio-Cultural* (Petrópolis: Vozes, 1979); D. H. Lende and G. Downey, eds., *The Encultured Brain: An Introduction to Neuroanthropology* (Cambridge: MIT Press, 2012); J. M. Lochman, "Theology and Cultural Contexts," *Reflections: Center of Theological Inquiry* 2 (1999): 24–41; and O. Espín, "Culture," in *An Introductory Dictionary of Theology and Religious Studies*, ed. O. Espín and J. Nickoloff (Collegeville: Michael Glazier Books, 2007), 302. And consider the theoretical argument regarding culture in L.-G. Tin, *The Invention of Heterosexual Culture* (Cambridge: MIT Press, 2012).

[22] Hence, without culture we are not human. Yet culture remains a human construct.

[23] The influence of A. Gramsci's thought is evident here. See A. Gramsci, *Literatura e vida nacional* (Rio de Janeiro: Civilização Brasileira, 1978; transl. of *Letteratura e vita nazionale*); Gramsci, *Concepção dialética da história* (Rio de Janeiro: Civilização Brasileira, 1981; transl. of *Il materialismo storico e la filosofia di Benedetto Croce*); Gramsci, *Cadernos do cárcere* (Rio de Janeiro: Civilização Brasileira, 2001); Gramsci, *Cartas do cárcere* (Rio de Janeiro: Civilização Brasileira, 2005); and Gramsci, *Os intelectuais e a organização da cultura* (Rio de Janeiro: Civilização Brasileira, 1979; trans. of *Gli intellettuali e l'organizzazione della cultura*). See also L. Gruppi, *O conceito de hegemonia em Gramsci* (Rio de Janeiro: Graal, 1978) and H. Portelli, *Gramsci et le bloc historique* (Paris: Presses Universitaires de France, 1972). The idea of hegemony here is Gramsci's, but accompanied by the reading of E. Laclau. By or on the latter, see E. Laclau, *On Populist Reason* (London: Verso, 2005); E. Laclau and C. Mouffe, *Hegemony and Socialist Strategy*, 2nd ed. (London: Verso, 2001); and S. Critchley and O. Marchart, eds., *Laclau: A Critical Reader* (London: Routledge, 2004).

[24] J. Rancière's work is pertinent to this discussion. See J. Rancière, *Hatred of Democracy* (London: Verso, 2006); Rancière, *On the Shores of Politics* (London: Verso, 1992); Rancière, *Dis-agreement: Politics and Philosophy* (Minneapolis: University of Minnesota Press, 1999); Rancière, *The Intellectual and His People,* vol. 2, *Staging the People,* (London: Verso, 2012); and J.-Ph. Deranty, ed., *Jacques Rancière: Key Concepts* (Durham: Acumen, 2010). See also J. Baldwin, *Collected Essays* (New York: Library of America, 1998), 27–28.

[25] In western Catholic theology we find the categories "humanization" and "dehumanization." There has been an inclination to speak theologically of "humanness," "humanization," etc., in essential terms as if there were a set content or substratum identifiable as "humanness" toward which we strive ("humanization"). In the present volume, however, "humanness" is not essentially conceived, nor "humanization." These are *always and solely cultural constructs*. For important (historical or present) understandings of "humanization" (and "dehumanization") in western Catholic theologies, see, for example, J. Fuchs, *Moral Demands and Personal Obligations* (Washington: Georgetown University Press, 1994); K. A. Cahalan, *Formed in the Image of Christ: The Sacramental-Moral Theology of Bernard Häring* (Collegeville: Michael Glazier, 2004); and T. A. Salzman and M. G. Lawler, *The*

Sexual Person: Toward a Renewed Catholic Anthropology (Washington: Georgetown University Press, 2008).

²⁶ It is an extraordinarily scandalous affirmation to claim that God became human and that in a human we find God, specifically when these are not generic claims but are references to the life of a Galilean Jewish peasant, a day laborer from a small village, who was regarded as one of the "disposables" of his day and who was "disposed of" through a manner of execution inflicted mainly on vanquished or dismissible subversives. This claim, however, only becomes subversive and (religiously) credible if and when those making the claim actually *bet their own lives* on its *verosimilitud* (i.e., on its plausibility). Christianity, consequently, cannot discriminate against (i.e., dismiss as unimportant or rejectable) any human group on any grounds and still pretend to remain faithful to its origins.

²⁷ A very important contribution to the discussion of the relation of culture to doctrine-making is the work of Filipino theologian José de Mesa. For example, see J. de Mesa, "How Far Does Context Impinge on Truth?" in *Fundamentalism and Pluralism in the Church*, ed. D. T. González (Quezon City: Dakateo Publications, 2005), 29–70.

²⁸ Later in this chapter, we will see why today an *intercultural* approach is increasingly unavoidable (in theology and elsewhere). Such approach seems to be a crucial way to avoid the pitfalls of cultural self-idolatry and of renewed colonization of the other. An intercultural approach, it seems to me, can also make western Catholicism and western Catholic theology more methodologically "catholic" and more reflective of the faith and life of the *real* People of God (i.e., of the faith and life of the *real* Church), instead of merely re-inscribing the asymmetries of power and the interests of the dominant into theology and Church under the guise of orthodoxy or tradition.

²⁹ For everything that follows on globalization, see first (from the vast body of current literature) F. Jameson and M. Miyoshi, eds., *The Cultures of Globalization* (Durham: Duke University Press, 1998); J. Belnap and R. Fernández, eds., *José Martí's "Our America": From National to Hemispheric Cultural Studies* (Durham: Duke University Press, 1998); A. Cvetkovich and D. Kellner, eds., *Articulating the Global and the Local: Globalization and Cultural Studies* (New York: Westview, 1997); M. Waters, *Globalization* (New York: Routledge, 1995); A. B. King, ed., *Culture, Globalization and the World-System: Contemporary Conditions for the Representation of Identity* (Minneapolis: University of Minnesota Press, 1997); R. Wilson and W. Dissanayake, eds., *Global-Local: Cultural Production and the Transnational* (Durham: Duke University Press, 1996); E. Balibar and I. Wallerstein, *Race, Nation, Class: Ambiguous Identities* (New York: Verso, 1991); W. Mignolo, *The Darker Side of the Renaissance: Literacy, Territoriality, and Colonization* (Ann Arbor: University of Michigan Press, 1995); E. Mendieta and S. Castro-Gómez, eds., *Teorías sin disciplina: Latinoamericanismo, poscolonialidad y globalización en debate* (Mexico City: Porrúa, 1998); R. J. Schreiter, *The New Catholicity: Theology between the Global and the Local* (Maryknoll: Orbis, 1997); D. Hopkins, L. A. Lorentzen, E. Mendieta, and D. Batstone, eds. *Religions/*

Globalizations: Theories and Cases (Durham, NC: Duke University Press, 2001); and U. Narayan, *Dislocating Cultures: Identities, Traditions and Third World Feminism* (New York: Routledge, 1997).

[30] An earlier version of this section on globalization appeared as part of the first chapter in my *Grace and Humanness: Theological Reflections Because of Culture* (Maryknoll: Orbis, 2007).

[31] See B. Axford, *The Global System: Economics, Politics and Culture* (New York: St. Martin's, 1995); A. Giddens, *The Consequences of Modernity* (Stanford: Stanford University Press, 1990); F. J. Hinkelammert, *Cultura de la esperanza y sociedad sin exclusión* (San José, Costa Rica: DEI, 1995); P. Beyer, *Religion and Globalization* (London: SAGE, 1994); J. H. Mittelman, *The Globalization Syndrome: Transformation and Resistance* (Princeton: Princeton University Press, 2000); W. Dierckxsens, *Los límites de un capitalismo sin ciudadanía* (San José, Costa Rica: DEI, 1998); R. Fornet-Betancourt, ed., *Kapitalistische Globalisierung und Befreiung: Religiöse Erfahrungen und Option für das Leben* (Frankfurt a.M.: IKO/Verlag für Interkulturelle Kommunikation, 2000); Balibar and Wallerstein, *Race, Nation, Class*; N. Goodman, *Ways of Worldmaking* (Indianapolis, IN: Hackett, 1995); S. Sassen, *Guests and Aliens* (New York: New Press, 1999); and Sassen, *Globalization and Its Discontents: Essays on the New Mobility of People and Money* (New York: New Press, 1998).

[32] Schreiter, *The New Catholicity*, 5.

[33] Although, since at least 2008, we have become increasingly aware of the fragility of the western (and now globalized) economic system. This fragility and its ongoing dangers are one complex and important example of the interconnectivity we call globalization.

[34] I readily acknowledge that, as a citizen of a First World nation, I benefit from the dynamics and consequences of globalization, although I also acknowledge that, as a member of an ethnic-cultural minority in a First World country, I belong to a community which can be (has been, and still is) the object of racist, xenophobic and other discriminatory prejudices. It would be unethical for me to claim to be in the same situation as theologians (and as the people in general) in most countries of the Third World; but it would be just as naïve for me (or for the reader) to think that First World citizenship has brought real and effective equality in U.S. society (or within the Church) to racial, ethnic, and LGBTQ communities. Bigotry and racial stereotyping, unfortunately, are also globalized.

[35] This, in my view, is a very serious critique which must be raised to European and especially to U.S. theologians who seem to engage postmodern philosophers without further consideration of the real-life consequences which such philosophers' theories might have for large portions of the world's populations (when the theories are appropriated, as they have been, by the ideological forces of globalization). Most Third World scholars have strongly and consistently found significant ethical and theoretical lacunae (to put it mildly) in many of the postmodern philosophies which U.S. (and other Eurocentric) theologians use without prior rigorous ethical analysis. Simply as examples from Latin America, see E. Dussel, *Apel, Ricoeur, Rorty y*

la filosofía de la liberación (Guadalajara: Universidad de Guadalajara, 1993); A. Gómez-Müller, "¿Qué universalidad para los derechos humanos?" *Cuadernos Latinoamericanos* 12 (2000): 1–21; H. Cerutti, *Filosofar desde nuestra América* (Mexico City: Porrúa, 2000); Dierckxsens, *Los límites de un capitalismo sin ciudadanía*; R. Fornet-Betancourt, ed., *Kapitalistische Globalisierung und Befreiung* (with contributions by several Latin American scholars); and Castro-Gómez and Mendieta, *Teorías sin disciplina.*

[36] See Dierckxsens, *Los límites de un capitalismo sin ciudadanía.*

[37] See O. Espín, "Immigration, Territory, and Globalization: Theological Reflections," *Journal of Hispanic/Latino Theology* 7, no. 3 (2000): 46–59; and Espín, "La experiencia religiosa en el contexto de la globalización," *Journal of Hispanic/Latino Theology* 7, no. 2 (1999): 13–31.

[38] See Espín, "Immigration, Territory, and Globalization" and "La experiencia religiosa en el contexto de la globalización"; Dierckxsens, *Los límites de un capitalismo sin ciudadanía*; Cvetkovich and Kellner, *Articulating the Global and the Local*; Sassen, *Guests and Aliens*; and Sassen, *Globalization and Its Discontents.*

[39] See Espín, "Immigration, Territory, and Globalization" and "La experiencia religiosa en el contexto de la globalización" and the bibliographies cited there.

[40] To question, on cultural and theological grounds (as we do in this volume), the universal validity claims of dominant societies and of the dominant in societies is not the same as globalization's relativization of truth claims, although clearly the results might at times appear to be similar. The ethical intent and purpose, and the means, nevertheless, are clearly different. Globalization seeks dominance and a new colonization, and for that it requires relativizing truth claims that could obstruct its aims, while our argument here intends the subversion of that very dominance and the prevention of the new colonization. (Our argument understands this subversion to be anchored in the core message of Jesus of Nazareth.) The truth claims we relativize are the ones that feed the hegemony of the few at the expense of the humanness and dignity of the vast majority.

[41] The bibliography on immigration is immense. The following works are merely examples. See the excellent book by Sassen, *Globalization and Its Discontents.* See also D. R. Maciel and M. Herrera-Sobek, eds., *Culture across Borders: Mexican Immigration and Popular Culture* (Tucson: University of Arizona Press, 1998); K. McCarthy and G. Vernez, *Immigration in a Changing Economy: California's Experience* (Santa Monica: Rand Institute, 1997); J. P. Smith and B. Edmonston, eds., *The New Americans: Economic, Demographic and Fiscal Effects of Immigration* (Washington, DC: National Research Council, 1997); and M. M. Suárez-Orozco, ed., *Crossings: Mexican Immigration in Interdisciplinary Perspective* (Cambridge, MA: Harvard University Press, 1998). For a very good introduction to Roman Catholic social teaching on immigration, as well as for extensive bibliography on official Roman Catholic views on immigration, see W. R. O'Neill and W. C. Spohn, "Rights of Passage: The Ethics of Immigration and Refugee Policy," *Theological Studies* 59, no. 1 (1998): 84–106.

[42] See F. J. Hinkelammert, *Cultura de la esperanza y sociedad sin exclusión*; A. Sojo, *Mujer y política: Ensayo sobre el feminismo y el sujeto popular* (San José, Costa Rica: DEI, 1985); A. Serbin and D. Ferreyra, eds., *Gobernabilidad democrática y seguridad ciudadana*

en Centroamérica: El caso de Nicaragua (Managua: Coordinadora Regional de Investigaciones Económicas y Sociales, 2000), and especially in that book the excellent paper by D. M. Téllez, "Nicaragua: Entorno económico y social," 17–116.

[43] See Axford, *The Global System*; Mittelman, *The Globalization Syndrome*; Wilson and Dissanayake, *Global/Local*; King, *Culture, Globalization and the World-System*; Cvetkovich and Kellner, *Articulating the Global and the Local*; and Jameson and Miyoshi, *The Cultures of Globalization*.

[44] Although globalization is not identical to or coextensive with colonization, it would be naïve (and analytically unacceptable) to ignore the myriad connections, mutual influences, and similarities between globalization and colonization, and indeed the evident colonizing thrust of globalization. It is no exaggeration to suggest that globalization is an analogy for colonization. I found postcolonial theory (recognizing its distinctive character and its own internal diversity) useful in further understanding globalization and its effects in the contemporary world. See B. Moore-Gilbert, *Postcolonial Theory: Contexts, Practices, Politics* (London: Verso, 1997); P. Williams and L. Chrisman, eds. *Colonial Discourse and Post-Colonial Theory* (New York: Columbia University Press, 1994); R. Guha and G. C. Spivak, eds., *Selected Subaltern Studies* (Oxford: Oxford University Press, 1988); Bhabha, *The Location of Culture*; E. W. Said, *Orientalism* (New York: Vintage, 1979); and B. Ashcroft, G. Griffiths, and H. Tiffin, eds., *The Post-Colonial Studies Reader* (London: Routledge, 1995). No author, however, have I found more insightful on globalization's colonizing thrust than de Souza Santos, *Una epistemología del sur*. See also de Souza Santos, ed., *Another Knowledge Is Possible: Beyond Northern Epistemologies* (London: Verso, 2008).

[45] Although the forces of globalization might at times appear to foster cooperation (or so it is claimed) in order to oppose another obstacle to their dominance, only to be followed by the discrediting of those who cooperated.

[46] I occasionally suspect that some First World theologians assume that their colleagues in the Third World, as well as minorities in the First World, are theologically "underdeveloped," requiring of First World "assistance" or "guidance" in becoming "sufficiently proficient" in professional theology. I suspect this because I have, in fact, heard such comments. I need not argue against such colonial mentality: its racist and ethnocentrist assumptions are morally and doctrinally unacceptable and unfounded, even when disguised under apparently supportive or "progressive" language. Not surprisingly, many of those who display this attitude have rarely, if ever, taken the time to study seriously the publications and thought of the very authors they consider theologically underdeveloped. Self-appointed "mainstream" theology is mainstream only among the dominant or among the colonized, because the very notion of "mainstream" as well as its assignation are expressions of ideological hegemony.

[47] To attempt to diminish or ignore human diversity, or to treat it as an inconsequential component of human reality, is similar to diminishing or ignoring time and history. In theology this would be irresponsible, to say the least. Unfortunately, the Eurocentric theological mind seems to deal with diversity by claiming the center of thought, reason, history and culture for itself—thereby justifying (to itself) its dismissal of most of humankind and, thus, of most human experience. The

Eurocentric theological mind, therefore, only manages to tribalize (or provincialize) itself through its imperial logic.

   [48] Nevertheless, the "disposables" must ethically struggle not to reinscribe, in *their* self-affirmation and in *their* construction of meaningful humanness, the bias implied in today's dominant list of the "non- . . ." (non-white, non-male, non-heterosexual, non-western, etc.). The struggle for diversity and self-affirmation cannot be turned into a new chapter of self-colonization.

   [49] See L. Rowntree et al., *Globalization and Diversity: Geography of a Changing World* (Upper Saddle River, NJ: Prentice Hall, 2007).

   [50] Theologically, and especially in the long history of western Catholicism, there has been an attempt to deal with diversity by claiming that there is *a* (in the singular) "natural law" inscribed in "human nature"—a "nature" shared by all who are human because it is what makes them human. Ultimately, it is claimed, "human nature" is God's act (at creation) and thus "natural law" is also from God. Convenient to this argument is the further claim that the contents and implications of this "natural law" can easily be discerned and reasoned, for all to follow (implying, thereby, that only the "unreasonable" would choose not to follow what is so evidently required by "natural law"). Historically, and all too frequently, it seems that many who claim to discern the evident in "natural law" are themselves members of groups benefitting from cultural dominance. However, there are today significant difficulties with such argument on behalf of "natural law," "human nature," and their origin in a sovereign act of God (beyond the contemporary argument against essentialism). First of all, and as we will see shortly, all talk or claims about God can only be (at best) analogical. When analogy is interpreted "literally" we begin to descend into the realm of idolatry, and more specifically self-idolatry (of *our* constructs of the analogy and its meaning). To think that what *we* understand of God or of what is said *by us* to come from God is the only possible understanding is, mildly put, idolatrous. History also demonstrates the scandalous crimes committed by this self-idolatrous attitude (the justification of slavery by "natural law" is very relevant here). Secondly, any claim regarding a "human nature" and a "natural law" cannot avoid being a *human* claim, and thus inescapably, a *culturally constructed* claim. And again, lest we fall into the idolatrous, we must acknowledge that no culture escapes time, transience, and the particularity of its context. There is *no universally valid or universally needed culture*—and certainly not in reference to God! This, however, does not mean that at some moments in history, and in some specific contexts, such analogical language might not have made sense to some in some human societies. Lastly, the struggle to respect and affirm diversity is not just about "diversity" but it is also *a profoundly prophetic stance*—against demonstrably idolatrous claims, as well as against the also idolatrous and imperial dynamics of colonization implicated in globalization. Needless to add that this struggle for diversity demands relentless self-critique and discernment. More on idolatry later.

   [51] Apophatic theology is as old as theology. Apophatic thought is older and certainly broader than western Catholic theology. See, for example, W. Franke, ed., *On What Cannot Be Said: Apophatic Discourses in Philosophy, Religion, Literature, and the Arts*, vols. 1 and 2 (Notre Dame: University of Notre Dame Press, 2007); D. Turner,

The Darkness of God: Negativity in Christian Mysticism (Cambridge: Cambridge University Press, 1998); M. A. Sells, *Mystical Languages of Unsaying* (Chicago: University of Chicago Press, 1994); Gregory of Nyssa, *The Life of Moses* (New York: HarperCollins, 2006); C. Keller and C. Boesel, *Apophatic Bodies: Negative Theology, Incarnation, and Relationality* (New York: Fordham University Press, 2009); and J. A. Vélez de Cea, *The Buddha and Religious Diversity* (London: Routledge, 2012).

[52] The transcendence of the Mystery is obviously implied in this discussion. Yet the category "transcendence" (in reference to the Ultimate Mystery) is a human, cultural construct to say what ultimately cannot be said. The transcendence of God is not available to us, obviously. So how can we reflect on it? Our inability to "say" or understand the transcendence of God, however, is *ours*. See J. McIntyre, "Transcendence," in *The Westminster Dictionary of Christian Theology*, ed. A. Richardson and J. Bowden (Philadelphia: Westminster, 1983), 576–77.

[53] At one point in the second half of the twentieth century there was a divide among many western Catholic and Protestant theologians over the "knowability" of God. Although the reasons for the divide were understandable during those decades, today this seems to be an immensely less important problem or question. The issue, reformulated, now confronts all Christians (and all believers in theistic religions) vis-à-vis modern atheism or secularism and the growing theological challenge posed by non-theistic religious traditions. For a serious discussion on the issues raised during the twentieth century, see H. Bouillard, *The Knowledge of God* (New York: Herder and Herder, 1968).

[54] In reference to this question and the real-life consequences of *not* asking it, see G. Gutiérrez, *Hablar de Dios desde el sufrimiento del inocente* (Lima: CEP, 1986). The question is theologically urgent: see A. Bentué, *¿En qué creen los que creen?* (Barcelona: Claret, 2010) and Bentué, *La opción creyente* (Santiago de Chile: San Pablo, 2001).

[55] As when we began to discuss these inescapable contexts, it is still important to remember that "I cannot address everything that could or should be said or discussed about each of the various contexts and topics discussed in this chapter, or about the thought of the scholars I engage. This chapter focuses *only* on *some* specific issues about a *few* (albeit crucial) specific contexts raised here because of the succeeding chapters." This new section on the "unsayability" of the Mystery, with its various parts, is no exception. The reader should not expect here, therefore, a full discussion of "God talk" or of the logical or rational possibility of "speaking of God."

[56] *Verosimilitud* is not analogy or metaphor. More later on these two words.

[57] *Verosímil* is the Castilian adjective, and *verosímilmente* is the adverb. The etymologies of the Latin terms *verosimilitudo* and *simil* (both at the root of the Castilian) further lead us to the pre-classic term *semol* ("alike" because it is "next to" or "close to"). See V. J. Emery, "On the Definition of Some Rhetorical Terms," *American Journal of Philology* 18 (1897): 206–13; F. Corripio, *Diccionario etimológico general de la lengua española* (Mexico City: Bruguera, 1996); R. Barcia et al., *Diccionario general etimológico de la lengua española*, 8 vols. (Charleston and Seattle: Nabu Press, 2010; originally published in Madrid, 1880–1923); L. R. Palmer, *The Latin Language* (London: Faber & Faber, 1954); and S. Santiago, *The Space In-Between* (Durham: Duke University Press, 2001), 64–78.

[58] Within the field of statistics there are theories of *verosimilitud*, which might suggest too the point of relationship, although they do not enter the more philosophical or theological discussion. See J. Bescos Sinde, "El paradigma de la verosimilitud," *Estadística Española* 44, no. 149 (2002): 113–28.

[59] Reasonableness (and its concomitant reason and logic), therefore, cannot be assessed by outsiders to the contexts—unless colonization or the imperial is the aim.

[60] Very importantly, see de Souza Santos, *Una epistemología del sur* and de Souza Santos, *Another Knowledge Is Possible: Beyond Northern Epistemologies*. Despite the apparent similarities of these two volumes' titles, one is not the translation of the other; these are two distinct contributions, the latter collective.

[61] Is it ethically and logically or rationally acceptable among theologians (and other scholars, church leaders, and the like) to dismiss two-thirds of humankind, and thereby most of Christianity, and still pretend that *the* universal concerns or claims of humanity are only those that come from the world's dominant societies and, more precisely, from the dominant groups within them (whites, men, heterosexuals, etc.)? I think not.

[62] See T. S. Kuhn, *The Structure of Scientific Revolutions* (Chicago: University of Chicago Press, 1970); S. Arbesman, *The Half-Life of Facts: Why Everything We Know Has an Expiration Date* (New York: Penguin, 2012); E. Laclau, *Misticismo, retórica y política* (Buenos Aires: Fondo de Cultura Económica, 2002); Laclau, *On Populist Reason*; S. Buck-Morss, *Hegel, Haiti and Universal History* (Pittsburgh: University of Pittsburgh Press, 2009); M.-R. Trouillot, *Silencing the Past: Power and the Production of History* (Boston: Beacon, 1995); W. Mignolo, "Decolonizing Western Epistemology, Building Decolonial Epistemologies," in *Decolonizing Epistemologies: Latina/o Theology and Philosophy*, ed. A. M. Isasi-Díaz and E. Mendieta (New York: Fordham University Press, 2012), 19–43; O. Maduro, "An(other) Invitation to Epistemological Humility: Notes toward a Self-Critical Approach to Counter-Knowledges," in ibid, 87–106; and R. Kusch, "Creer en algo," in *Obras completas*, vol. 1, 543–76, and all of vol. 3; Kusch's *Obras completas* bring together his main works on epistemology and autochthonous thought. Also of interest to the discussion in this section on *verosimilitud* is G. Vattimo, *Creer que se cree* (Buenos Aires: Paidós, 2008).

[63] For those claimants, and only for them, at least as expressed within their cultural perimeter of reasonableness.

[64] There is, in some circles within western philosophy, a view that *seems* close to what I have said here regarding *verosimilitud*, but which is certainly not the same because, and emphatically so, of its Eurocentric contextualization and interests. See, for example, T. Black, "Contextualism in Epistemology," *Internet Encyclopedia of Philosophy*, http://www.iep.utm.edu/contextu/.

[65] See G. Agamben, *The Signature of All Things: On Method* (New York: Zone Books, 2009), 7.

[66] Indispensable for any (western) discussion of analogy is its confrontation with non-western forms and dynamics of analogical thought that challenge the western proven inclination to self-universalize. See, for example, D. B. Zilberman et al., *Analogy in Indian and Western Philosophical Thought* (Dordrecht: Springer, 2006) and M. León Portilla, *La filosofía Náhuatl*, 3rd ed. (Mexico City: UNAM, 1979).

[67] I found this fascinating interview with Wheeler (of Princeton University) and Linde (of Stanford University) in T. Folger, "Does the Universe Exist if We're Not Looking?" *Discovery* 23, no. 6 (2002): 44–48. Professor Wheeler passed away in 2008.

[68] This, the reader will recall, is precisely what we were discussing on the perspectival character of all knowledge and life in Chapter One.

[69] For this section on analogy, see C. Shelley, *Multiple Analogies in Science and Philosophy* (Amsterdam: John Benjamins, 2003); E. Melandri, *La linea e il circolo: Studio logico-filosofico sull'analogia* (Macerata: Quodlibet, 2012; originally published in 1968); P. A. Rolnick, *Analogical Possibilities: How Words Refer to God* (Atlanta: Scholars, 1993); R. M. White, *Talking about God: The Concept of Analogy and the Problem of Religious Language* (Burlington: Ashgate, 2010); S. Vosniadou and A. Ortony, eds., *Similarity and Analogical Reasoning* (Cambridge: Cambridge University Press, 1989); and J. F. Ross, *Portraying Analogy* (Cambridge: Cambridge University Press, 1981). See also Z. Kövecses, *Metaphor* (Oxford: Oxford University Press, 2010); G. Lakoff and M. Johnson, *Metaphors We Live By* (Chicago: University of Chicago Press, 1980); and Lakoff and Johnson, *Philosophy in the Flesh: The Embodied Mind and Its Challenge to Western Thought* (New York: Basic Books, 1999).

[70] See C. Brown, *Philosophy and the Christian Faith* (Downers Grove, IL: InterVarsity, 1968), 30–32 and E. J. Ashworth, "Medieval Theories of Analogy," in *Stanford Encyclopedia of Philosophy* (2009), http://plato.stanford.edu/entries/analogy-medieval/.

[71] There are numerous histories of the concept of analogy in western and non-western thought. Most of the titles mentioned in this section's notes include such histories. I am here focusing mainly on western notions of analogy because this volume's perspective (as previously explained) is western Catholic.

[72] The reader should note that I am not involving myself here in the continuing discussion regarding best uses and types of analogy (i.e., of proportionality, of attribution, of being, etc.) and which, if any, is "best" in reference to God. Although some types of analogy assume some sort of symmetrical relationship, in reference to God it is obvious that no analogy can be symmetrical. See R. M. White, *Talking about God*, 173–192. Tempting is E. Jüngel's justification of analogy, although it still seems (to me) not to distance itself enough from the symmetric. See E. Jüngel, *God as the Mystery of the Word* (Edinburgh: T&T Clark, 1983). The demonstrable fact remains that humans cannot know without analogy.

[73] This, of course, from the perspective of the ones undergoing the experience. Everyday examples of experiences that often escape defining could be love and the aesthetic experience, or hate and violence. The experience of the Mystery too.

[74] Is there, we may reasonably wonder, a "universal" (transcultural but nevertheless cultural) structure in human language and reasoning for what we call "analogy"? Is there a shared grammar of "analogizing" or of "myth-making"? R. Bellah, in *Religion in Human Evolution: From the Paleolithic to the Axial Age* (Cambridge: Harvard University Press, 2011), suggests that the biggest historical leap forward into "modern" humanity came from and because of our ancestors' ability to "mythify"—which

is a crucial way of finding and affirming life's meaning beyond the immediate, and that *life is meaningful*. This leap, according to Bellah, precedes language and is the very condition for language. A parallel argument appears in J. Cauvin's *The Birth of the Gods and the Origins of Agriculture* (Cambridge: Cambridge University Press, 2007), where Cauvin proposes—based on recent archaeological evidence—that the origin of civilizations is not to be found in agriculture or town-making but in religion, and more specifically in communal ritual and myth-making (and, consequently, in temple-making too).

[75] I have found many contemporary discussions of the analogical also in works on the metaphorical, on the paradigmatic, and on the exemplar. This is frequent in M. Foucault, W. Benjamin, G. Agamben, C. Ginzburg, E. Melandri, P. Ricoeur, et al. I hasten to note, however, the (probably unconscious and unchosen) Eurocentric character of these discussions. Necessary antidotes to this Eurocentric tendency might be A. Jardines in *El cuerpo y lo otro*; "Analogía," in *Diccionario de filosofía latino-americana*, http://www.cialc.unam.mx/pensamientoycultura/biblioteca virtual/dic-cionario/analogia.htm; M. Beuchot, "Los márgenes de la interpretación: Hacia un modelo analógico de la hermenéutica," in *Diálogos sobre filosofía contemporánea*, ed. M. Aguilar Rivero (Mexico City: UNAM, 1995); and E. Dussel, "El método analéctico y la filosofía latinoamericana," in *Hacia una filosofía de la liberación latinoamericana*, ed. R. Ardiles et al. (Buenos Aires: Bonuni, 1973).

[76] See Lakoff and Johnson, *Metaphors We Live By*.

[77] G. Agamben, *Idea of Prose* (Albany: SUNY Press, 1995), 107.

[78] An earlier version of this section on intercultural thought and dialogue appeared as part of the first chapter in my *Grace and Humanness*.

[79] The International Society for Intercultural Philosophy was founded in 1992; its statement of principles can be found in *Concordia: Internationale Zeitschrift für Philosophie* 23 (1993): 27–128. Among the early works on intercultural thought, and solely as examples, see R. Panikkar, "La visió cosmoteándrica: El sentit religiós emergent del tercer milleni," *Qüestions de Vida Cristiana* 156 (1991): 78–102; H. Kimmerle, *Philosophie in Afrika: Annäherungen an einen interkulturellen Philosophiebegriff* (Frankfurt a.M.: IKO/Verlag Interkulturelle Kommunikation, 1991); F. Wimmer, *Interkulturelle Philosophie: Geschichte und Theorie*, 2 vols. (Vienna: Verso Verlag, 1990); R. A. Mall, *Intercultural Philosophy* (London: Rowman and Littlefield, 2000; collection of earlier essays by the author which had appeared mostly in Germany, England, and India); J. Estermann, "Hacia una filosofía del escuchar: Perspectivas de desarrollo para el pensamiento intercultural desde la tradición europea," in *Kulturen der Philosophie*, ed. R. Fornet-Betancourt (Frankfurt a.M.: IKO/Verlag Interkulturelle Kommunikation, 1996); G. Bollème, *El pueblo por escrito: Significados culturales de lo "popular"*; D. Sobrevilla, ed., *Filosofía de la cultura* (Madrid: Trotta, 1998); and the works by R. Fornet-Betancourt to which I refer below in n. 80. On an earlier and still fascinating pertinent model of intercultural thought, proposed by the late Argentinean philosopher R. Kusch, see C. M. Pagano Fernández, *Un modelo de filosofía intercultural: Rodolfo Kusch, 1922–1979* (Frankfurt a.M.: IKO/Verlag Interkulturelle Kommunikation, 1999).

[80]   Professor R. Fornet-Betancourt has written extensively on the history of Latin American philosophies, and their contributions. He has also published significant analyses on the philosophical work of José Martí. Cuban-born Fornet-Betancourt is professor of philosophy at the University of Bremen, Germany. His publications (specifically on intercultural philosophy and theology) are many, frequently translated into Spanish, Portuguese, German, and French, depending on the original language of publication. Among his works specifically on intercultural thought are: *Theologien in der Sozial- und KulturgeschichteLateinamerikas: Die perspektive der Arme*, vol. 1, *Interdisziplinäre und interkulturelle Forschung in der Theologie: Autochthone Theologien und Kulturen* (Eichstätt:Verlag des Katholische Universität, 1992); *Theologien in der Sozial- und KulturgeschichteLateinamerikas: Die Perspektive der Arme.*, vol. 2, *Theologien in der Praxis von Mission und Kolonialisierung: Ethnizität und nationale Kultur* (Eichstätt: Verlag des Katholische Universität, 1993); *Kulturen der Philosophie* (Frankfurt a.M.: IKO/ Verlag Interkulturelle Kommunikation, 1996); *Lateinamerikanische Philosophie zwischen Inkulturation und Interkulturalität* (Frankfurt a.M.: IKO/ Verlag Interkulturelle Kommunikation, 1997); "Aprender a filosofar desde el contexto de las culturas," *Revista de Filosofía*, 90 (1997): 365–82; *Kapitalistische Globalisierung und Befreiung*; "Tradición, cultura, interculturalidad: Apuntes para una comprensión intercultural de la cultura"; "Aproximaciones a la globalización como universalización de políticas neoliberales, desde una perspectiva filosófica," *Revista Pasos* 83 (1998), electronic edition at: www.dei-cr.org/pasos.htm#83; "La existencia como resistencia," *Concordia: Internationale Zeitschrift für Philosophie*, 7 (1985), 95–101; *Kulturen zwischen Tradition und Innovation* (Frankfurt a.M.: IKO/ Verlag Interkulturelle Kommunikation, 2001); Fornet-Betancourt and J. A. Senent, eds., *Filosofía para la convivencia: Caminos de diálogos norte-sur* (Seville: MAD, 2004); and Fornet-Betancourt et al., *El discurso intercultural: Prolegómenos a una filosofía intercultural* (Madrid: Biblioteca Nueva, 2002). For this section I have especially, but not exclusively, relied on Fornet-Betancourt's three (in his estimation and mine) best contributions on intercultural thought: *Interculturalidad y globalización: Ejercicios de crítica filosófica intercultural en el contexto de la globalización neoliberal* (Frankfurt a.M.: IKO/ Verlag Interkulturelle Kommunikation, 2000); *Hacia una filosofía intercultural latinoamericana* (San José, Costa Rica: DEI, 1994); and *Transformación intercultural de la filosofía* (Bilbao: Desclée de Brouwer, 2001).

[81]   See Fornet-Betancourt, *Hacia una filosofía intercultural latinoamericana*, 17–18, 33.

[82]   There are obviously other perspectives on inculturation, although they all admit the existence of a "canonical something." I view inculturation, consequently, as too close (or too open) to colonization. For a recent study on inculturation which disagrees with my views, see D. Irarrázaval, *Inculturation: New Dawn of the Church in Latin America* (Maryknoll: Orbis, 2000).

[83]   It is important to again remember what I have discussed above regarding *verosimilitud* and analogy in all God-talk.

[84]   It should be noted, here as elsewhere in this volume, that I am *not* proposing this "contrasting dialogue" only or mainly as an exercise among individual scholars. Real everyday communities are the key indispensable subjects of the contrasting

dialogue, aided by intellectuals to the degree that this aid might prove helpful to the communities' dialogue needs. I should further add that Antonio Gramsci's notion of the "organic intellectual" is very pertinent when deciding *who* are the "helpful" scholars in the contrasting dialogue, as well as in determining the scholars' role therein. Consequently, institutional recognition of a role (e.g., ordination) is not, by itself, what I am speaking of here, and it has little to do with Gramsci's notion. It is engagement and participation within, and "betting one's life" with, a concrete community that may lead to recognition of the role of "organic intellectual." See Gramsci, *Literatura e vida nacional*; Gramsci, *Concepção dialética da história*; and Gramsci, *Os intelectuais e a organização da cultura*.

   [85] See Fornet-Betancourt, *Hacia una filosofía intercultural latinoamericana*, 23–24.

   [86] See ibid, 24–25. See also Fornet-Betancourt, *Interculturalidad y globalización*, 14–17, 24–25, 27; Fornet-Betancourt, *Transformación intercultural de la filosofía*, 173–90, 273–84; and also D. Hervieu-Léger, *Religion as a Chain of Memory* (New Brunswick: Rutgers University Press, 2000); H. Lefebvre, *Critique de la vie quotidienne, I: Introduction* (Paris: L'Arche, 1958); and M. de Certeau, *La culture au pluriel* (Paris: Seuil, 1994).

   [87] This, however, seems to be one of the non-spoken premises of Eurocentrism (and of Eurocentric theologies).

   [88] On "universal validity" and "universal relevance" see O. Espín, "An Exploration into the Theology of Grace and Sin," in *From the Heart of Our People: Latino/a Explorations in Catholic Systematic Theology*, ed. O. Espín and M. Díaz (Maryknoll: Orbis, 1999), 121–52. See also Fornet-Betancourt, *Transformación intercultural de la filosofía*, 191–218, 273–84.

   [89] See Gruppi, *O conceito de hegemonia em Gramsci*; O. Maduro, *Religión y conflicto social* (Mexico City: Centro de Reflexión Teológica, 1980); and Bhabha, *The Location of Culture*. I found very fruitful the reflections on the construction of knowledge and truth (even religious truth) by philosopher X. Zubiri in his *El problema filosófico de la historia de las religiones* (Madrid: Alianza Editorial/Fundación Xavier Zubiri, 1993) and *Inteligencia sentiente: Inteligencia y realidad* (Madrid: Alianza Editorial/Fundación Xavier Zubiri, 1980).

   [90] See Gruppi, *O conceito de hegemonia em Gramsci* and Portelli, *Gramsci et le bloc historique*.

   [91] See Fornet-Betancourt, *Hacia una filosofía intercultural latinoamericana*, 25.

   [92] See the preceding section on diversity.

   [93] Which is not to be understood as being the same as the inescapable diversity we find in the world.

   [94] Professor Fornet-Betancourt is highly critical of postmodern philosophers on several grounds, the most important of which is their apparent ethical naïveté vis-à-vis globalization, as well as their apparent disregard of the substantive theoretical questions raised (for postmodern philosophies) by scholars from the Third World. The main works by Fornet-Betancourt (i.e., *Hacia una filosofía intercultural latinoamericana*, *Transformación intercultural de la filosofía*, and *Interculturalidad y globalización*, and especially the last named) are fierce in their critique of postmodern philosophies. Throughout the present volume I refer to postmodern philosophy on

a number of occasions. The philosophies I have specifically in mind when making these comments on postmodernism are mainly (but not only) those by R. Rorty and D. Davidson. I have focused on these two philosophers because they seem to be the preferred dialogue partners of some or many First World theologians of tradition and traditioning, especially U.S. theologians (but see below, in this same note, for other postmodern authors). Let this note stand as clarification for all references to postmodern philosophical thought in this chapter, unless otherwise stated. A magnificent volume by B. de Sousa Santos which I already cited, is (with Fornet-Betancourt's works) an excellent and most coherent critique of the postmodern and the postcolonial while in no way legitimizing dominance or coloniality, see de Sousa Santos, *Una epistemología del sur*. By R. Rorty, see *Philosophy and the Mirror of Nature* (Princeton: Princeton University Press, 1979); *Philosophy and Social Hope* (London: Penguin, 1999); *Achieving Our Country* (Cambridge, MA: Harvard University Press, 1998); *Contingency, Irony, and Solidarity* (Cambridge: Cambridge University Press, 1989); *Objectivity, Relativism and Truth: Philosophical Papers I* (Cambridge: Cambridge University Press, 1991); and *Truth and Progress. Philosophical Papers II* (Cambridge: Cambridge University Press, 1998). Engaging and critiquing Rorty are Norman Geras, *Solidarity in the Conversation of Humankind: The Ungroundable Liberalism of Richard Rorty* (London: Verso, 1995) and E. Dussel, *Apel, Ricoeur, Rorty y la filosofía de la liberación*. D. Davidson's bibliography is vast, with much of his most important thought in articles. The best introduction to his thought, with detailed listing of his works, and with significant essays on Davidson by other authors, is L. E. Hahn's massive edited volume, *The Philosophy of Donald Davidson* (Chicago: Open Court, 1999). But see also, by Davidson, *Inquiries into Truth and Interpretation* (Oxford: Clarendon, 1984) and *Essays on Actions and Events* (Oxford: Clarendon, 1980). Obviously, postmodern thought is broader than Rorty's and Davidson's theories. For example, see also R. Barthes, *A Barthes Reader* (London: Fontana, 1982); J. Baudrillard, *Selected Writings* (Cambridge: Polity, 1988); J. Derrida, *Writing and Difference* (Chicago: University of Chicago Press, 1967); Derrida, *Margins of Philosophy* (Chicago: University of Chicago Press, 1972); Derrida, "Living on: Borderlines," in *Deconstruction and Criticism*, ed. H. Bloom et al. (London: Routledge and Kegan Paul, 1979), 75–176; T. Eagleton, *The Crisis of Contemporary Culture* (Oxford: Clarendon Press, 1993); J.-F. Lyotard, *La Condition postmoderne: Rapport sur le savoir* (Paris: Minuit, 1979); Lyotard, *Le Postmoderne expliqué aux enfants: Correspondence, 1982–1985* (Paris: Galilée, 1986).

[95] By "need," here, I want to say "requirement," "condition or demand *sine qua non*," or some such ethical obligation. I am not assuming, however, a universally valid principle or ethical "essence" or moral imperative underlying the obligation; rather, I am referring to the internal need of particularities (perceived precisely as need by and within the particularities) for their own ethical subsistence and coherence.

[96] Fornet-Betancourt, in his *Hacia una filosofía intercultural latinoamericana*, arrives at a very clear and emphatic conclusion: "El mismo posmodernismo particularista, al decretar que no existe más nada fuera o más allá de sí, no hace sino repetir de modo aparentemente nuevo la misma mentalidad occidental colonizante que decreta que su particularidad es la verdadera universalidad. El posmodernismo particularista no

es más que la nueva faz de la colonización, que establece al Occidente como quien tiene y conoce la verdad de manera mejor, más clarividente y convincente" (p. 38). See also Fornet-Betancourt, *Interculturalidad y globalización*, 83–84 and again, de Sousa Santos, *Una epistemología del sur*.

⁹⁷ See Geras, *Solidarity in the Conversation of Humankind*.

⁹⁸ This has been a repeated theme in the writings of R. S. Goizueta. See, of course, his *Caminemos con Jesús: Toward a Hispanic/Latino Theology of Accompaniment* (Maryknoll: Orbis, 1995), as well as his article, "Fiesta: Life in the Subjunctive," in Espín and Díaz, *From the Heart of Our People*, 84–99.

⁹⁹ See Said, *Orientalism*; Young, *White Mythologies*; and F. Jameson, *Postmodernism, or, The Cultural Logic of Late Capitalism* (Durham, NC: Duke University Press, 1997).

¹⁰⁰ On "foundationalism" and "nonfoundationalism," see J. E. Thiel, *Nonfoundationalism* (Minneapolis: Fortress, 1994). See also M. Steup, *An Introduction to Contemporary Epistemology* (Upper Saddle River, NJ: Prentice Hall, 1996); M. E. John, *Discrepant Dislocations: Feminism, Theory, and Postcolonial Histories* (Berkeley: University of California Press, 1996); and S. Benhabib et al., *Feminist Contentions: A Philosophical Exchange* (New York: Routledge, 1995), especially, in that volume, J. Butler's essay, "Contingent Foundations: Feminism and the Question of 'Postmodernism,'" 35–58.

¹⁰¹ See Fornet-Betancourt, *Hacia una filosofía intercultural latinoamericana*, 34–35 and Fornet-Betancourt, *Interculturalidad y globalización*, 33–39.

¹⁰² See Fornet-Betancourt, *Interculturalidad y globalización*, 151–53 and Fornet-Betancourt, *Transformación intercultural de la filosofía*, 173–218.

¹⁰³ See Fornet-Betancourt, *Hacia una filosofía intercultural latinoamericana*, 36–38, 73–98 and Fornet-Betancourt, *Interculturalidad y globalización*, 9–20, 51–58.

¹⁰⁴ In the western Catholic theologies of tradition and traditioning the usual "objects of study," or sources, have been the Bible, ecclesial creeds, decisions and definitions by ecumenical councils, the works of the early bishops and theologians of the Church (Patristics/Patrology), the *sensus fidelium*, joint statements by bishops (or papal magisterium), the works of medieval and post-Reformation theologians (all the way to more contemporary authors), and, especially since the mid-nineteenth century, the history of the development of doctrines. I propose, in this volume and elsewhere—for example, in my *The Faith of the People: Theological Reflections on Popular Catholicism* (Maryknoll: Orbis, 1997)—that popular Catholicism, daily life, and popular epistemologies (and others) must be included in the list of authoritative sources. An intercultural theology would include all of the above, as well as the cultural perspectives and experiences of western Catholic communities worldwide (with much to be said and to be nuanced on the former and the latter) engaged in the significant "contrasting" dialogue which would yield the universally relevant truth(s) which can be labeled as "Tradition" by the western Catholic faith communities. These faith communities, because they exist only in specific cultures, have produced their own "theologizing subjects" (communities and individuals in communities). The notion of theologizing subjects, as used here, is therefore closely related, but not identical, to Gramsci's notion of organic intellectuals. On Gramsci's thought, see earlier notes.

[105] See Fornet-Betancourt, *Interculturalidad y globalización*, 99–106 and John, *Discrepant Dislocations*.

[106] See Fornet-Betancourt, *Interculturalidad y globalización*, 12–17 and Fornet-Betancourt, *Transformación intercultural de la filosofía*, 173–218.

[107] See M. J. Mejido, "A Critique of the 'Aesthetic Turn' in U.S. Hispanic Theology: A Dialogue with Roberto Goizueta and the Positing of a New Paradigm," in *Journal of Hispanic/Latino Theology* 8, no. 3 (2001): 18–48. In this article, it seems to me, Mejido makes a very valid argument for grounding theology on social conditions and reality; although his reading and evaluation of Goizueta's work do not convince.

[108] See the preceding section on culture above in this chapter (and the related endnotes). Also, see Fornet-Betancourt, *Interculturalidad y globalización*, 13–50 and Fornet-Betancourt, *Kulturen zwischen Tradition und Innovation*.

[109] See Fornet-Betancourt, *Transformación intercultural de la filosofía*, 285–98, 349–70.

[110] See Fornet-Betancourt, *Interculturalidad y globalización*, 25–50; E. Dussel, *Arquitectónica de una ética de la liberación en la edad de la globalización y la exclusión* (Mexico City: Siglo XXI, 1998), especially chapter 6; J. Ortega y Gasset, *Meditaciones del Quijote* (Madrid: Espasa-Calpe, 1964); Gruppi, *O conceito de hegemonia em Gramsci*; Portelli, *Gramsci et le bloc historique*; M. McGergen, ed., *Feminist Thought and the Structure of Knowledge* (New York: New York University Press, 1988); and S. Fleischacker, *The Ethics of Culture* (Ithaca, NY: Cornell University Press, 1994).

[111] Consider again Agamben's wise insight: "The only true representation is one that also represents its distance from the truth," in Agamben, *Idea of Prose*, 107.

[112] I remind the reader of our discussion (above, in the present chapter) on *verosimilitud* and on the *verosímil*. And, more importantly, of the discussion on Jesus and his message with which we opened Chapter One.

[113] I remind the reader of the distinction I made in the preceding section between "universally valid" and "universally relevant" claims. The distinction is important here too.

[114] See F. Krantz, ed., *History from Below: Studies in Popular Protest and Popular Ideology* (Montreal: Concordia University Press, 1985); Gramsci, *Os intelectuais e a organização da cultura*; J. C. Scott, *Weapons of the Weak: Everyday Forms of Peasant Resistance* (New Haven: Yale University Press, 1986), and Scott, *Domination and the Arts of Resistance* (New Haven: Yale University Press, 1990).

Chapter III

[1] I refer the reader to the first section of this volume's Chapter One.

[2] See J. D. Newsome, *Greeks, Romans, Jews: Currents of Culture and Belief in the New Testament World* (Philadelphia: Trinity, 1992); F. J. Murphy, *The Religious World of Jesus: An Introduction to Second Temple Palestinian Judaism* (Nashville: Abingdon, 1991); and E. P. Sanders, *Judaism: Practice and Belief, 63 BCE-66 CE* (London: SCM, 1992).

[3] See R. L. Wilken, *The Christians as the Romans Saw Them* (New Haven: Yale University Press, 1984), 105–08.

[4] An ancient Greek term referring to the opportune or right moment—the moment that needed to be seized in order to come to pass. It has been used by more recent philosophers to mean the moment of opportunity for an unexpectedly better future—the "breaking" of the future into the present—that also needs to be seized in order to become reality.

[5] As L. C. Schneider has demonstrated in *Beyond Monotheism: A Theology of Multiplicity* (London: Routledge, 2008), monotheism is not the only possible human understanding or expression of the Ultimate Mystery. Other scholars (in theology and religious studies) have also insisted on this, stressing that even theism is not the only necessary or possible understanding and expression of the Ultimate Mystery. My colleague L. Komjathy has often and wisely reminded me of Daoism; M. G. Ramos has reminded me of the Afro-Cuban Lukumí experience of the Mystery, monotheistic and yet not in a western sense or experience of the "divine one." Obviously, as a western Catholic Christian I assume the monotheistic option and experience of the Christian religious tradition, while reminding the reader that this tradition cannot dismiss key insights in its trinitarian, incarnational claims and that Christianity's truth claims cannot be understood idolatrously. See also L. C. Schneider's *Re-Imagining the Divine: Confronting the Backlash against Feminist Theology* (Cleveland: Pilgrim, 1998).

[6] See Ex. 20:2–6 and Deut. 5:6–10. In my references here to Israel in biblical times, and especially during the time of Jesus, I will frequently use the past tense of verbs, because I will be mostly referring to those historical periods. In no way should this be construed to mean disregard or disrespect for later Judaism, including today's.

[7] And so Jews and Christians still hope.

[8] Even during that period, before the fourth century BCE, when Israel's religion was monolatric and not yet monotheistic. See n. 9 below.

[9] It is well known that the earliest Israel was not monotheistic, as today we understand the term. "Monolatric" would be a more accurate adjective to describe the earliest Israel: there was only one God (the God of Abraham and of Israel's Exodus) who could be worshipped by Israel and with whom Israel had established a covenantal relationship. No other God was allowed for Israel—although a growing number of scholars believe that there were more Gods tolerated by Israel prior to the fourth century BCE. Later, post-exilic Israel became monotheistic. Because of these changes (i.e., monolatry to monotheism, over several centuries), anti-idolatry cannot be claimed in the same way, and with the same understanding, over the entire history of biblical Israel. On "monotheisms" in biblical Israel's history, see R. Albertz, *A History of Israelite Religion in the Old Testament Period* (Louisville: Westminster/John Knox, 1994); B. Becking et al., *Only One God? Monotheism in Ancient Israel and the Veneration of the Goddess Asherah* (Edinburgh: T&T Clark, 2002); D. V. Edelman, ed., *The Triumph of Elohim: From Yahwisms to Judaisms* (Kampen, The Netherlands: Pharos, 1995); G. Fohrer, *History of Israelite Religion* (Nashville: Abingdon, 1972); and R. K.

Gnuse, *No Other Gods: Emergent Monotheism in Israel* (Sheffield: Sheffield Academic Press, 1997). See also M. Maimonides, *Guide for the Perplexed*, pt. 1 (Greensboro, NC: Empire, 2011); Y. Kaufmann, *The Religion of Israel: From Its Beginnings to the Babylonian Exile* (New York: Shocken, 1972); D. Novak and N. Samuelson, eds., *Proceedings of the Academy for Jewish Philosophy* (Lanham, MD: University Press of America, 1992); P. C. Finney, *The Invisible God: The Earliest Christians on Art* (Oxford: Oxford University Press, 1997); D. F. Ford, *Self and Salvation: Being Transformed* (Cambridge: Cambridge University Press, 2000); G. K. Beale, *We Become What We Worship: A Biblical Theology of Idolatry* (Westmont, IL: IVP Academic, 2008); S. Barton, *Idolatry: False Worship in the Bible, Early Judaism, and Christianity* (Edinburgh: T&T Clark, 2007); and very importantly, D. Tracy, "The Hidden and Incomprehensible God," *Reflections, Center of Theological Inquiry* 3 (2000): 62–88.

[10] W. R. Herzog, *Prophet and Teacher: An Introduction to the Historical Jesus* (Louisville: Westminster/John Knox, 2005), 125–52; and J. D. Crossan, *Jesus: A Revolutionary Biography* (San Francisco: HarperCollins, 1994).

[11] See Matt. 25:31–46 and a long list of New Testament texts that would confirm the early Church's agreement.

[12] Agamben, *Idea of Prose* (Albany: SUNY Press, 1995), 107.

[13] "If you understand, it isn't God." In his Sermon 52.

[14] R. Fornet-Betancourt, "Tradición, cultura, interculturalidad: Apuntes para una comprensión intercultural de la cultura," keynote paper presented at the *XII Corredor das ideias do Cone Sul*, Universidade do Vale dos Sinos (Unisinos), São Leopoldo, RS, Brazil, Sept. 2011.

[15] As the intercultural was discussed in the preceding chapter.

[16] The "scandal" of Christianity certainly involves the claim that the Mystery became "enfleshed" ("incarnate") in Jesus of Nazareth. This "incarnation" is equal to "humanization": a human life historically became hermeneut, effective analogy, real presence of the Mystery—as Nicaea and Chalcedon proclaimed. The full humanity of Jesus is in no way compromised or diminished by the hypostatic union. And if he was "human like us in *all* things but sin," then let us take this Chalcedonian affirmation seriously and reflect on its consequences as well.

[17] See E. Schillebeeckx, *Revelation and Theology*, vol. 1 (New York: Sheed and Ward, 1967); A. Dulles, *Models of Revelation* (Maryknoll: Orbis, 1983); R. Latourelle, *Theology of Revelation* (Cork: Mercier, 1968); F. J. van Beeck, *God Encountered*, vol. 2/1 (Collegeville: Michael Glazier, 1993); and J. Haught, *The Revelation of God in History* (Eugene: Wipf & Stock, 2009).

[18] Christianity is not the only religion that claims a revelation from and of the Mystery (as the Mystery and revelation might be experienced and named in each religion that claims a revelation). This being a volume on and of Christian theology, I will limit myself to a Christian theological reflection on revelation. It will become clear, however, that much that is said here is shared by other religions—but their theologians will have to make that assessment in their name.

[19] See, for example, Phil. 2:7 and 2 Cor. 6:2. The reader should be aware that my understanding and use of the Greek term *kairos* has been influenced both by Paul's

use of the term in his New Testament texts and by G. Agamben's explanation(s) of the term, in turn influenced by the work of W. Benjamin. See G. Agamben, *"What Is an Apparatus?" and Other Essays* (Stanford: Stanford University Press, 2009); Agamben, *The Coming Community* (Minneapolis: University of Minnesota Press, 1993); and especially Agamben, *The Time That Remains: A Commentary on the Letter to the Romans* (Stanford: Stanford University Press, 2005). Benjamin's notion of "messianic time" is behind much of Agamben's reflections on this point, on *kairos* and on his reinterpretation of both (messianic time and *kairos*) through each other. Therefore, see also W. Benjamin, "Theses on the Philosophy of History," in *Illuminations* (New York: Shocken, 1968), 253–64.

²⁰ I refer the reader to the first discussion on revelation that is part of Chapter One. That discussion is assumed and expanded here.

²¹ In other words, studying revelation from the perspective of experience and from the perspective of contents, both always contextual, if humans are to experience and understand revelation as revelation.

²² See E. Jüngel, *Dios como misterio del mundo* (Salamanca: Sígueme, 1984).

²³ Again, consider the comments by physicists John Wheeler and Andrei Linde, cited in the preceding chapter.

²⁴ All Christians will also say that this "crossing" is not the result of our doing, our praying, or our religion, but the totally free and surprising initiative of the Mystery.

²⁵ Even then, given what we have been discussing (and much more) regarding *our* inability to "say" or "know" the Mystery, there remain a wide range of other honorable and arguable human attempts at saying and knowing the Mystery.

²⁶ Christian faith is because of God, and therefore there must somehow be (in the always contextual and perspectival manners possible to humans) an encounter with God to authorize the claim of faith for us.

²⁷ Regardless of denomination or ecclesial tradition. Evidently, without a real, clearly observable *life of compassion*, the experience of the Mystery would be betrayed and its consequent self-unveilings and contents aborted. No amount of doctrinal affirmations can ever supersede, in western Catholicism (or in any other strand within Christianity), a life of compassion—because doctrines are not God, while God *is* compassion. Sometimes, in their quest for doctrinal orthodoxy, Christians dismiss God.

²⁸ More later on hope and faith.

²⁹ Christians, however, have fiercely disagreed with each other over their respective (and sometimes contradictory) claims regarding this content. Sometimes they arrive at the conclusion that their disagreements were grounded on misunderstandings of each other (see the 1999 Lutheran-Roman Catholic "Joint Declaration on the Doctrine of Justification"), but at other times they persist in endorsing their differences (e.g., the 2000 Roman Catholic declaration "*Dominus Iesus*: On the Unicity and Salvific Universality of Jesus Christ and the Church"). Many Christians, for example, still hold fast to the notion that only Christians can be saved, yet it is typical among many other Christians to affirm that all (including non-Christians)

who act compassionately and follow their consciences may be saved. In their disagreements and agreements, Christians always appeal to the "knowable" contents of revelation. Unfortunately, this appeal has often turned the human assumptions and explanations of the contents of revelation into idols.

[30] No Christian doctrinal affirmation or moral requirement can replace or contradict the core message of Jesus. I here refer the reader to the opening section of Chapter One.

[31] See the bibliography cited and referred to in the first section of Chapter One.

[32] Jesus' Galilean Jewish peasant listeners must have actually thought that he was right, that his radical interpretation of Torah reflected the faith of the people, and that this was good news worth betting one's life for. If what Jesus was saying and doing had not attracted a significant following among Galilean peasants, the abused backbone of Palestine's economy at the time, his message would not have worried the religious elites in Jerusalem or the Herodians in Galilee, or led the Romans to execute him.

[33] N. T. Wright states: "The key message of Easter is not 'Jesus is alive again, and therefore we're all going to heaven.' If you look at the gospel resurrection narratives in Matthew, Mark, Luke, and John and the beginning of Acts, none of them say 'Jesus is alive again, and therefore we're all going to heaven.' Later on in the New Testament, it says it again and again: Our future is bound up with what happened – *the point about the resurrection is that 'Jesus has been raised from the dead, and therefore God's New Creation has begun, and therefore we have a job to do.'*" (italics mine) N. T. Wright, "Christian Origins and the Resurrection of Jesus: The Resurrection of Jesus as a Historical Problem," *Sewanee Theological Review* 41, no. 2 (1998). Text used here at http://ntwrightpage.com/.

[34] See J. L. Segundo, "Revelation, Faith, Signs of the Times," in *Mysterium Liberationis*, ed. I. Ellacuría and J. Sobrino (Maryknoll: Orbis, 1993), 328–49. Important, too, in the *Mysterium Liberationis* volume, are the articles by G. Gutiérrez ("Option for the Poor"), I. Ellacuría ("The Historicity of Christian Salvation"), and J. Sobrino ("The Central Position of the Reign of God in Liberation Theology").

[35] "Reasonable" is not equal to "credible." Credibility can be attained through *verosimilitud*. See Chapter Two's section on *verosimilitud*.

[36] Some Christians, unfortunately, will not even notice how crucial the preceding question is. Credulity, however, is not credibility; the latter must be reasonable and respond to reason too, while credulity is infantile wishful thinking. The challenge raised by someone like L. Berlant in *Cruel Optimism* (Durham: Duke University Press, 2011), although not specifically directed at the credibility I speak of here, is a serious challenge to the credulity of many who (perhaps sincerely) think of themselves as Christians. The credibility I am speaking of is reflected in and responds to reason. See, for example, J. B. Metz, *Faith in History and Society* (New York: Crossroad, 2007).

[37] See the discussion on hope that immediately follows this section on revelation.

[38] It is pertinent to remember that individualism, as we know it today in North Atlantic cultures, is still foreign to most of humankind (including many in western

cultures). It was clearly not present in Jesus' Galilean culture. This is not to say that there was no awareness of each human person's being each human person, or no awareness that persons had rights and dignity, but this is different from the individualism that begins (perhaps, as M. Weber claimed) as one of the more recent consequences of several (especially Calvinist) sixteenth century European reformations. It becomes an influential social philosophy and later cultural assumption (especially in the Eurocentric dominant centers) with the nineteenth century. See J. Harrison. *Quest for the New World Order: Robert Owen and the Owenites in Britain and America* (New York: Scribners, 1969). And M. Weber, *The Protestant Ethic and the Spirit of Capitalism*, rev. ed. (New York: Oxford University Press, 2010; German original, 1905).

[39] Exactly the same must be said of the claims of every other religion (theistic or not), and also (by logical necessity) of all the claims that would refute religion. "Definitive," in reference to any religion or revelation, consequently becomes a problematic claim if we remind ourselves of our inescapable human contextualizations and of the utter otherness and mystery of the Mystery.

[40] The hearing I am referring to here is of the historical Jesus as best reconstructed by the most rigorous historical and contextual scholarship. The message and meaning of the historical Jesus, nevertheless, are not proclaimed or heard (in the process that leads to the call to faith) as an academic, scholarly argument. They are proclaimed and heard as Christianity proclaims its gospel, but with the non-negotiable condition that the proclaimed Jesus and his message actually reflect the historical Jesus.

[41] I again repeat that I have no difficulty with doctrinal affirmations, as these might be and have been important or necessary for clarity. But no doctrine, and no sum of doctrines, are the "object" of Christian faith. *Credo in unum Deum* is clearly not a denial of the value of doctrine, but only of the idolatrous claims of many who would benefit from determining and controlling doctrinal orthodoxies.

[42] For well-known and documented historical reasons, it is impossible to claim that Jesus' message was about saving our souls. Such claim completely ignores or disregards the linguistic, religious, and cultural contexts among the peasants of rural Galilee at the time of Jesus. I refer the reader again to the bibliography noted in the opening section of our Chapter One.

[43] For millennia the totally reasonable, observable, and well-documented perception of humankind was that the Earth was flat. And humankind was wrong. Christian arguments cannot dismiss the documented perceptions even when the arguments include other reasonable elements; therefore, Christian claims cannot make Jesus a-human or super-human—ever. The ancient council of Chalcedon realized this. See G. Macy, "Chalcedonian Definition," in *An Introductory Dictionary of Theology and Religious Studies*, ed. O. Espín and J. Nickoloff (Collegeville: Michael Glazier, 2007), 218.

[44] On what follows on hope, see D. Tracy, *Plurality and Ambiguity: Hermeneutics, Religion, Hope* (San Francisco: Harper and Row, 1987); J. B. Metz, *Faith in History and Society*; G. Girardi, *Teología de la liberación y refundación de la esperanza* (Mataró, Spain: Viejo Topo, 2004); J. Moltmann, *The Crucified God: The Cross of Christ as the*

Foundation and Criticism of Christian Theology (Minneapolis: Fortress, 1993); Moltmann, *Theology of Hope* (Minneapolis: Fortress, 1993); Moltmann, *Ethics of Hope* (Minneapolis: Fortress, 2010); R. A. Neal, *Theology as Hope: On the Ground and Implications of Jürgen Moltmann's Doctrine of Hope* (Eugene: Pickwick, 2008); R. Alves, *A Theology of Human Hope* (Washington: Corpus, 1969); J. A. de Aldama, ed., *Teología de la liberación. Conversaciones de Toledo* (Burgos: Aldecoa, 1974); J. B. Libânio, "Hope, Utopia, Resurrection," in *Mysterium Liberationis: Fundamental Concepts of Liberation Theology*, ed. I. Ellacuría and J. Sobrino (Maryknoll: Orbis, 1993), 716–28; L. Boff, *Teologia do cativerio e da libertação* (Petrópolis: Vozes, 1980); R. Vidales and L. Rivera Pagán, eds., *La esperanza en el presente de América Latina* (San José: DEI, 1983); A. Nolan, *Hope in an Age of Despair* (Maryknoll: Orbis, 2009); A. Giambusso, *"The Most Precious Refuge of Hope": Herbert Marcuse, Alienation and the Space of Possibility in American and European Social Philosophy* (Ann Arbor: UMI Dissertation Publishing, 2012); H. Marcuse, *The Essential Marcuse* (Boston: Beacon Press, 2007); Marcuse, *El final de la utopía* (Barcelona: Planeta, 1986); G. Marcel, *Homo Viator: Introduction to the Metaphysic of Hope* (South Bend: St. Augustine Press, 2010); and E. Bloch, *The Principle of Hope*, vols. 1–3 (Cambridge: MIT Press, 1995), esp. vol. 1. Also very relevant here are R. Horsley, *Jesus and the Powers: Conflict, Covenant, and the Hope of the Poor* (Minneapolis: Fortress, 2010); G. S. Harak, "Hope, in Christianity," in *An Introductory Dictionary of Theology and Religious Studies*, 585; M. J. Scanlon, "Hope," in *The New Dictionary of Theology*, ed. J. Komonchak, M. Collins, and D. Lane, 492–98; and H. Desroche, *Sociología de la esperanza* (Barcelona: Herder, 1976). A very good contribution to the discussion on hope and eschatology is S. M. Rodenborn, *Hope in Action: Subversive Eschatology in the Theologies of Edward Schillebeeckx and Johann Baptist Metz* (Ann Arbor: UMI Dissertation Publishing, 2010).

[45] An early tradition now incorporated into the canonical gospels suggests that it was hope indeed that sustained Jesus during the crucifixion. It quotes from Ps. 22 (retained in Aramaic in Mark). I am *not* saying that Jesus actually repeated a verse from Ps. 22 while on the cross. The early Christians, however (the writer of Mark and his community, for example), thought it important to incorporate this verse— whether because it represented a memory of what occurred or as their invented didactic text—as part of the crucifixion narrative. For early Christians, this was a non-flattering portrayal of Jesus during his execution. Nevertheless, it showed him sustained by a hope that God was still listening and still cared. See Mark 15:34 ff. Unless we are ready to claim (but on which grounds?) that Jesus despaired as he was being crucified, the human alternative would have been hope.

[46] In his *Faith in History and Society*, and in subsequent publications, Metz has convincingly demonstrated the crucial importance of *memory* (as in "dangerous memory" or "subversive memory" of Jesus, his message, and his cross) for a Christianity that would avoid being doctrinified, romanticized, and in any way made to ignore the suffering of the world and its marginalized majority. I certainly agree with Metz. But I have focused here more on the *hope* than on the *memory* because it seems that to remember (indispensable as it obviously is for Christians) is not as ultimately crucial (for action and for betting one's life) as *the hope that arises from the*

dangerous memory of Jesus. This takes Metz's insight a subversive step forward. See also Metz's *Por una cultura de la memoria* (Madrid: Anthropos, 1999). It enriches the reflection on memory (as discussed by Metz) to interpret or re-read it together with the philosophy of the cross by S. Breton and the theology of the cross by V. Westhelle, especially Breton's *The Word and the Cross* (New York: Fordham University Press, 2002) and Westhelle's *The Scandalous God: The Use and Abuse of the Cross* (Minneapolis: Fortress, 2006). A very serious, difficult, but still mutually enriching conversation (again, on memory) would also occur by confronting Metz's *Faith in History and Society* with Agamben's *The Church and the Kingdom* (London: Seagull, 2012).

[47] The expression is from Aquinas in his *Summa Theologiae* (*Prima secundae*, q. XL). See D. Doyle, "Changing Hopes: The Theological Virtue of Hope in Thomas Aquinas, John of the Cross, and Karl Rahner," *Irish Theological Journal* 77 (2012): 18–36.

[48] Very incisive and insightful (and pertinent to our discussion) are Metz's fundamental remarks on the practical structure of the Christian claims about God. See Metz, *Faith in History and Society*, 62.

[49] There is no attempt on my part here to repeat Pascal's wager. His bet was for God's existence, while I am very explicitly suggesting that the bet is for compassion—even if God did *not* exist. See B. Pascal, *Pensées* (Oxford: Benediction Classics, 2011), pen. 233.

[50] For what follows on faith, see R. P. Carbine, "Faith," in *An Introductory Dictionary of Theology and Religious Studies*, 443–45; C. Clements, "Faith," in *The Westminster Dictionary of Christian Theology*, 207–08; K. Rahner et al., "Fe," in *Sacramentum Mundi: Enciclopedia Teológica*, vol. 3 (Barcelona: Herder, 1976), 95–147; A. Dulles, "Faith and Revelation," in *Systematic Theology*, vol. 1, ed. F. Schüssler Fiorenza and J. P. Galvin (Minneapolis: Fortress, 1991), 89–128. But see also S. Critchley, *The Faith of the Faithless: Experiments in Political Theology* (New York: Verso, 2012); S. Zizek and B. Gunjevic, *God in Pain: Inversions of Apocalypse* (New York: Seven Stories, 2012); G. Agamben, *The Kingdom and the Glory: For a Theological Genealogy of Economy and Government* (Stanford: Stanford University Press, 2011); and Agamben, *The Church and the Kingdom*, 1–45. For what preceded on hope and for this section on faith, see also the very important S. C. Sullivan, *Living Faith: Everyday Religion and Mothers in Poverty* (Chicago: University of Chicago Press, 2011). I admit that Kierkegaard's leap, and not Pascal's wager, is an influence here.

[51] Although never denying that faith is in the triune God, western Catholicism has often enough appeared to demand (as of equal importance) faith in doctrines said to have been revealed. Indeed, most other Christians have too when they demanded assent to *their* biblical interpretations as "obviously the meaning" of the texts, etc.

[52] And as we can continue to learn from G. Agamben's insight, the only true representation is one that also represents its distance from the truth. See Agamben, *Idea of Prose*, 107.

[53] Not, please note, of faith. A consequence of this is the need to ask if the terms and assumptions of the centuries-long intra-Christian discussions regarding

justification and faith (as well as the *pro* and *contra* issues surrounding "justification by faith alone") might not need to be re-thought and perhaps abandoned. The discussion is better moved to "hope in compassion" and thus to "justification by hope and compassion alone." Salvation, then, is for those who bet for the hope, a bet that requires not the "correct saying" (i.e., orthodoxy or baptism) but the "correct doing" (i.e., living lives of compassion towards all—like Jesus'—without limits, without conditions and without exceptions). Jesus "saves" if and when we accept his dare for the transformation of this world into a world according to God's compassionate will. Jesus does not "save" when we dismiss this world or attempt to find salvation only for our individual souls. Salvation, consequently, is less about religious acts, feelings, or commitments and immensely more about subverting this world by daring it with and toward compassion.

[54] See R. I. Moore, *The Formation of a Persecuting Society: Authority and Deviance in Western Europe, 950–1250* (London: Blackwell, 2007); L. Lambert, *Medieval Heresy: Popular Movements from the Gregorian Reform to the Reformation* (London: Blackwell, 2002); G. Macy, "Gregorian Reforms," in *An Introductory Dictionary of Theology and Religious Studies*, 516–17; Macy, "Gregory VII," in ibid, 520; Macy, *The Hidden History of Women's Ordination: Female Clergy in the Medieval West* (Oxford: Oxford University Press, 2008); J. Boswell, *Christianity, Social Tolerance, and Homosexuality: Gay People in Western Europe from the Beginning of the Christian Era to the Fourteenth Century* (Chicago: University of Chicago Press, 1980). Historians suggest that, based on the best evidence available, the Gregorian Reform led to the clericalization of western Christianity. It was the response of the episcopate led by Gregory VII (d. 1085) to the growing power and abuse of the aristocracy in matters ecclesiastical. The many canonical changes associated with the Gregorian Reform led to the growing centralization of authority (in matters religious) in the hands of the clergy. This, in turn, required theological and doctrinal justification—whence the denial of ordination to women, the demonization of lesbian women and gay men, and especially the reinterpretation of "Church" and of "the faith of the Church" to coincide with the doctrinal and moral affirmations of the episcopate in union with the bishop of Rome. Even after the Reformations of the sixteenth century, the churches that flowed from that century (Roman, Anglican, Lutheran, and others) continued to use the expressions "Church" and "faith of the Church" in ways that still evoked their use since the Gregorian Reform. Today the more common public (and scholarly) usage of these two expressions limit their meaning to the various denominational clergies and/or the institutions led by them. I am not saying anything new, therefore, when I suggest that the clericalization that flowed from the Gregorian Reform was a consequence of a late medieval struggle for power (between the episcopate led by Rome and the aristocracies of the time). The reinterpretation of "Church" and "the faith of the Church" was then perhaps inevitable; what remains remarkable is that the original participatory meanings of those two expressions was never forgotten (not before and not after the sixteenth century).

[55] "At all times and in every race, anyone who fears God and does what is right has been acceptable to him. He has, however, willed to make men holy and save

them, not as individuals without any bond or link between them, but rather to make them into a people who might acknowledge him and serve him in holiness. He therefore chose the Israelite race to be his own people and established a covenant with it. He gradually instructed this people. . . . All these things, however, happened as a preparation for and figure of that new and perfect covenant which was to be ratified in Christ . . . the New Covenant in his blood; he called together a race made up of Jews and Gentiles which would be one, not according to the flesh, but in the Spirit." Second Vatican Council, *Lumen Gentium* ("Dogmatic Constitution on the Church") 2.9, in *Vatican Council II: The Conciliar and Post-Conciliar Documents*, ed. A. Flannery, rev. ed. (Collegeville: Liturgical Press, 1992; the non-inclusive language and androcentric references to God are in the original). Important also is K. A. Locke, *The Church in Anglican Theology: A Historical, Theological and Ecumenical Exploration* (Burlington: Ashgate, 2009).

[56] The hermeneutical role of the episcopate does not contradict the fact that the faith of the Church is the faith *of the People of God*, or that the Church *is* the *entire People of God*. The bishops cannot claim that they alone received revelation, or that they alone are the necessary witnesses of revelation, or that they alone understand revelation, without adulterating revelation. See O. Espín, *The Faith of the People: Theological Reflections on Popular Catholicism* (Maryknoll: Orbis, 1997); E. Schillebeeckx, "The Catholic Understanding of Office in the Church," *Theological Studies* 30, no. 4 (1969): 567–87; and P. Casaldáliga, "Another Way of Being Church," http://www.shc.edu/theolibrary/resources/sedos_casalda.htm.

[57] It should not surprise, then, that the Nicene creed expressly includes the affirmation that we "believe in the Church." This also indicates the importance of the infallibility of the *entire* Church. See G. A. Lindbeck, *Infallibility* (Milwaukee: Marquette University Press, 1972). Equally as important, however, is the admission that historically not all communities and/or generations in fact traditioned the hope or witnessed to it by faith (as the hope and the faith are understood in this volume). Unfortunately, for many the subversive dimension, demand and consequence of the hope were misplaced or ignored; and in consequence their faith became individualistic and focused on personal benefit (e.g., "to save my soul"), wrapped in doctrine or in individual piety.

[58] See Espín, *The Faith of the People*, 63–90 and O. Espín, *Grace and Humanness: Theological Reflections Because of Culture* (Maryknoll: Orbis, 2007), 2–50, as well as the section on the *sensus fidelium* in this book's Chapter One and the bibliography cited there. In *The Faith of the People*, I also tried to make clear that what is often called (and dismissed as) "popular Catholicism" is, in fact, the main bearer of the People of God's (i.e., the Church's) *sensus fidelium*. The dismissal of the faith of the People of God, furthermore, unveils the social, cultural and religious interests of the hegemonic and their allies.

[59] It has, however, always been diverse.

[60] See Espín, *The Faith of the People*, 63–90. It is obvious, and I am not claiming otherwise, that no one aphorism can be said to have universal validity or demand universal acceptance. The aphorism I am about to mention simply serves as an ex-

ample, because other popular sayings, in many other cultural settings, can also be acknowledged as embedding the same insight as the Spanish aphorism I refer to here.

[61] *Dime con quién andas y te diré quién eres*: "Tell me whom you walk-with and I'll tell you who you are." M. H. Díaz has done a theological analysis of this popular saying (specifically in the context of a particular devotional practice) and unveiled some of the faith insights embedded in it. I still find Díaz's insights extremely on target and valuable. See M. H. Díaz, "*Dime con quién andas y te diré quién eres*: We Walk-with Our Lady of Charity," in O. Espín and M. Díaz, *From the Heart of Our People: Latino/a Explorations in Catholic Systematic Theology* (Maryknoll: Orbis, 1999), 153–71. See also G. Diez Barrio, *Los refranes en la sabiduría popular* (Valladolid: Ed. Monte de Piedad, 1985); J. G. Healey, "Proverbs and Sayings: A Window into African Christian Worldview," *Service* 3 (1988): 1–35; A. García-Rivera, *St. Martin de Porres: The "Little Stories" and the Semiotics of Culture* (Maryknoll: Orbis, 1995); J. Rodríguez, *Stories We Live, Cuentos que vivimos: Hispanic Women's Spirituality* (New York: Paulist, 1996); S. Hauerwas and L. G. Jones, eds., *Why Narrative: Readings in Narrative Theology* (Grand Rapids: Eerdmans, 1989).

[62] *Andar con* and *caminar con* are two ways, in Spanish of saying "to walk with." For further theological unpackings of these insights, see Díaz's "*Dime con quién andas y te diré quién eres*"; see also R. S. Goizueta, *Caminemos con Jesús: Toward a Hispanic/Latino Theology of Accompaniment* (Maryknoll: Orbis, 1995) and Goizueta, *Christ Our Companion: Toward a Theological Aesthetics of Liberation* (Maryknoll: Orbis, 2009).

[63] *Kenosis* is "emptying" or "depletion." There is an evident subversive claim in and when connecting *kenosis* to the Incarnation, because the Logos did not (does not) just "become human"—as if a "human" were ever generic. The Logos historically became enfleshed in and among the disposables of the Earth. This, therefore, makes the doctrinal claims regarding the Incarnation profoundly subversive of those who benefit from "disposing of" most of humanity, as well as subversive of those who religiously benefit from, adulterate, or dismiss the connection. Obviously, see Phil. 2:6.

[64] It should not surprise, then, that the early Christians called the discernably faith-full witnesses by the Greek *martyr*, which not only means "witness" but also connotes "one who remembers."

[65] This wager or bet, I have already noted, is faith. *Constatablemente* is the adverb derived from the verb *constatar* and is much stronger and more proof-demanding than the mere "observable."

[66] I proceed now to define and reflect on doctrine and its roles. Within this discussion I will bring up what I have called "doctrinification." By the latter term, I mean not only the understandable process of "making doctrine," but also, and more specifically, the inclination and attempt to turn revelation (and hence the subversive hope, and its traditioning) into a doctrinal corpus, which eviscerates faith of its dangerous demands.

[67] For what follows on doctrine, see J. L. González, *A History of Christian Thought*, 3 vols., rev. ed (Nashville: Abingdon, 1987); Gonzalez, *Christian Thought Revisited: Three Types of Theology* (Maryknoll: Orbis, 1999); J. Pelikan, *The Christian*

Tradition: A History of the Development of Doctrine, 5 vols. (Chicago: University of Chicago Press, 1975–1991); J. L. Segundo, *El dogma que libera* (Santander: Sal Terrae, 1989); G. A. Lindbeck, *The Nature of Doctrine: Religion and Theology in a Postliberal Age* (Louisville: Westminster/John Knox, 1984); J. Granier, "Saber, ideología e interpretación," in *Iniciación a la práctica de la teología*, vol. 1, ed. B. Lauret and F. Refoulé (Madrid: Cristiandad, 1984), 25–42; J. F. Malherbe, "El conocimiento de fe," in ibid., 92–122; Y. Congar, "Teología histórica," in ibid., 238–69; F. Jacques, "El estudio analítico de los enunciados teológicos," in ibid., 508–32; A. C. Thiselton, *The Hermeneutics of Doctrine* (Grand Rapids: Eerdmans, 2007); and C. Geffré, *Le christianisme au risque de l'interprétation: Essais d'herméneutique théologique* (Paris: Cerf, 1983). J. H. Newman's *An Essay on the Development of Christian Doctrine* (Seattle: CreateSpace, 2012; original, 1878) is still important. It is of utmost importance that we understand the role of performance when discussing doctrine because doctrine can be and has also been "performed" among Christians. The Hellenic and Eurocentric type of conceptual affirmation is not and has not been the most common manner of expressing the doctrinal claims associated with Christian revelation, if we mind our ecclesiology and remember that the Church is the People of God. See J. C. Scannone, *Evangelización, cultura y teología* (Buenos Aires: Guadalupe, 1990) and also K. J. Vanhoozer, *Faith Speaking Understanding: Performing the Drama of Doctrine* (Nashville: Westminster John Knox, 2013) and E. Bell, *Theories of Performance* (Thousand Oaks, CA: Sage, 2008).

[68] Unfortunately, the mutual persecution of those involved in doctrinal disputes is ancient among Christians. Being doctrinally right became more important than being compassionate. After 313 CE, imperial power entered the Christian context as doctrinal enforcer, and under one guise or another it remains.

[69] See Matt. 7:21.

[70] By "language" here I do not only mean languages like Spanish, Portuguese, Yoruba, Nahuatl, Tagalog, Quechua, Chinese, English, French, German, or Latin. I mean here the various cultural ways in which human societies and groups evidently express themselves to themselves and among themselves—most frequently not through written texts but through live conversations. This is very important when considering the role of doctrine within Christian traditioning.

[71] The critique of Eurocentrism is certainly pertinent here, and also the critique of clericalism and of other such "privileged languages" within western Christianity: androcentrism, white privilege, heterosexism, etc.

[72] See O. Espín, "Reception of Doctrine," in *An Introductory Dictionary of Theology and Religious Studies*, 1133–34.

[73] See, in the Chapter Two, the explanation of inter-discursive dialogue and particularities, in the section on intercultural thought.

[74] Lindbeck (see *The Nature of Doctrine*) suggests that doctrines act as parameters or identity markers and much less as statements of what is true. I agree. But I think that historically doctrines have been crafted and employed within Christianity as more than parameters or markers. They are "internal conversations" for clarity and understanding, only analogically pointing to truth, while serving as parameters or markers as a real but unintended consequence.

[75] Or whatever is said or claimed about doctrine or doctrinally would be another exercise of dominance and exclusion. This, ethically, is not innocent.

[76] See Espín, *The Faith of the People*; Espín, "An Exploration into the Theology of Grace and Sin," in Espín and Díaz, *From the Heart of Our People*, 121–52; T. Bamat and J.-P. Wiest, eds., *Popular Catholicism in a World Church: Seven Case Studies in Inculturation* (Maryknoll: Orbis, 1999), esp. 249–302. More and more theologians, across the world, are paying closer "dogmatic" attention to popular Catholicism. Social scientists are also focusing more research on it. For a more complete bibliographies on it, see the titles just cited, as well as the bibliography in my *Grace and Humanness* and the bibliographies (theological and/or social scientific, for example) at http://anthropology.ua.edu/Faculty/murphy/419/Cathbib.htm and http://www.sandiego.edu/cas/latino-cath/resources/bibliographies.php.

[77] I use this expression, but I will not quarrel with alternative labels that might (and do) correctly name and explain "popular" western Catholicism. I do not mean it here as a part of denominational Roman Catholicism, although it obviously exists there too. I should also clarify that by "popular" I do not mean "widespread" (although popular Catholicism is certainly very widespread). By the adjective "popular" I mean to focus on the noun "people"—the subjects, crafters, and sustainers of most of western Catholicism are the real "people" in Rancière's sense, or the subaltern in Gramscian terms, which coincide with much in the theological understanding of "People of God."

[78] In the following discussion I will be using the term "hegemony" (and its variants) in a Gramscian sense. For the best study of the notion of hegemony in the work of A. Gramsci, see Gruppi, *O conceito de hegemonia em Gramsci*. For an unsurpassed social scientific application of Gramsci's analysis of hegemony, see O. Maduro, *Religión y conflicto social* (Mexico City: Centro de Reflexión Teológica, 1980).

[79] There are numerous studies that underline the determining role(s) played by "popular Christianity" during the sub-apostolic and later patristic periods. The reader need only remember, for example, the Arian crisis and the different roles played (in its development and resolution) by the Arian doctrines of most of the episcopate and the orthodox faith of most of the people. As an excellent example on the second century, see J. O'Callahan, *El cristianismo popular en el Egipto antiguo* (Madrid: Cristiandad, 1975); see also J. H. Newman, *The Arians of the Fourth Century* (Notre Dame: University of Notre Dame Press, 2001; original, 1833).

[80] I refer the reader to the pertinent sections on culture, history, et al. in Chapter Two.

[81] Nevertheless, I admit that there have been important exceptions in western Catholicism's history but, being exceptions, these only prove the rule. There are such exceptions today too. However, most ecclesiastical documents (regardless of denominational provenance) "talk down," as if all "conversation" had ended by decision of the dominant, instead of conversationally engaging the hope and faith of the People of God as this hope and this faith are lived and expressed through the symbols, practices, and internal conversations of the real People of God. Furthermore, and also on the point made in the text, we cannot dismiss as theologically irrelevant the

fact that throughout most of its history Christianity has been a religion of illiterate majorities. Literacy, therefore, has been mostly a privilege of hegemony.

[82]   See González, *History of Christian Thought.*

[83]   It is transparently obvious that most western Catholics do not use the terminology I employ here because, as I have mentioned before, the vocabulary and the doctrines of scholars do not replace, and are not coextensive with, the hope, the faith, or the compassion of the People of God. Nor do I claim to represent here what millions of young and old western Catholics believe—nor to give adequate voice to the real pain inflicted on so many of them by ecclesiastical normativities more fascinated with their own authority and power than with necessary compassion the Gospel demands of all Christians. Intellectuals have ethical choices to make as they construct their scholarship. I do hope, however, that this intellectual's work can help challenge the unethical naïveté of many theologians, philosophers, and social scientists, who continue to assume that their work is about "books talking with books" and thus continue to dismiss (by ignoring) the faith of the real Church. I am neither the first nor last to point to the need for new theological methodologies, responsive to the academy but also responsive to the real-life experience and faith of the real-life majority of Christians (and of the real-life human majorities).

[84]   Here and in the preceding chapters.

[85]   However, the frequent appeal to "evident" biblical interpretation, or to "evident" or "obvious" interpretations of divine law (often understood as "natural law"), seem effectively (conveniently?) to reaffirm the authority and superiority of the hegemonic decisions and prior interpretations. It is extremely rare that arguments from "natural law" are used to dismantle dominance, oppression, or injustice.

[86]   See, in Chapter One, the section on apostolic succession.

[87]   I am speaking of western Catholicism as a whole. One barely need add that among ecclesiastical denominations within the western Catholic tradition there are significant variants regarding the specifics of the episcopal role in doctrinal discernment. Most western Catholics, however, appear to concur with what I am stating in the text, although we must be aware that not all western Catholics might be in full agreement with the "official normativity" of their respective denominations. This raises other issues.

[88]   Just as there cannot be an "apostolic succession" without the People of God, because only the entire People of God are the Church of God and the apostolic ministry exists only in and for the Church. The episcopate, therefore, only has its existence *within* the People of God and *as its servant*, never above or apart from the People of God. It is clear, nevertheless, that all sorts of theories can be crafted (and have been crafted) in order to rob the episcopate of its role as servant, by reinterpreting it in a way that reinscribes in apostolic succession and in the episcopal ministry the power asymmetries that correspond to the world the Reign of God is subverting. The *sensus fidelium* of the People of God can discern that such reinterpretations and reinscriptions are not reflective of the Reign of God and of the God of the Reign, and while this ecclesial discernment may be public today in the globalized means of information, and in other ways, it has always and just as publicly been

expressed over many centuries by the various forms of "popular Catholicism" that continue (under this or other labels) in the various denominations within western Catholicism. "Official [denominational] normativity," in western Catholicism, has often enough been the claim of the hegemonic who have had social and cultural power to silence the public recognition of the real faith of the real People of God.

[89] I do admit that there have been episcopally proposed doctrines that have effectively justified the subversion of dominance and hegemonies. On a historical balance, nevertheless, my assertion in the text still stands. Two relatively recent examples of episcopally proposed explanations that justified the subversion of the hegemonic status quo are the Latin American Roman Catholic bishops' statements commonly known as *Conclusiones de Medellín* (1968) and *Documento de Puebla* (1979).

Chapter IV

[1] Chapter Three's final section, on doctrine and doctrinification, is obviously pertinent to this chapter as well.

[2] Although it is evident that Kusch did not engage in theology, he did philosophically reflect on religious claims as these are constructed, appear, and are conveyed in and through Latin American popular cultures. His philosophical analyses, especially his philosophical anthropology, are pertinent here. See R. Kusch, *Obras completas* (Córdoba, Argentina: Fundación Ross, 2000), esp. vol. 3, 241–551 ("Esbozo de una antropología filosófica americana"). Fruitful here too, but for a different reason, is E. Laclau, *On Populist Reason* (London: Verso, 2009), 65–172.

[3] See G. Agamben, *Idea of Prose* (Albany: SUNY Press, 1995), 107 and Augustine of Hippo, Sermon 52.

[4] Humans can only understand as transient beings understand, individually and communally. Consequently, even what humans might claim to understand as "eternal" can only be *verosímilmente* claimed if, as "eternal," we only claim what is possible within the understanding of exclusively transient beings (i.e., human understanding).

[5] Evidently, then, all traditioning occurs only in our respective *cotidianos*.

[6] This understanding of *lo cotidiano* which I am proposing here helps translate the category of "universal particularity" and/or "particular universality." I borrow these terms from the work of R. Fornet-Betancourt. See my discussion, as well as the bibliography by Fornet-Betancourt, in the extensive section on intercultural thought in Chapter Two. Furthermore, my understanding of *lo cotidiano* here builds on the work of several Latino/a theologians over the past few decades. See my "Exploration into the Theology of Grace and Sin," in *From the Heart of Our People: Latino/a Explorations in Catholic Systematic Theology*, ed. O. Espín and M. Díaz (Maryknoll: Orbis, 1999), 121–52, for a more complete bibliography. Furthermore, among the pioneering authors on the critical study of daily life are A. Heller, *Historia y vida cotidiana* (Mexico City: Grijalbo, 1972); Heller, *Sociología de la vida cotidiana* (Barcelona: Península, 1977); Heller, *La revolución de la vida cotidiana* (Barcelona: Península, 1982); T. de Barbieri, *Mujeres y vida cotidiana* (Mexico City: Fondo de

Cultura Económica, 1984); A. Sojo, *Mujer y política: Ensayo sobre feminismo y sujeto popular* (San José, Costa Rica: DEI, 1985); M. de Certeau, *The Practice of Everyday Life* (Berkeley: University of California Press, 1984); L. K. Kerber, "Separate Spheres, Female Worlds, Woman's Place: The Rhetoric of Women's History," *Journal of American History* 75 (1988): 9–39; and, of course, A. M. Isasi-Díaz, *En la lucha/In the Struggle: A Hispanic Women's Liberation Theology* (Minneapolis: Fortress, 1993) and Isasi-Díaz, *Mujerista Theology* (Maryknoll: Orbis, 1996), 66–73. Very pertinent to this discussion, and to any reflection on *lo cotidiano*, is the third chapter ("*Nosotros*: Community as the Birthplace of the Self") in R. S. Goizueta's excellent book *Caminemos con Jesús: Toward a Hispanic/Latino Theology of Accompaniment* (Maryknoll: Orbis, 1995), 47–76.

[7] What is "launched" and what is "received" (i.e., the "conversations" that occur in the "locations of interlocution") are always transmitted by inescapably cultural, historical, and transient testimony and life.

[8] See Chapter Two on contexts.

[9] I beg the reader to forgive the perhaps annoying repetition of expressions like "real," "daily living," "real life," etc., throughout this chapter. The repetitions are intended to make sure we do not miss the "real-ness" and "daily-ness" of life and reality, and the fact that neither exists except in each other as lived by real people.

[10] As implied by the Spanish verbs *saber* and *conocer*. Both can be translated into English as "to know." In Spanish, however, they are distinct as they name the "factual knowing" (*saber*) on the one hand or the "understanding" implied and involved in every act of knowing (*conocer*) on the other. The connection between *lo cotidiano* and these two Spanish ways of referring to the act of knowing were brought to my attention by Prof. Nancy Pineda-Madrid.

[11] See my reflections on history and transience in Chapter Two.

[12] See M. A. DiGiovine, *The Heritage-scape: UNESCO, World Heritage, and Tourism* (Lanham, MD: Lexington, 2009), 261.

[13] It is certainly not irrelevant to suggest that this "re-inscription" is very much part of the dynamic that Christian doctrine has attempted to understand under the expression "original sin" and by the doctrinal claim that the latter affects all humans and all that is human (including, we must conclude, doctrine and traditioning). See O. Espín, "Sin, Original," in *An Introductory Dictionary of Theology and Religious Studies*, ed. O. Espín and J. Nickoloff (Collegeville: Michael Glazier, 2007), 1290–91 and J. L. Segundo, *Grace and the Human Condition* (Maryknoll: Orbis, 1973), vol. 2 of Segundo's series *A Theology for Artisans of a New Humanity*. Segundo addresses, in his masterful discussion of original sin, not only the re-inscription but also the social structures and ideologies that accompany it.

[14] See W. Benjamin, *The Arcades Project* (Cambridge, MA: Harvard University Press, 1999); U. Steiner, *Walter Benjamin: An Introduction to His Work and Thought* (Chicago: University of Chicago Press, 2010), 145–53, 165–72; and M. P. Steinberg, "The Collector as Allegorist: Goods, Gods, and the Objects of History," in *Walter Benjamin and the Demands of History*, ed. M. P. Steinberg (Ithaca: Cornell University Press, 1996), 88–118. See also my reflections on history in Chapter Two, and, in the same chapter, my discussion of M. de Certeau's philosophy of history and of daily life.

[15] In a personal electronic message sent to me in December 2010 as part of our ongoing conversation on many of the topics discussed in this book, Prof. E. Ortega-Aponte of Drew University stated: "I see a reaction to the colonizing paradigm of the 'gifts of the poor.' The use of the faith and struggles of those at the margins, as spiritual therapeutic for the privileged, is repulsive. You know the line: 'The faith of those poor people sustains me! How wonderful is their faith in God!' Instead of seeing that faith—and the narratives that come with and out of it—as a challenge to the dominant world system (in Habermas' sense). So, for me, when we say with the hymn, *cuando el sediento tiene sed y agua nos da, va Dios mismo en nuestro mismo caminar,* cannot be other than a kenotic act. I think we would be right to say that, in this sense, it would also be a kairotic event. But not one of salvific grace for the colonizing paradigm, but a transgression of it that announces a new reality that overturns it." I wholly agree with Prof. Ortega-Aponte. This insight, in my estimation, puts Agamben's notion of the kairotic on its head. Ortega-Aponte clearly suggests that there is no moment of revelation as kairotic moment (i.e., as moment of opportunity to be seized) except and unless it is *also* (and inseparably) a moment of *kenosis,* of self-giving . . . which is precisely what is claimed about revelation: God's *self-donation,* which also implicates Jesus' cross as the greatest act of God's *self*-revelation because it is God's greatest act of *self-donation* (without in any way diminishing or denying my insistence on the cross and the crucified as "effective analogy"). I am very grateful to Prof. Ortega-Aponte for many and invariably insightful suggestions. Interestingly, see also J. B. Metz, *Faith in History and Society* (New York: Crossroad, 2007), 62–70 and P. Fenves, *The Messianic Reduction: Walter Benjamin and the Shape of Time* (Stanford: Stanford University Press, 2011).

[16] This, we recall, is the meaning of *metanoia*: not "repentance" primarily (because this could only be a consequence of *metanoia*) but "drastic change in direction."

[17] See Chapter Three's reflections on revelation, hope, and faith.

[18] The Christian claim and hope are not and cannot be, therefore, a *gnosis* reserved for the powerful, the educated, or the pious. The idol can build fences around itself, preventing access by establishing conditioning categories among its human followers, but not so God's grace. "Conditioning fences" must be carefully analyzed and critiqued in Christian claims and traditioning.

[19] It is sadly obvious that among the marginalized there are strata of suffering and of "disposability." It is also sad and obvious that the abuse of the weaker also occurs among the marginalized and by the marginalized who (arguably instrumentalized by hegemonic ideology) do not hesitate to inflict on others what is inflicted on them. Although the marginalized abusers cannot escape their moral responsibility for their choices, this book focuses on the world structures of abuse created by and for the "grand" abusers. Nevertheless, our discussion of "truthfulness" as part of compassion (below) is also applicable to the abusers among the marginalized, be they rapists, drug dealers, or LGBTQ whites who do not hesitate to be racist and xenophobic, or racial minorities who act as if other minorities were their enemies, or white feminists who seem to fight for equal participation in a world built on the backs of non-white women. There are other examples.

[20] See Chapter Two.

[21] Apparently not directly about this, but undoubtedly also about it, see. E. A. Johnson, *Quest for the Living God: Mapping Frontiers in the Theology of God* (New York: Continuum, 2007), 141–52.

[22] Again, *metanoia*.

[23] Obviously, I assume in this statement the understandings of hope and faith developed throughout this volume. It is also important to recall that the core content of Christian revelation is, emphatically, the hope that Jesus was right about the Reign of God and about the God of the Reign.

[24] "Seminal meanings" or "seminal reasons." The Greek noun *logos* is from the verb *lego*, which means "I say." Therefore, *logos* is an "utterance" before it is a "word," and more precisely a "meaningful utterance" that we *then* call a "word" or "reason." "Meaning" seems (for example) closer to *logos* as used in John 1. Ancient Greek philosophy (from Heraclitus onward) thought of the *logos* as the grounding principle of reality, while our contemporaries J. Piaget and N. Chomsky have employed the expression in their theories of generative epistemology. Early Christian writers (especially Cyril of Alexandria) used the expression *logos spermatikos* almost as equivalent to "the planting of *the* meaning" of life (by God, outside of the identifiable perimeters of Judaism and Christianity), which came to full fruition in Christ. Evidently, as Christians these early thinkers understood "*the* uttered meaning" to be Jesus (and his message). Very pertinent here are S. Breton, *El porvenir del cristianismo* (Bilbao: Mensajero, 2002), 75–102 and Breton, *The Word and the Cross* (New York: Fordham University Press, 2002).

[25] Thus, the *Letter of Clement to the Corinthians* uses the term to describe as homeless pilgrims the Christian communities of Clement's day. See *Letter of Clement to the Corinthians, The Apostolic Fathers*, vol. 1 (Cambridge, MA: Loeb Classical Library, 2003), 17–152

[26] And here I do mean to use "among" and not "between."

[27] Explaining it not as doctrine but as the expected bet of one's life for the hope. This, obviously, requires thought and responsible consideration if it is to become a lifetime commitment to compassion and justice, with their dangerous consequences. The faith is not an excuse for fanaticism.

[28] And of traditioning.

[29] "Can" is not the same as "will." To expect that *any* human construct (such as an analogy) *will* tradition the hope and the faith is an idolatrous and groundless expectation.

[30] See the distinction between the "universally valid" and the "universally relevant" in the first chapter of my *Grace and Humanness*: O. Espín, *Grace and Humanness: Theological Reflections Because of Culture* (Maryknoll: Orbis, 2007). The present section of this chapter also assumes the discussions on intercultural thought in Chapter Two above.

[31] An effective analogy that is also anti-idol because, as analogy, it is sacramental and even paradoxical, never claiming to *be* the truth. The three main idols of humankind, historically, seem always to be power, wealth, and prestige, with their

greatest ideologically justifying tool being the "explanation" that renders toothless and irrelevant the crucifixion and the crucified as effective analogy, transforming these into a tool for renewed dominance. Zizek reminds us that the critique of ideology must recognize that it is possible to lie under the guise of truth: S. Zizek and N. Abercrombie, eds., *Mapping Ideology* (London: Verso, 2012), 1–33.

[32] We should take very seriously Matt. 25's insight, "what you did to the least, you did to me." See X. Alegre, *Memoria subversiva y esperanza para los pueblos crucificados* (Madrid: Trotta, 2003); J. Moltmann, *Religion, Revolution and the Future* (New York: Scribner's, 1969); C. Mesters, *A missão do povo que sofre* (Petrópolis: Vozes, 1981); and of course J. Sobrino, *Fuera de los pobres no hay salvación* (Madrid: Trotta, 2007); Sobrino, *Jesús en América Latina: Su significado para la fe y la cristología* (Santander: Sal Terrae, 1982); and H. Samour, *Voluntad de liberación: La filosofía de Ignacio Ellacuría.*

[33] "The originality of Christian faith is incontestable to the extent that it is defined by the Cross and solely by it." S. Breton, *The Word and the Cross* (New York: Fordham University Press, 2002), 28.

[34] See J. Rieger and Kwok P.-L. *Occupy Religion: Theology of the Multitude* (Lanham: Rowman & Littlefield, 2012); and J. Rieger, *God and the Excluded: Visions and Blind Spots in Contemporary Theology* (Minneapolis: Fortress, 2001). A very much needed (and hopeful) contemporary critique of dominant theological blindness is expressed, for example, by M. Althaus-Reid, *The Queer God* (London: Routledge, 2003) and P. S. Cheng, *From Sin to Amazing Grace: Discovering the Queer Christ* (New York: Seabury, 2012).

[35] See Matt. 7:21; Matt. 25:31–46; Mark. 9:38–39; Acts 10:15; etc. The patristic notion of *logos spermatikos* is also an indication of this early Christian attitude: denying nothing they claimed about Jesus, the early Christians too realized that there were very many compassionate and courageous non-Christians, and that these could not be dismissed, in theology or in life.

[36] And we hope to be welcome by them. "Hope—a new constellation, waiting for us to map it, waiting for us to name it, together." (Poet Richard Blanco, at the 2013 U.S. presidential inauguration.)

[37] The Latin, in turn, seems to have been borrowed from the earlier (and similar in meaning) Greek term *sympatheia*, "to feel with." Recall, in Chapter Two's discussion of intercultural thought, how *convivir* was indispensable.

[38] The text of Mary's *Magnificat*, in Luke's gospel (1:46–55), is a didactic announcement of the drastic subversion brought by Mary's son. The early Christians understood this well.

[39] I am not making light of the desperate real-life needs and options that are a crucially indispensable part of the answer. What follows is proposed not instead of, or even prior to, the urgent options, but as a set of concomitant issues that may not be ignored throughout the entire struggle for compassion.

[40] A phrase from César Chávez (1927–93), the great Latino/a leader and organizer of farmworkers across the U.S.

[41] See A. Gramsci, *Literatura e vida nacional* (Rio de Janeiro: Civilização Brasileira, 1978; transl. of *Letteratura e vita nazionale*); Gramsci, *Concepção dialética da história*,

(Rio de Janeiro: Civilização Brasileira, 1981; trans. of *Il materialismo storico e la filosofia di Benedetto Croce*); Gramsci, *Cadernos do cárcere* (Rio de Janeiro: Civilização Brasileira, 2001); Gramsci, *Cartas do cárcere* (Rio de Janeiro: Civilização Brasileira, 2005); and Gramsci, *Os intelectuais e a organização da cultura* (Rio de Janeiro: Civilização Brasileira, 1979; trans. of *Gli intellettuali e l'organizzazione della cultura*). Also, and indispensable as well for an arguable notion of "organic intellectual" in this context, is Rancière's contribution: see Rancière, *Hatred of Democracy* (London: Verso, 2006); Rancière, *On the Shores of Politics* (London: Verso, 1992); Rancière, *Dis-agreement: Politics and Philosophy* (Minneapolis: University of Minnesota Press, 1999); Rancière, *The Intellectual and His People*, vol. 2, *Staging the People* (London: Verso, 2012); and Rancière, *The Philosopher and His Poor* (Durham: Duke University Press, 2003). See also J.-Ph. Deranty, ed., *Jacques Rancière: Key Concepts* (Durham: Acumen, 2010).

[42] P. Freire, *Pedagogia do oprimido* (Rio de Janeiro: Paz e Terra, 2011; originally published in 1968). Others also come to mind, for example C. Sandoval, *Methodology of the Oppressed* (Minneapolis: University of Minnesota Press, 2000) and C. Nanko-Fernández, *Theologizing en Espanglish: Context, Community, and Ministry* (Maryknoll: Orbis, 2010).

[43] As explained above, *logos* as "meaningfulness."

[44] By these I am pointing to (for example) aphorisms, popular theater and poetry, ritualized behaviors, dance, reasons and occasions for festivities and for mourning or praying, means of decorating domestic and public spaces, symbols, etc., including the colors of skin, dress, and manners of speech chosen for or expected from the dramatic characters in religious plays. Popular religions, in their internal expressive diversity, are very important and frequent means of expression among the disposables of the world. All of these are the "languages" through which thought, reason, et al. are expressed. See J. C. Scott, *Domination and the Arts of Resistance: Hidden Transcripts* (New Haven: Yale University Press, 1990); Scott, *Weapons of the Weak: Everyday Forms of Peasant Resistance* (New Haven: Yale University Press, 1987); A. Ashford and D. Poole, eds., *Anthropology in the Margins of the State* (Santa Fe: School of American Research, 2004); and also J. Rancière, *Mute Speech* (New York: Columbia University Press, 2011); S. Vosniadou and A. Ortony, eds., *Similarity and Analogical Reasoning* (Cambridge: Cambridge University Press, 1989), 199–241, 298–312; and O. Espín, *The Faith of the People: Theological Reflections on Popular Catholicism* (Maryknoll: Orbis, 1997). See also the many works by philosopher R. Kusch cited throughout this volume.

[45] Assistencialism, a term originating in Latin American social movements, refers to treating the person as a passive recipient of aid rather than an active transformer of his or her environment.

[46] Audre Lorde very wisely understood and bluntly stated this. Audre Lorde, "The Master's Tools Will Never Dismantle the Master's House," in *Sister Outsider: Essays and Speeches* (Freedom, CA: The Crossing Press, 1984), 110–13.

[47] I refer the reader to some (among many other) important theological studies that ground and significantly expand what I have just mentioned *in nuce*: M. de França Miranda, *Libertados para a práxis da justiça: A teologia da graça no atual con-*

texto latino-americano (São Paulo: Loyola, 1980); L. Boff, *A graça liberadora no mundo* (Petrópolis: Vozes, 1977); J. L. Segundo, *Gracia y condición humana* (Montevideo: C. Lohlé/Centro Pedro Fabro, 1969); M. H. Díaz, *On Being Human: U.S. Hispanic and Rahnerian Perspectives* (Maryknoll: Orbis, 2001). Of course, see K. Rahner, *Foundations of Christian Faith* (New York: Crossroad, 1990) and Rahner, *Nature and Grace: Dilemmas in the Modern Church* (New York: Sheed and Ward, 1964). Useful are Q. Quesnell, "Grace," in *New Dictionary of Theology*, ed. J. Komonchak, M. Collins and D. Lane (Wilmington: Michael Glazier, 1987), 437–50; O. Espín, "An Exploration into the Theology of Grace and Sin," in Espín and Díaz, *From the Heart of Our People*, 121–71; and Espín, "Grace," in *An Introductory Dictionary of Theology and Religious Studies*, 503–09.

⁴⁸ See Matt. 7:21 and 25:37–40; Rom. 8:38–39; 1 Cor. 13:3–7. Pertinent here are important insights in Elaine Padilla's 2011 doctoral dissertation, successfully defended at Drew University (*A Passionate God: Constructing a Theology of Divine Enjoyment*). The dissertation was directed by Prof. Catherine Keller.

⁴⁹ It would be close to impossible to demonstrate that among the villagers in rural Galilee, in Jesus' day, there was any belief or expectation of "saving their souls" by going to "heaven," especially when the notions of "soul" and "heaven" did not exist among the Jewish peasants of Galilee. It would be equally impossible to show that Jesus announced a message that would simply not have been understood by his fellow villagers. None of this, however, prevented later generations of Christians from reinterpreting his message, in and for their contexts. The question is not whether the *possibility* of re-interpretation or development is legitimate within Christianity (yes, it is); the issue is whether any re-interpretation or development can *change* what was the core message of Jesus so that it would be no longer important or central in Christianity (no, it can't).

⁵⁰ The stage is this volume. *Paroikousa* is homeless journeying. The twenty statements that follow synthesize what I am proposing as adequate (never sufficient or final) understanding of western Catholic traditioning. These statements synthetically incorporate the reflections present throughout this entire book, but they are by no means "conclusions."

Index